Directing

A handbook for emerging theatre directors

Rob Swain

methuen | drama

Methuen Drama

1 3 5 7 9 10 8 6 4 2

First published in 2011

Methuen Drama is an imprint of Bloomsbury Publishing Plc

Methuen Drama
Bloomsbury Publishing Plc
49–51 Bedford Square
London W1CB 3DP

www.methuendrama.com

Copyright © Robert Swain 2011

Robert Swain has asserted his rights under the Copyright, Designs
and Patents Act, 1988, to be identified as the author of this work

A CIP catalogue record for this book is available from the British Library

PB ISBN: 978 1 408 12765 0
EPUB ISBN: 978 1 408 15662 9

Available in the USA from Bloomsbury Academic & Professional,
175 Fifth Avenue/3rd Floor, New York, NY 10010
www.BloomsburyAcademicUSA.com

Typeset by Country Setting, Kingsdown, Kent CT14 8ES
Printed and bound in Great Britain by CPI Cox & Wyman, Reading, Berks

Contents

Acknowledgements

With thanks to all those who gave of their time, experience and wisdom and who agreed to be interviewed for this book. With thanks to all the directors in training on the Master of Fine Arts in Theatre Directing at Birkbeck University of London, and the practitioners who have contributed to the programme, from whom I have learnt a great deal. With thanks to Andrew McKinnon for all his support and advice. With special thanks to my wife Shelly for limitless amounts of support, advice and encouragement.

Introduction

This book is primarily written for those considering a future as a theatre director. It sets out with the reader in mind who has directed productions at university or with groups of friends, and now wants to increase their knowledge of theatre, the director's craft and what directing entails. By the end it is aimed at someone who has directed one or two pieces, perhaps with a professional cast, and who wants to know how to establish a sustained career as a director. The chapters in between discuss key sources of information and key considerations in working with a number of collaborators that may be useful to directors at many stages of their work. It is also intended to be useful to someone who is an actor, stage manager, or an artist in a related field of theatre, who has experience of working in performing arts but who feels that they need additional skills and knowledge to direct.

Theatre directing is one of the most open professions to enter, since there is no necessity for formal qualifications and there are no prescribed career routes; yet this very openness can also make it seem a secretive and daunting world to the outsider. Where do I begin? How do I find theatres and organisations that support emerging directors? How do I contact professional actors, designers, lighting designers and stage managers? How can I put on a piece of work that will be professionally recognised? Should I consider further training or learn by trial and error?

As this is intended to be a 'handbook' for directors which can be referred to in practical situations, the level of detail has been gauged to give the director a guide through processes and situations where there is little readily available information outside the experience of professional practice. It may also be of interest to those with a broader desire to know more about how theatre is being made today.

By viewing the director's role through his or her key relationships – with the actor, the author, the designer, the industry, the production, and finally, the work of directing itself – this book will offer a sense of the geography of the theatre as it is practised in the UK today, outlining the key factors in each relationship and giving enough information for an emerging theatre director to increase their knowledge and under-standing of each area.

Each chapter will:

➢ Introduce key theories, practitioners and reading to provide an overview of the knowledge necessary to understand historic and current practice in the area.

➢ Discuss the key factors and considerations in the relationship.

➢ Include interviews with leading and emerging directors, and with actors, designers, writers and producers about their work and relationships with directors.

➢ Suggest exercises to develop the director's own approach and practical skills.

➢ Provide a reading list and weblinks where further information can be found.

The book is not intended to give primacy to any particular genre of theatre or theatrical aesthetic, but to provide an overview of the myriad approaches that theatre directors are employing today, so that a director can pursue those ideas and study those theatre-makers who are of most interest in developing their own synthesised methods of working. I have outlined a wide variety of theories about acting and theatre-making, but only in so far as they are possibly useful tools in gathering the courage to stand up in a rehearsal room and start to make things happen. Hopefully, knowing what other directors are thinking and doing, and what they might do when facing daunting challenges, will help reduce the sense of working in a void, in ignorance and in fear – although the fear never quite goes away, however experienced you become.

This book is based on my experience of being a freelance director and artistic director for over twenty years, and on training theatre directors for the past eight years; many of the questions which I attempt to answer are the practical ones that demystify the pragmatic craft of the director, as posed by successive groups of directors about to embark on professional careers.

Many of those directors have come from countries across the world, and although this book is rooted in theatre-making in the UK today, its references are international, and many of the approaches outlined here are applicable to theatre-making the world over.

1 I'm a theatre director

This chapter is intended for someone who is considering a career as a theatre director who may have directed one or two pieces, but perhaps without the attention of professional peers. It therefore covers some fundamental information and considerations that may be helpful in developing your thinking and practice before reaching the stage where you invite other directors and professionals to your productions. Chapter Seven, the final chapter, is aimed at those who are ready to engage fully with the industry and to commit to a sustained level of work as a director.

With nearly 800 members of widely varying levels of experience, the Young Vic Genesis Directors' Network allows directors to network with each other, find out about workshops, explore assisting and directing opportunities, and promote their work. The criteria for becoming a member are UK residency and a commitment to being a professional director; the only bar is being a student in full-time education, as this limits availability. This acknowledges that directors come from a wide range of backgrounds and will have to forge their own individual paths to establish a career as a director. In an intensely competitive field the key qualifications for success are desire, determination, a knowledge of current theatre-making, a well-articulated sense of the theatre you wish to make and an ever-growing circle of collaborators. Then hopefully the work speaks for itself, and you.

Some directors are ex-stage managers or technicians, such as Howard Davies and Jonathan Church; many are actors, such as Michael Grandage and Samuel West; some, such as Kerry Michael, come from music and live art backgrounds rather than theatre. One of the commonest routes is through university – not necessarily following a theatre-related degree. The National Student Drama Festival is held every spring in Scarborough; it not only showcases the best student productions from around the country, but also offers advice and workshops for student directors, and can provide a valuable bridge between university and professional work. Other directors begin with little practical experience in theatre but with the desire to mount one particular production, and then find they want to do it again. Although the section below outlines training opportunities, there are no training requirements for directors, and in the end there is no substitute for working with the best group of collaborators it is possible to bring together, putting on a piece of work and inviting your peers to see it. Many people say, 'I want to be a theatre director'; fewer people say, 'I am a theatre director'; but the only real difference between them is that the latter group of people have actually gone and done it – after that it is simply about becoming a better director, or as Samuel Beckett said, learning to 'fail better'.

Director training

In 1986 the Calouste Gulbenkian Foundation funded a report into the lack of training for directors: *A Better Direction*, written by Kenneth Rea, was followed by *The Training of Theatre Directors* by Andrew McKinnon in 1996. Since then, a number of drama schools have launched director training programmes, and RADA and LAMDA, Bristol Old Vic and Drama Centre have long-established programmes. Some of the programmes are three-year BAs and some are one-year MAs. They all offer the opportunity to gain an understanding of directing by participating in and observing classes being taught in the schools' acting courses, as well as the opportunity to assist on productions and take classes which focus on directing. Some of the courses, such as Drama Centre's, also cover directing for film and TV, and offer secondments to theatre or film companies; some, such as RADA's, offer well-publicised productions at the end of the programme.

There are also a growing number of university-based directing programmes, providing different combinations of theoretical and practical work and varying levels of production opportunity. There is now a wide choice of training programmes for directors, easily researched through a web search: the courses at drama schools can be searched via the Conference of Drama Schools (CDS) website. However, all of these programmes have different focuses: some will be best suited for studying directing as an academic subject; some will be more vocationally orientated and better suited for practising as a professional director. Anyone researching these courses will wish to identify those that most closely match their knowledge and skills requirements, but it is also worthwhile trying to discover the 'graduate destinations' – the actual work that the courses' graduates are now doing.

In addition to these full-length courses, there is also a growing number of short courses and one-off workshops, many led by prominent directors, being offered by theatres that support emerging directors, particularly the Young Vic, the Old Vic and the Directors Guild of Great Britain.

Many directors have effectively constructed their own training programmes, while still trying to earn a living and put on work, by attending talks and workshops by directors, writers, actors and designers they admire. Katie Mitchell and Emma Rice are prime examples of directors who identified directors and companies whose work they wanted to learn more about, so went to Russia and Poland to meet and work with them. In the UK it is possible to simply write to directors and either to ask to meet them and talk about their work, or to observe some of their work: they may say no, but many directors are extremely helpful to emerging directors who clearly have a serious interest in their work.

The rest of this chapter indicates what it might be useful to learn about while trying to construct a career. In the end there is no substitute for doing it, and it is perfectly possible to direct work without any of this knowledge, but it might offer a historic and current context for developing your own work, aesthetics and ethos.

Seeing work

Recently I heard of a director who went to see a show at a leading fringe theatre and happened to see the artistic director in the bar afterwards, so decided to introduce himself. The artistic director was very friendly and she began to ask the director about the directors', writers' and actors' work he had seen lately and enjoyed. But when the conversation went on to designers and lighting designers, the director realised that he had not really noted who had designed or lit the productions he admired, and could not voice an informed opinion about designers' or lighting designers' work.

Keeping notes on people whose work you see will not only build up a database of possible future collaborators, but also help identify and articulate your own tastes and work; discussing in some detail the work you have seen is often the first way in which other directors, or those who might be able to help you, or be interviewing you, will try to find out about your ideas and work.

As a director rather than an interested theatregoer, it is worthwhile going to productions you would not naturally choose to see. As part of building up a knowledge of the breadth of theatre-making it is worthwhile making a point of seeing work by those who are considered to be influential in their field; for example, seeing a piece by director Rupert Goold or playwright Simon Stephens if you've not seen their work; going to at least one big West End musical, a scratch night at BAC or a production in a found space, if these types of theatre lie outside your current knowledge and tastes. As well as building up lists of the productions, build up lists of key directors, writers, actors, designers and theatre companies who are influencing how theatre is being made.

The Stage, the *Guardian* and *Whatsonstage* websites are particularly useful in finding out not only what is on, but what is going to be on. For £165 a year, a subscription to *Theatre Record* offers the most detailed information on future productions across the country, as well as all the reviews of productions that receive more than one national review, and all the cast and production details of those productions. It comes out fortnightly and can also be bought issue by issue. The cheaper option is to add several of the independent theatre websites to your favourites list or RSS feeds, such as those mentioned above and others which might include *Up The West End* or *UK Theatre Web*.

Understanding the industry

It is also useful and easy to keep up to date with current debates about theatre-making through websites and blogs. The *Guardian*'s site includes blogs and articles by Lyn Gardner, Michael Billington and other commentators, and there are numerous independent blogs, and review or discussion websites set up by theatregoers, such as *A Younger Theatre*.

The above websites will give you a familiarity with the work of many of the leading theatre companies, and even companies that exist for only one production. It is useful to construct your own mental map of theatre companies in terms of their size, location, specific audiences and artistic policies, and how they relate to one another. The map might include the permanent and ever-visible companies, such as the National Theatre and the RSC; the national network of subsidised regional theatres; the national and regional touring companies; the companies creating work with, or by, young people and children; companies creating work with circus artists, digital artists, aerialists; the London, Manchester, Glasgow and Bristol fringes; those who specialise in street arts, site-specific or site-sympathetic work; companies creating work that actively involves the audience in its creation; and festivals such as Edinburgh, Latitude, HighTide and Forest Fringe. The boundaries between separate art forms are breaking down and definitions such as 'physical theatre' and 'devised theatre' seem inadequate and clumsy when describing companies who combine, say, text, movement, projection and music, and since the map constantly changes it is essential to keep up with these changes by visiting websites that discuss how theatre is made as well as those sites that review theatre.

Through visiting a few websites it is possible to get an overview of how government policy affects funding and the whole subsidised theatre ecology. From the Department of Culture, Media and Sport's site, through the Arts Council of England, the Creative Scotland, Arts Council of Wales, Arts Council of Northern Ireland sites, which list all the companies they fund, to a theatre's individual website, it is possible to build up a picture of the whole subsidised theatre structure and how that structure is changing. From that, it is interesting to compare work that is subsidised and work that is produced commercially, or through profit sharing and the director's overdraft or a canny independent producer. Even looking at the logos on a seasonal brochure or production flyer can reveal a lot about how a piece of theatre was financed and made.

It is also useful to begin to analyse the artistic policies of one or two theatres in more detail, to gain a better understanding of how work is made and the decisions behind individual play choices. For example, the Royal Court Theatre, the Bush, the Gate and the Lyric Hammersmith are all leading new-writing theatres in west London, but each has a distinctive engagement with new writers. The Royal Court has a strong writer development programme, mainly focused on writers under twenty-six, and an international department that engages with new writers from around the world, and this is reflected in their programming. The Bush and the Gate are both small theatres and although both often defy the physical limitations of their spaces by mounting some extraordinarily large productions, the Bush's focus tends to be on emerging UK writers while the Gate's is on international writers. The Lyric Hammersmith's artistic director, Sean Holmes, mixes revivals of twentieth-century classics with new commissioned work from writers such as Simon Stephens and co-productions with companies such as Filter, who radically reimagine classics such as Chekhov's *Three Sisters* with a strong emphasis on soundscapes. Similarly, it is enlightening to compare the programmes of theatres of similar size around the country. Although they are all serving large urban populations and are roughly comparable in size, the West Yorkshire Playhouse in Leeds, the Royal Exchange in Manchester and the Bristol Old Vic have very distinctive artistic policies, and it is interesting to ask to what extent these differing policies are the product of their artistic directors' artistic vision and tastes, the profile and tastes of their local audiences, their outreach and creative learning policies, and the physical shape and sizes of their main auditoria and studios.

The Young Vic and the Old Vic often put on events where current issues affecting how directors work are discussed, and other theatres occasionally mount similar events: the above 'what's on' and blog sites are good sources of information about one-off events. Improbable Theatre organises *Devoted and Disgruntled*, a democratic 'open space' forum for discussion and debate between theatre artists about whatever the artists wish to discuss. There is a large three-day event in London every January and meetings in other cities during the year plus smaller monthly meetings in London. The sites mentioned above often have details of future events such as these.

The directory *Contacts*, published each year in October, is regarded as a useful reference tool for anyone creating professional work. It contains the contact details for agents and personal managers, casting directors, drama schools, audition and rehearsal rooms; contacts for television, film and radio, as well as stage; scenery makers, and even vintage vehicle hire companies. It also contains the contact details for probably 80 per cent of the theatre companies in the UK, conveniently divided into categories. Although it is a photograph of a moving image, it is a really useful way of acquiring an overview of the UK's theatre companies.

Knowledge of the 'canon'

Of course, no one is going to consider a career as a director without some knowledge of the rich and wide range of extant plays from the Greeks to Harold Pinter. As was suggested above, as a director rather than a theatre lover it is surprising and stimulating to go to see theatre we might not have a natural taste for; and so it is worth mapping out our knowledge and ignorance of the main periods and places of the flowering of theatre, and to go sightseeing. First stop might not be single plays, but books which give an overview of the history of theatre, perhaps beginning with those which have the widest and broadest overview, such as Phyllis Hartnoll's *The Theatre: A Concise History*, which covers the most significant points in theatre history from Dionysus to the first half of the twentieth century; although this is now becoming dated, it offers a general overview of two millennia of theatre-making, with fullest detail on the nineteenth and twentieth centuries.

From there, it might be useful to read at least one Greek tragedy, a Roman comedy, a play by a contemporary of Shakespeare – and of course a play or two by Shakespeare himself – a Jacobean or Caroline play, a Restoration comedy, a play in the Italian *commedia dell'arte* tradition, a play by Molière and Racine, a play by Schiller and Goethe, a nineteenth-century melodrama, a play by Chekhov, Ibsen, Strindberg and Brecht. I have deliberately missed out Irish dramatists, from Congreve to Shaw, and the Spanish Golden Age, but this is my reading list – the essential exercise is getting to know the geography of what is regarded as the 'canon' – and then to map out an individual journey through that terrain. Books with the widest sweep are very good atlases: at least you know what you don't know.

Richard Eyre and Nicholas Wright's *Changing Stages* is a comprehensive, witty and wise account of the most significant plays, playwrights, directors and companies in English-speaking theatre in the twentieth century, and even contains a year-by-year list of the most influential plays and productions. From Harley Granville Barker to Sarah Kane, it is the most enjoyable and accessible to way to become familiar with the twentieth-century canon and influential theatre-makers.

Dominic Dromgoole's *The Full Room* provides pithy and irreverent sketches of over 100 playwrights active in the UK now and over the last fifty years to the mid-noughties. These two books are not about theory, they are about people, and they provide brilliant guides to our recent history and allow a director to navigate a personal journey through that history while having a sense of the broad movements in theatre-making.

There are also books which are 'readers' on directors: books which contain either short extracts from other publications or interviews with significant directors, such as *The Twentieth Century Performance Reader*, edited by Michael Huxley and Noel Witts, and *In Contact with the Gods?*, edited by Maria M. Delgado and Paul Heritage. These offer a quick insight into the work of directors such as Peter Brook, Ariane Mnouchkine, Peter Stein, Lev Dodin and Robert Lepage, allowing you quickly to build up an overview of directors considered to be of world significance.

Although they consist of authored chapters rather than interviews, Edward Braun's *The Director and the Stage* and Robert Leach's *Makers of Modern Theatre* offer a similar overview of the key European directors of the nineteenth and twentieth centuries, including figures such as Meyerhold, Gordon Craig, Artaud, Piscator and Brecht. The interview with Irving Wardle which follows in this chapter offers a genealogy of the UK theatre director from its nineteenth-century European roots.

As was mentioned at the outset, there are no easy or recognised pathways to becoming a theatre director, and the point at which you call yourself a theatre director is as much about aspiration and assertion as it is about credits on a CV, although at some point there is a need to create work with professional practitioners, and to invite professional practitioners to see it, in order to begin a sustained career as a professionally recognised director.

But it is also about developing an attitude to theatre as a theatre-maker: recognising just how hard it is to make theatre and that no piece of theatre was ever created in perfect conditions. It is a mental 180-degree change in point of view, by which you are no longer just an audience member but also the empathetic colleague of the people making the work. By being involved in the continuing dialogue around theatre-making and considering the real and changing contexts in which you see a single production, you will develop a much deeper relationship with the work and find new, practical sources of inspiration that help you define and refine your own work.

Interviews

Interview with Irving Wardle

Irving Wardle was chief theatre critic for The Times *newspaper for over thirty years. During this time he also interviewed numerous leading directors, writers and actors. He is the author of* The Theatres of George Devine, *published by Jonathan Cape in 1978, and of* Theatre Criticism, *published by Routledge in 1992. He is also the author of two plays:* The Houseboy, *produced at the Open Space Theatre in 1974, and* A Kurt Tucholsky Cabaret, *produced at the Arcola Theatre in 2010.*

Directing started with the birth of the modern theatre – and by the modern theatre I mean something quite specific. As I understand it, it means the mood of dissatisfaction with existing theatrical practice which spread across mainland Europe in the second half of the nineteenth century. Decline in religion was a factor. There was a widespread feeling among a lot of highly intelligent people for whom the theatre was an important part of civilised existence that somehow it had gone to the dogs. It just consisted of melodramas, extravaganzas, leg shows and plays about society which told lies in the last act, and altogether that something elemental like air or food had been stolen from the people and then resold back to them in a diluted or polluted form and that it was time to clear out the Augean Stables and make a space for something fresh to happen. In that time people who went to theatres became spectators or consumers, whereas in the past when you went to the theatre you went as a citizen or as a celebrant or as a worshipper and these have active and more useful roles in relation to what you're seeing, instead of filling in the time between supper time and bedtime, as Duke Theseus defines playgoing in *A Midsummer Night's Dream*.

So people like Otto Brahm, Jacques Copeau, Georg Fuchs, August Strindberg and André Antoine started clearing space for something new and what they thought more truthful to happen, almost always in a very small way but it was truthful because it had roots in the spirit of the time, and so it survived.

There are two sources that are worth mentioning here. Firstly, the influence of Greek theatre, which started looming large in the 1890s. There is a paradox in that theatre, which is perhaps the greatest invention of democracy, only functions successfully under a dictatorship – a director. The theatre usually functions most successfully when there's one guy running it. It needn't be the same guy: the trouble with the theatre they wanted to get rid of was that it was largely run by star actors who just wanted the attention on themselves and in a picturesque environment. So it wasn't so much a question of saying we want a democratic theatre, but we want a theatre which is not so much about the egocentric performer.

Naturalism was also becoming a strong influence in the theatre, as it already was in the novel. This started when the Duke of the small German Duchy of Saxe-Meiningen formed a troupe with his own money – he was an amateur, and what's important about amateurs is not that they are amateurs but that they are not compromised by the profession. The thing about working in the industry is that you become job-conscious and very nervous about making any serious changes in case your livelihood collapses. But if you're Duke Saxe-Meiningen in your nice pepperpot castle with tons of money, who cares if they don't like *Julius Caesar*? And so you make more of where that came from, which I think is the thing that enabled him to go ahead and do what he did, with the aid of a German director called Ludwig Chronegk. The Duke was also an amateur draughtsman and used to do lots of costume, architectural and choreographic drawings for the plays which were then translated beautifully into fabric, scenery canvas and bodies on the ground. Spectators who saw this were really astonished with the verisimilitude, not only of costume and environment, but also the minute choreography of the crowd scenes: everyone in the crowd was distinguished in great detail by trade and by particular mannerisms. Naturalism was associated with Darwinism, the idea being that your behaviour is affected by your environment, and on stage if you get the environment right that lessens the possibility of false representation of human behaviour and human feeling, because if you do something false in an environment which is correct it's more likely to look like a falsehood.

So the director appeared initially just to clear a space where the theatre could regain contact with its high name and civic function and maybe religious function; but in doing so, from a more negative point of view, the movement also gave birth to a monster, because the director was a very different sort of character from the nineteenth-century stage manager. This new figure of the director started doing things no one had ever heard of before with ensemble and spectacle; and as time went on his demands became more and more excessive. In Russia in the 1920s you find Meyerhold putting on Gogol's *The Government Inspector* and billing himself as the author because he regarded his creative input as being so much greater than Gogol's.

This movement was one which started on mainland Europe, and England was very slow to latch on to it. There were hopeful beginnings. William Poel started to look into the circumstances of Shakespearean and Elizabethan productions, and tried to produce historically accurate versions of Shakespeare down to the technique of verse speaking. Then there was Harley Granville Barker, who did in fact have continental links because he had contact with Jacques Copeau. Copeau came over and very much admired Barker's version of *Twelfth Night,* of which he produced his own version at the Vieux Colombier in Paris. Barker and Copeau had certain very important things in common, not least the idea of a continuous action, because Victorian and Edwardian productions of Shakespeare took up a long time because they were highly pictorial and elaborate. They also used to change the running order of scenes. So Barker started to revive respect for Shakespeare, and it took a long time actually to get respect of Shakespeare back, as he had been heavily rewritten: you had all these happy endings of what were meant to be tragedies.

Copeau was a professional critic and he developed a programme for what he wanted to do. His vision was of an ensemble company based on the idea that you had one continuous stage design which was minimally altered from one show to another; Georg Fuchs had much the same idea in Munich. They did some modern works, but mainly it was French and English classics which were staged with the idea of showing what a serious thing comedy is. Antagonists of the Vieux Colombier used to refer to them as Les Folies Calvin – the Calvinistic follies. Copeau became more and more dissatisfied with the existing audience: 'Why do the audience keep wanting entertainment when I'm doing something so serious?' So he left Paris, gave up the Vieux Colombier and went to ground in Burgundy and had all his talented actors there doing the equivalent of scales and arpeggios in preparation for a show that was never quite ready to be put on. The frustration amongst the company who had been accustomed to working in Paris was such that when Copeau's nephew Michel Saint-Denis turned up on the scene and said, 'Let's piss off and do some proper shows,' the company said, 'Yes, yes!' and out of this came Le Compagnie des Quinze, which became very influential among the cognoscenti. It was a great success and toured internationally, but put down its roots in England where it had a very considerable effect on acting and on theatre training. Saint-Denis had two schools here: one before the war, the London Theatre Studio in Beak Street; and one after the war, the Old Vic School, which trained a whole generation of talented theatre people, including Michael Elliott. Saint-Denis was a big figure who became very unpopular in England. The English had always been ready to welcome visiting geniuses as long as the visiting geniuses didn't stay too long. Theodore Komisarjevsky and Michael Chekhov were only around for a few years, but Michel Saint-Denis had the disconcerting habit of sticking around.

Theodore Komisarjevsky had run the Alexandrinsky Theatre in St Petersburg, which was where Chekhov's *The Seagull* was first produced. He wasn't here very long, but long enough to make a huge splash, partly in a little theatre in Barnes, London, where he introduced Chekhov in a big way, and had young actors like Alec Guinness, John Gielgud and Edith Evans. They did unheard-of things. In the first act of *The Seagull* they're sitting outside after Kostya's play has just flopped, he's flounced out and nobody quite knows what to say and they sit there, and it's Edith Evans's cue, and they sit there, and three minutes went by with nobody speaking – an unprecedented length of stage time – and eventually Edith Evans just shrugs her shoulders and says: 'It's getting a bit chilly, shall we go in?' and evidently the audience just sat there with tears streaming down their faces.

Partly this had to do with the use of the pause, which was a novelty in England. When Chekhov's nephew, Michael Chekhov, came to England he mainly taught at Dartington Hall, teaching people like Deborah Kerr and Paul Rodgers in the 1930s before he went to Hollywood. And he too was teaching unheard-of stuff: 'What happens if you pause before a speech?', 'What happens if you pause after a speech?', 'When does an expression turn into a grimace?', 'When does a grimace turn into a mask?', 'When is it legitimate to use a mask?', and 'How do you learn to fill a pause, so that it's not just an empty stretch of time but a space in which the audience's imagination is working all the way through?'

What Edith Evans must have felt to keep her going for three minutes is unimaginable. Komisarjevsky introduced all these things that Russian directors were doing: at one point he wanted a bit of colour so he got the local fire service involved, and had a big brass band – and he did the plays very fast and English viewers were outraged by this. They had to acknowledge the huge theatricality of it, but it wasn't at all the gentlemanly entertainment they were accustomed to, and he left a great big echoing vacuum when he went off to America.

Saint-Denis's educational venture was also the foundation of modern design, because there were these three clever girls: two sisters, Margaret (aka Percy) and Sophie Harris, and their pal Elizabeth Montgomery who started doing drawings of actors in costumes and launched themselves as costume designers, Motley Design, and they became Gielgud's regular designers. They did *Richard of Bordeaux* by Gordon Daviot, a huge hit in the 1930s that turned Gielgud into a star. After the war Saint-Denis came back from France and started the Old Vic School with Glen Byam Shaw and George Devine, and the Motleys, and this was very influential. It was a very cruel school in some ways because the theory was that you reduced the acting students to zero and then gradually built them up, but opinions are divided about this.

The reason for the Old Vic School's demise was largely Saint-Denis, who kept insisting on what he wanted to fulfil, which was the vision of his uncle Copeau, not only to have a functioning theatre and a school but also an experimental theatre of his own – a self-sufficient, autonomous unit which would train actors, put on its own shows and create its own work. Such was the mistrust of the governors towards this guy who was always talking about theory, always talking about style, that while the Old Vic company was in Australia, Lord Esher, the chairman, just fired the lot, including Laurence Olivier and Ralph Richardson, and torpedoed the entire Old Vic School, with the authority of Tyrone Guthrie, who was the leading director at the time. Saint-Denis went on to the Juilliard School afterwards.

By and large if you wanted to be a director at that time, you had to have money; you had to be someone like Barry Jackson, Frith Banbury or Terence Gray – the legacy of rich eccentrics to the English theatre is quite important. These were the class of people who elsewhere in Europe had produced Otto Brahm, Stanislavski and Saxe-Meiningen, but the rich

English eccentrics who went into theatre did not have talents on that scale. Tyrone Guthrie was one of the few who came through by being an actor. He was an extremely effective director. He was a great advocate of the open stage and was extremely influential in getting the stage built at Stratford, Ontario, and then the Guthrie Theatre in Minnesota. He was a perceptive director of lesser-known Shakespeare. One of the most exciting productions from that era that I can remember was Guthrie's *Troilus and Cressida*, then rarely staged but appropriate at the end of the war, and he portrayed the Trojans as impractical romantic Ruritanians and the Greeks as field-grey-uniformed ant-like combatants who had irresistible resemblances to Germans. He loved doing crowd scenes, he was good at that and good at what they call 'Guthrie-isms' because he would often resort to vulgaris-ing scenes in order to make them palatable. But if Guthrie, Terence Gray and Frith Banbury were the only English directors we had to show for it, we wouldn't be discussing English directing.

Next came the almost simultaneous arrival on the scene of arguably the two most talented directors of all we've discussed so far - Joan Littlewood and Peter Brook, who arrived at the end of the war. Littlewood arrived on the scene in 1945 and Brook in 1946, and the effect of this conjunction was not noted at the time, partly because Littlewood's debuts were Molière's *The Flying Doctor* and a piece called *Johnny Noble* which happened at the Keswick High School for Girls, without any input and money from anyone else, whereas Brook's production of *The Brothers Karamazov* happened at the Lyric Hammersmith under the wing of the leading producer H. M. Tennent and started with the discharging of a duelling pistol in a darkened theatre in which even the exit signs had been illegally blacked out.

Brook is the prototype of the non-acting director; we hadn't seen such a character before. He was a self-made director who, when he started at Oxford, had really wanted to make films, but he began, as so many Oxford directors have, with a production of Marlowe's *Faustus* and in this case typically he went to the top. He wanted an adviser on magic, so he went to Britain's number-one black magician, Aleister Crowley, otherwise known as the Great Beast, who supplied all sorts of effects and said: 'This would raise the devil even on a Saturday matinee', and Brook carried on from there. In his twenties he was installed in the West End. He got to be director of productions at the Royal Opera House, but he found he was in an institution that was more powerful then he was, so it didn't last very long – but long enough to engage Salvador Dali as a designer. He himself said he started with a box of tricks, with a little toy theatre in his attic, and I think that element remains – the box of tricks with which he can do absolutely amazing things that you don't even see coming.

Unlike these rather puritanical, 'let's get back to the high essence of theatre' characters, Brook had no compunction whatsoever about going straight into the fleshpots. He was in with the 'New Look' crowd with all the glamour of post-war England. He did a famous piece by Christopher Fry adapted from Anouilh called *Ring Around the Moon* which had designs by Cecil Beaton, the most fashionable designer at the time – it was like a fashion parade. Brook right from the start knew who he was and what he wanted to do – he could sup with the devil without becoming damned. He could go into the West End with leading West End managers, particularly with Binkie Beaumont who was regarded as horrifying by all the puritan types, and come out with his soul intact, to do something completely individual and not with commercial theatre afterwards. He could take advantage of the West End rather than being exploited by it.

The other side of him is the alertness he has to the times he's living in, like a barometer to political and social opinion. He saw the arrival of the Theatre of Cruelty, which took place under the aegis of Antonin Artaud. It was experimental theatre that directly reflected modern events in the world such as the full implications of the Holocaust and what had happened in Cambodia – taking in the full atrociousness of twentieth-century experience. The fact that the two absolutes, love for art and love for music, could co-exist with committing the most unspeakable crimes in your daily life was suddenly percolating the consciousness of people in this country. Brook's production of *Love's Labour's Lost*, which had entirely dropped out of the Shakespearean repertory, revealed it to be a wonderfully spontaneous, colourful, funny and yet death-haunted play. At a stroke it was recognised as one of the masterpieces, thanks to Brook. A few years later that's no longer in the air – he has his antennae up to what's in the air and so he gets to *Titus Andronicus*, for which he wrote the music himself. As always it contained things that he and Olivier, playing Titus, who was also a great magician, liked to put in just for the sake of pulling off a great stunt. There was one point where the Emperor says to Titus: 'Well, if you're in earnest about wanting to help me, just send me a sign of your allegiance by chopping off your left hand and sending it to me.' Olivier reads this, there's a blare of electronic music, he turns away and there's the unmistakable sound of an axe going through bone, he turns about and gives this hand to the messenger and tells him to take it off – it was a fantastic stunt, done with total realism. It had its own vocabulary of violence.

That was one extreme, the absolute direct naked violence, but then, when Titus's daughter is raped and has her tongue ripped out in the woods by Tamara's sons, what you had was the girl turning up with long strips of blood-coloured silk coming from her mouth, so that it was done almost in a Japanese style and in an elegant symbolic way as opposed to grotesque sick-making realism. So you had a kind of stylistic spectrum by which the atrocities of that play could stay interesting and it wouldn't be monotonous as if it was all on one realistic or one poetic level. It was a masterpiece. That was in 1955 and it foreshadowed where the theatre was going to be in another five or six years' time, under the shadow of Artaud and with an increased preoccupation with man's inhumanity to man. On the whole, in that period, Brook tends to work with classics, with the big exception of works he conjured into existence himself, like *US*. I don't know if you can call it a play at all – it was an approach to questions aroused by Vietnam, ranging from the re-enactment of atrocities to the response of the English to people a long way off. It was all written by different people, who hadn't a clue what the other ones had contributed. They all came in with their material and then Brook edited it into a final shape, often to the extreme anger and resentment of those who had contributed these different parts. So this is another example of the director who cannot write or doesn't write himself but conceives a work and conjures it into existence by engaging different artists to cover different aspects of the subject as he envisioned it. I loved it, but lots of people detested it, including some of the people who had written it. The English career of Brook effectively came to an end with the 1971 *A Midsummer Night's Dream* at Stratford, and after that he departed to Paris.

My first contact with Joan Littlewood was a piece called *Johnny Noble*. Written by Littlewood's long-time partner Ewan MacColl, it was about a merchant fleet during the war being tracked by a German U-boat. It was set on the deck and all there was on stage was a bit of rope, but what the very good lighting revealed – it was dark, happening at night – was a port light and a starboard light which were going up and down. Such was the rhythm you felt you were on a ship, almost seasick looking at it, and the feeling of being at sea was total. Then the bombardment started. They had a Bofors gun on the deck and they were firing through darkness at the unseen Germans. At that point you saw what was happening, because it was light enough to see that it wasn't metal, it was people – four actors. That was a big night out for me at the age of fifteen.

But that was already quite a way through Littlewood's career. Born in 1914, she went to RADA briefly, then in the late thirties she heard that the German expressionist playwright Ernst Toller had gone into exile and was working at the Rusholme Rep near Manchester. So she left RADA and walked to Manchester, not realising that the German pioneer in dance notation, Rudolf Laban, was also there, and she found that, unlike London, around Manchester it was a very politicised area because it was in the middle of a textiles strike – you couldn't go on a factory site without finding two Poles in top hats entertaining the workers, with advanced expressionist avant-garde agit-prop techniques. Then she came into contact with an outfit called the Red Megaphones, an agit-prop outfit run by Mr Miller and his son, Jimmie (aka Ewan MacColl). They were playing to the workers and Littlewood teamed up with them. They said they were fired by two things at that time, which were depression politics and the hunger for information. The Red Megaphones morphed into Theatre Union and they were either rehearsing breathing techniques, and Laban and Piscator and Meyerhold's biomechanical exercises, or they were out trying to get the cheapest possible food from local markets. Then they morphed again into Theatre Action, by which time they left agit-prop behind, because, as Ewan MacColl said, 'We can't presume to tell the workers anything, unless we can do it with the same skill as a girl working a Jacquard loom.'

In other words they didn't underestimate the skills of the people they were talking to. So their repertory then changed, into one that either consisted of works by MacColl or classics by the world's greatest people's dramatists, like Molière, Aristophanes and Lope de Vega, which formed the core repertory of what became Theatre Workshop. But when they moved to the Theatre Royal, Stratford East, Ewan MacColl saw them as having taken the 'bourgeois' option of bricks and mortar, and he split off and pursued the rest of his career as a folk singer. Most of the actors were living in the theatre, they had no money and they were changing the bill every fortnight or so. Their way of rehearsing, according to people I've talked to, was orthodox Stanislavski, which is interesting in the way it shows that agit-prop was not everything for Littlewood. The difference was that the rehearsal began with action and the text followed, and the settings were determined by the shapes which the actors' bodies made, so that instead of having a model brought in by a designer which the actors then had to fit themselves into, the shapes they made in rehearsal would become the matrix from which the designer, usually John Bury, would contract the set. He was almost always more a builder than a designer; it was usually something architectural.

We're now coming to the great playwriting revolution, when England started finding new writers, the way it hadn't done for a long time. Littlewood participated in this first of all with the discovery of Brendan Behan, somebody who'd actually been in jail, who'd been in prison for IRA activities, who first wrote *The Quare Fellow*. This was a very good text, the like of which hadn't been seen on the English stage before; it was about the reality of prison life before an execution. Behan followed this up with *The Hostage* which was again brilliant and became a commercial hit.

Then Shelagh Delaney wrote *A Taste of Honey*, and Lionel Bart's *Fings Ain't Wot They Used T'be* was a Cockney knees up about fun in the East End, but success brought downfall – Littlewood suddenly felt she hadn't got a company any longer because all her best actors were playing to an audience she really despised up in the West End. The new actors she was engaging were not real actors at all; they'd never done Muller breathing exercises, they knew nothing about units and objectives – they knew about East End life and that was it. All the traditional discipline of the theatre had gone to hell, and it was just turning into a fun palace. The whole tragic irony I think is that she started off from exactly the opposite position to Brook. He had no fixed political position, but was alert to the currents in the air, night, darkness, magic and respect for the West End audience. Littlewood stood for a fixed political position and the open air, never night time, and character development from social circumstances rather than individual psychology, so they were absolute opposites.

By the end of her life, she'd done all the right things: she'd tried to build a new audience from people who didn't go to the theatre, whereas Brook was working for an existing audience. She was working for an imagined, ideal audience, and although she'd done all the right things she'd delivered herself straight into the mouth of the commercial dragon. She'd worked through a stage when her actors were highly disciplined, then entertainers, then clowns, and then just anybody having fun, so in the end there wasn't really a theatre there at all. It went up like a puff of smoke and she disappeared from the scene to the south of France, never to direct another show. From the outside it was the spectacle of the system taking its toll and also a parable about what happens to directors who want to develop a new audience. It's this strange thing: the more you do work about the starving of the world the greater the bourgeois audience, the more you despise the bourgeois audience the more they come along and ask for more. As Dario Fo says: 'The bourgeois audience loves being spanked.'

The English Stage Company at the Royal Court Theatre was formed in 1956 under the artistic direction of George Devine, and that was the dawn of a writer's theatre. What's not so often heralded when people talk about this famous date is that it saw the arrival of some really remarkable new directors whose main aims were not immediately apparent because they did something which is very uncharacteristic for directors – they subdued their talents for those of the playwrights, in a theatre devoted to new writing – a practically unheard-of thing in English theatre history. Devine, who is a difficult person to pin down, is certainly very clear cut in that situation – the writer leads, the writer comes first. When anything was coming on it was always 'the new Osborne', 'the new Jellicoe'. He collected directors mainly from Oxford. The Royal Court was almost entirely Oxford in its directorate, while the Royal Shakespeare Company was almost entirely Cambridge. The remarkable thing was that Devine was a veteran who had gone through the London Theatre Studio and Old Vic School and now was hoping that having got command of this writer's theatre that he would bring some of the Saint-Denis message into genuine day-to-day theatrical experience in London.

Then he appointed Tony Richardson, who was about a third his age – just down from Oxford, and without much experience – not as his assistant director but as his associate, and Tony Richardson loathed and detested everything Saint-Denis stood for. So it seemed like an absolutely impossible partnership. They had this room full of assistant directors, all very young, all very ambitious and all faced with the task of subduing their ravenous ambition to the ravenous ambition of the playwrights – none of whom was more ravenous of course than John Osborne. He promptly paired up with Tony Richardson, William Gaskill with John Arden, John Dexter with Arnold Wesker, and a little later on Lindsay Anderson with David Storey. This is a very unusual thing, because if you think about the history of direction, whatever directors have said they've always sorted it out so that they're on top, usually specialising in old plays with an author who can't answer back.

Laurence Oliver had formed an attachment to the Court, partly because he was very alert to the way theatre was going and realised that the old star system was on the way out and that new writing was what was going to bring audiences in. So he migrated to the Court and had one of his greatest successes in Osborne's *The Entertainer*, directed by Richardson. When he took over the National Theatre he purloined two of the Court's best directors, William Gaskill and John Dexter. These were not heroic figures but they were very interesting and talented people and very contrasting. One thing they had in common was their ability to act as midwives to playwrights: Gaskill in the case of Barry Keeffe and Dexter in the case of Wesker and Peter Shaffer. Otherwise they were very different characters.

Gaskill came from Shipley in Yorkshire, from a family of teachers, and he had a very Socratic method of teaching but at the same time there was the showman in him which took over in the last stages of rehearsals. So instead of asking questions he supplied the tempo and the orders. He was also highly political; you can read through the lives of some directors and see a sort of concealed biography through what they did, and if you look at what Gaskill did, from his early work with John Arden through his work with Brecht and Pirandello, you can see someone looking for a political position on which he can take a stand. Politics in the Royal Court is a subject in itself and people used to refer to it as a 'kitchen sink' theatre or a 'left-wing' theatre, but you never ever managed to get a policy statement out of the Royal Court, partly I think because of its lineage through France. Devine was running it, as a devotee of Saint-Denis, and so of Copeau, who would never ever write a manifesto, saying that to declare that your aim was a left-wing theatre of the people was a death knell: stay quiet and you might achieve it, state it through a manifesto and you certainly won't. Trying to work out the policy of the Royal Court is like trying to scrape custard off the wall: it's in the left-wing good-chap ethos with varying degrees of stringency and Calvinism. Nobody summed it up better than Gaskill: I said, 'What is the policy?' and he said, 'Policy just means the people you're working with.'

Gaskill was one of the few directors of that period who still clung to the idea that it was possible to have such a thing as a democratic theatre, and when he ceased to be a figurehead at the Royal Court, he set up a company called Joint Stock with Max Stafford-Clark, which they did to achieve a democratic set-up, in the sense that they would work in a similar way to Brook in *US*. They would decide on a subject to be investigated, for example, the Levellers in the seventeenth century, extending a newspaper story beyond its normal duration. The technique would be to engage the company to go out and research this, create characters, create storylines, come back, hand the material over to a writer to write it and then take away the character that each member of the group had investigated for themselves and give it to another member of the group so that they wouldn't have the feeling of possessing the character. It produced some interesting results, but it still left the director in the position of the editor, so it wasn't democratic in the sense of some of the extreme would-be German democratic theatres like Peter Stein's, where everyone including the cleaner would have a casting decision.

Gaskill also produced some extraordinarily effective little-known old plays. His revival of Farquhar's *The Recruiting Officer* was one of the great events at the National Theatre, likewise his revival of Granville Barker's *The Voysey Inheritance* and *The Madras House*. Gaskill took them and looked at them microscopically and realised just how alive their theatre language was: he found what the music was in the language and brought it back to life. He had a wonderful ear for what will come to life in terms of rhythm and language and appearance on stage. He also backed the writer Edward Bond, and said: 'He knows what he's doing. And if you follow exactly the stage directions it will work.'

Gaskill completely abdicated himself and did exactly what the stage directions said, and it had an extraordinary vitality. Gaskill also has a belief in real theatrical basics: doors, traps, ropes – the physical, traditional equipment of a playhouse. He is not at all interested in what Macbeth thinks: 'I'm interested only in what he does.' He had one foot in the French camp, and also learnt an awful lot from Brecht.

Dexter was another playwright's midwife. Dexter's immediate strength was a Guthrie-like ability to organise and arrange crowds. He was also a hugely precise textual specialist. Perhaps because he hadn't been to a university he used to ransack every text until he knew every footnote backwards, and he had the ability to see what was deficient, what was lacking or how something could be restructured. He has this well-known line when Wesker in rehearsals was questioning something he was doing: 'If you don't shut up, I'll direct this play as you've written it.' He was the opposite to Gaskill in that sense. Dexter succeeded by saying to writers they'd forgotten what their own objective is. He was another liberator.

These guys are worth mentioning partly because of what they did and partly because of what they saw. Even if it didn't always come off, they had an idea of what could be. They could look at a text and say that you've not really fulfilled the potential of this script, or they could look at an old text and say, well, nobody's ever looked at cousin Ferdinand in *The Taming of the Shrew* before: it's not just a question of being faithful to the text, it's a question of being faithful to what the text could be.

Peter Gill was also a non-university candidate who turned up wild from Wales as a young playwright and director and the big thing he contributed to the Court tradition was the revival of naturalism. He did productions of his own work, things like *Small Change*, which were very beautiful, but their range was tiny. What really gave his plays the amplifying power they later had was his discovery of the plays of D. H. Lawrence, which had almost completely dropped out of sight. Peter Gill did a production of Lawrence's first play, *A Collier's Friday Night*, and showed how spellbindingly theatrical 'work plays' could be. These plays were written with a kind of authenticity to working-class life, not at all based on what workers were like at second hand, which is what most plays were like when they brought on working-class characters. They were based on ideas of how such characters talked. When Shaw, Pinero, Galsworthy, bring on working-class characters they've got all these clichés which are worlds away from what their actual speech is like. In Lawrence it's the authentic speech, the authentic action. I remember the excitement of seeing that collier come in covered in pit dirt and being stripped off and given a bath in the kitchen. It was absolutely electrifying and you thought, well (a) this is a great writer, and (b) this is what naturalism is for. It continued most successfully in *The Daughter-in-Law*. It had consequences particularly on that same stage when later people like David Storey started writing work plays. And in Wesker's *Four Seasons* the play came to a stop while someone demonstrated how to make an apple strudel – mesmerising.

The overwhelming figure of Peter Hall commands the history of the RSC. He arrived on the scene as a Cambridge undergraduate with a long list of plays he wanted to direct, and neglected all his academic work in order to put productions on and made friendships with people like Corin Redgrave and John Barton. One thing about Cambridge is that it had a two-pronged influence on people who wanted to direct: (a) it contained the figure of George (aka Dadie) Rylands, who was a theatrical don who had links with the West End theatre, and who had directed Gielgud in *The Duchess of Malfi*; and (b) the critical guru F. R. Leavis, who had a huge influence in terms of discrimination – what was important, what was 'significant'. In Leavis's special language 'significant' means that it's got some kind of moral fire power that's going to assist you in your life choices.

The Cambridge English school regarded itself as having 'rigour' – a special Cambridge word which has to do in part with Leavis. They regarded themselves as vastly superior to Oxford English practice at the Royal Court, which is fuzzy and soft round the edges. Rigour is achieved partly when doing a production by Shakespeare by counting the images, or even more by counting every single word and then doing a bit of mathematical calculation and thus arriving at what the play is 'about'. For example, John Barton did a production of *Troilus and Cressida* the main image of which turned out to be instability. So they set it in a sandpit. Hall himself had the Leavis experience, arrived in the West End, set up his own company and started to go through his list. Then he got appointed to be Alex Clunes's deputy at the Arts Theatre. Clunes said have a look at this, you might like it – turned out to be *Waiting for Godot*. Hall had never heard of Beckett, didn't understand the play, but thought it sounded quite interesting, put it on and it made him. Beckett came and said: 'It's not boring enough.'

The next thing that happened was that he got invited in his early twenties, only slightly older than Peter Brook, to be director of the Shakespeare Memorial Theatre. He told the Chairman, Fordham Flower, that they had a very nice little theatre company, and a guaranteed audience in tourists who want to see Shakespeare and Shakespeare's birthplace, and if they carried on as they were it would be absolutely stone dead because they were insulated from any theatrical development that was happening anywhere else – and he proposed that they take a London base where they would run a repertory of new plays whilst continuing to play Shakespeare and his contemporaries in Stratford. In addition, they would switch acting companies so that the classical company would add tradition and structure to the modern world, and the modern world would come in and refresh classic texts. Amazingly Fordham Flower swallowed this and they took over the Aldwych theatre and quite soon the governors' coffers were empty.

You might ask what role the new theatre had, as the Royal Court was already there putting on new plays. The answer was that the RSC London base would be there to gather up the slack of the post-war continental repertory. People like Beckett, Frisch and Dürrenmatt, who hadn't really got a hold on the English stage but whose work nevertheless was very good and relevant to the English experience. Hall was in his element and in financial direction he was very canny indeed. He deliberately spent all the money in order to put the squeeze on the Arts Council, who were then giving peanuts to the theatre, and got them to start giving out considerable sums of money. They'd started doing this in a small way for the Royal Court, but Devine was always a very careful budgeter and allowed himself to be constrained. Hall didn't. He said that thanks to the Court, thanks to the RSC, the theatre has been kicked into the centre of English cultural life – a position it hadn't occupied in three hundred years, and if the Arts Council let them die, it would create an enormous stink and bring the Council into disrepute and disgrace. So he started getting serious amounts of money, which also started coming to other parts of the theatrical scene, and to local municipalities who started to build new theatres, which spread all over the country.

It all started with the Court and the RSC, and thanks to this new breed – directors – theatre was coming to occupy a central position in the cultural landscape.

Interview with Walter Meierjohann

*Between 1995 and 1999 Walter Meierjohann studied directing at the
renowned Ernst Busch School of Dramatic Art in Berlin and spent a year at
St Hugh's College, Oxford. He works both in Germany and the UK. In
Germany, his productions include: Kleist's The Broken Jug, Schiller's Mary
Stuart, Miller's Death of a Salesman, Plath's The Bell Jar and devised
commissions in the Sophiensäle and the Maxim Gorki Theatre in Berlin.
In 2002 he was asked by Peter Stein to direct Thorton Wilder's A Long
Christmas Dinner with Stein's Ensemble in Berlin, and in the same year he
was nominated for a festival award for his production of Les Justes by
Camus. From 2004 to 2005 Walter was Artistic Director of Neubau, the
contemporary international line of the State Theatre of Dresden. Since
then he has worked on more than ten productions in Dresden, including
O'Neill's Long Day's Journey into Night; Adams's People Next Door; and
Paravidino's Genova 01. His production of Inkheart by Cornelia Funke
brought the 1,000-seat State Theatre of Dresden the best audience figures
of the last fifteen years.*

*In 2007 Walter joined the Young Vic as International Associate Director. In
autumn 2008 he directed the European premiere of In the Red and Brown
Water by Tarell Alvin McCraney on the main stage of the Young Vic and in
spring 2009 Kafka's Monkey, a new adaptation of Franz Kafka's Report to
an Academy, starring award-winning actress Kathryn Hunter. After a very
successful run in London, the production toured to Sydney, Melbourne,
Athens, and the Théâtre des Bouffes du Nord in Paris. In 2011 and 2012,
Kafka's Monkey will tour to Tokyo and New York. Most recently, Walter has
written and directed a short film, Dear Anna, which will premiere at the
Edinburgh Film Festival in 2011.*

I studied theatre directing in the middle of the 1990s in East Berlin at the
state school – the German equivalent of RADA. It was a four-year degree
and it was heavily based on a mixture of Stanislavski and Brecht. We
learnt a lot by working with professional actors. I then finished my degree
in 1999 and did my final production, *Baal*, in training as a professional
director in a small theatre in East Germany. I was given another production,
Les Justes by Albert Camus, and that was suddenly invited to a fringe
festival called Impulse: they invite the best ten fringe theatre shows from
around the country to the festival. That in a way proved my breakthrough,

and suddenly I was invited to work by lots of theatres. I directed Thornton Wilder's *The Long Christmas Dinner* for Peter Stein's Faust company in Berlin, and through Stein I met the director Klaus-Michael Grueber. He was called a magician and he really was a theatre magician, and I was fortunate enough to assist him twice on operas. I might have learnt more watching him rehearse than in four years' training.

In 2004 I was invited to the State Theatre in Dresden to direct a piece of contemporary writing, and then six months later the artistic director offered me the post of Artistic Director within his company. So within the big state theatre I was running the company for contemporary writing, which was called Neubau. After that I remained Associate Director in Dresden; for three years I was very privileged to be offered two guaranteed productions a year and I could therefore decide to live somewhere else for part of the time. That had to be London as my wife is English. After a while, while still mainly working in Germany, I wrote to theatres in London, and David Lan, the Artistic Director of the Young Vic, met me, and saw a show I did near Hamburg. He liked it and said, 'Would you like to join us?' So I've been an associate at the Young Vic since 2007.

Who are your heroes? Because they might be very different from a British director's heroes . . .

Probably people no one's heard of here. I think that Klaus-Michael Grueber was my biggest hero. He was the assistant of Giorgio Strehler in Milan. And Strehler was a big fan of Brecht, but in an Italian way. Grueber brought Brecht back to Germany in a very playful way – not the heavy intellectual German way, but a very sensual, Italian way. In the 1990s, when I was studying, the Volksbühne in Berlin became a temple for me. One of the directors working there was Christoph Marthaler. He's Swiss, and actually a musician. It was avant-garde devised work: he doesn't use much language, he used singing. His pieces were extraordinarily funny and extraordinarily slow – everything in life is becoming faster so he slowed everything down. He invented slowness on stage. It was like watching Jaques Tati's films but on stage. It's what you would expect from fringe theatre, but this was the Volksbühne, which seats about a thousand people, and it was packed.

And then I saw Frank Castorf who was the wildest theatre anarchist: it was vulgar, it was crude but it was beautiful. It's not my style but I always went there just to watch things that I could never come up with. I prefer the subtleties and the acting basics, but to watch his work was like going to a modern gallery and feeling this is 'now'. Sometimes I see shows and feel, 'Well, they're not "now", they're 1950s.' What I loved about these two directors, radical masters of anti-naturalistic theatre, was that they were really describing the 'now' but in very different ways: they were huge inspirations for me.

In Germany at that time were there any English-speaking directors or playwrights that you knew about?

In the 1990s Simon McBurney came over and did *The Caucasian Chalk Circle* and that blew me away – for me that was avant garde but with a heart. Also in the 1990s Thomas Ostermeier was running the Baracke, which was a small theatre where many of the plays were actually coming from the Royal Court. Within one or two years it was all Mark Ravenhill and Sarah Kane. I think they became bigger in Germany than here. More recently, the work of writers like Simon Stephens has been seen a lot in Germany. The idea of new writing came from Britain and suddenly the path of new German writers like Marius von Mayenburg was made possible because of the new English writers.

You've now worked with a wide range of English and German directors and actors. Can you identify any main differences in the way that English and German directors and actors work and think? I know there's a danger of generalising, but there must be some fundamental differences.

There are differences. The main difference is that the role of the director in Germany is much more the role of the *auteur*. The actors look at you and expect you to do something radical with the text. Here in England, I feel everyone looks to the writer and explores the play very fondly and very carefully, looking at the words. And that I would describe as like old-school theatre in Germany. Old actors still have this huge respect for writers; young directors in Germany don't care who's written it – they just want to do something with it.

I always feel like I'm stuck between the different ways of working here and in Germany. Here, I sometimes go to rehearsal spaces and I see all these biographies of the characters, all written on the wall. And I think, 'Why is everybody doing the same thing? Why is everyone drawing this backstory on the wall? How do they know this is the backstory?' So, the whole exploration of the piece, which is a very intellectual one, almost academic, is not being done in Germany. I sometimes find here that it's a bit frightening that everyone gets used to the idea of sitting around tables and just discussing the play – it can be wonderful, but it prolongs the time before actually doing something. In Germany the actors are expected to do that work themselves, and not the director.

I think the difference is that the director in this country wants to be on the same level as the actors: to be collaborative. In Germany, the director wants to create a myth around themselves a little bit. You would do all the research for the production with a set designer, and then go into rehearsals and start working from day one on your feet, and not sit around for a week. And another difference is that, with the set designer, you will have already established a sort of concept, which the actors will become part of, so you are always just one step ahead. You don't start at the same level. This can go as far as the costumes being ready on day one of rehearsals: so the actors are asked to fulfil your conceptual view.

Literally fit into the costumes that have been made for them?

Exactly, and I find that wrong. I don't believe in this whole German conceptual theatre: I find it too extreme, too intellectual, and I want to be moved, so I believe in collaboration with the actor. But on the other hand, when I see a piece in Britain I sometimes think, 'Why did they need a director? What is the role of the director? And could the director and designer not be more visionary?' As I said, perhaps I'm stuck in between these two worlds.

You talked about your own training being a combination of Stanislavski and Brecht. Do you think actors in Germany have a different skills base, or working method, than they have here?

Absolutely. When I first worked here I was a bit shocked by the lack of technique, as I would call it. And I think the actors I worked with here were shocked by the lack of psychological exploration. What I mean by technique is that an actor should be able to look at himself from the outside, not just ride on an emotional wave and move themselves to tears. You can actually think from the outside as a character and say, 'I can see myself like a director a little bit.'

That's what German actors are trained to do. It's the Brechtian influence, saying to actors, 'Actually you are not the character, but you are an actor who is going to play this character.' You always have the tool of distancing yourself from the character; but what I don't like about German actors is that they do that to perfection. And it really bores me because it's very safe; they're quite ironic and distanced with what they are doing. English actors, I sometimes feel, lack a bit of a distance to their role. However, if you then look at great actors, or actually Shakespearean acting, it's very Brechtian: you don't have to feel it emotionally the whole time, but you're steering your character, like a puppet. And great, older actors in this country are also doing that, so I'm sometimes amazed that the younger generation doesn't do that instead of trying to be one hundred per cent the role.

That's why I think our method of trying to link Brecht with Stanislavski is not a bad one. Of course I want a full character, and I want to be moved as an audience member, and I want an actor to really explore the whole character, but it also means looking at the character from the outside as well. Sometimes I have rehearsals here where I start on day one with a run-through and the actors say, 'What are you doing?' Or after day two, I say, 'I need high shoes for this character.' And the actor will say, 'Why?' and I say, 'Well, actually, you might find the character through this technical detail of just having her in high heels.' We were taught that these details are so important: by working, for example, from day two in high heels, without exploring the insecurities of the character, you might actually find the psychological depth of that character. And that's very Brechtian: theatre is about the inner world but it's also about observing something from the outside.

I said that English actors lack technique – on the other hand they do move me a lot, and German actors don't move me so much, so I'm quite critical of German actors as well.

What about German and British designers? Have you've worked with British designers as well as German designers?

I've worked only with German designers but I have worked with an English lighting designer. I tend to ask for German designers because I strongly believe the biggest strength of German theatre is design. I have this dream of having English actors and German set designers, to link these two worlds – of German aesthetics with actors who can be full characters and actually move you. I've worked with a lighting designer here twice – Mike Gunning. It was fascinating, watching him – how he was not saying, 'I'm going to use this light.' He was talking so much about the story and the characters, and I was amazed about his psychological approach – telling the story through light. I found that remarkable because I wouldn't find a German lighting designer who could talk so much about the dramaturgy and the characters. I realised that the detail in his lighting comes from an understanding of the story and not just from a technical understanding of how to light the show beautifully.

Talking of dramaturgy, what is the function of a dramaturg in Germany?

When I am preparing for a production I would have a dialogue partner in the dramaturg: we would work on and edit the script together, and it is very useful to have a dialogue going right from the beginning, not just between the designer and you. Then he or she would come into rehearsals once a week and give you notes. If you work together for the first time you can get quite paranoid because they normally don't say much, but it's very useful if you have a dramaturg you can work with well. They are considered to be the guardians of the text, and they normally have studied Theatre Science, German Literature and Philosophy – that's the classic profile. Directors are considered to be much more visual, and people who do practical things with the text, and dramaturgs are considered to be quite literary and more distant.

They also programme the theatre with the artistic director through weekly meetings. In Germany the programme is announced a year in advance. Dresden has five full-time dramaturgs, but Dresden is a very big theatre, with forty-four resident ensemble actors and 400 permanently employed people. The dramaturgs come up with the arc of the whole season and then they choose the directors for the productions. If, as a freelance director, you say, 'What about this new writer?' they would say, 'Sorry, but that's my job.'

They also have a psychological role to play. When actors are absolutely in tears, because rehearsals aren't going well, or because they hate the director, they would phone the dramaturg at three o'clock in the morning and say, 'Oh, please – I don't know what to do!' So they are almost the psychotherapist of the theatre. I very much like working with good dramaturgs, but I'm also quite critical of their role as they have more and more power now in German theatres: it's becoming a dramaturg's theatre.

Interview with Clare Shucksmith

Clare Shucksmith is a theatre-maker and creative producer who founded 2headedpigeon Theatre Company in 2003. The company is now resident at the Firestation Centre for Arts and Culture in Windsor. Their award-winning theatre has received five-star reviews at the Brighton and Edinburgh fringe festivals. The company have been described as 'a terrific young group' by the Guardian.

After graduating from East 15 Acting School she studied creative producing at Birkbeck College. Alongside her work on the fringe, Clare currently runs a children's theatre company and works with young people. I asked her about taking productions to the Edinburgh Festival.

The first show I took to Edinburgh was in 2004, for just one week, which is probably a good way of trying the fringe for the first time. We went in 2006, took two shows in 2008, and went again in 2009 and 2010.

What are the first steps and the planning cycle in taking a show?

The deadline for registration with the fringe festival is in the middle of April, because that's the deadline for the festival programme. Entry to the fringe costs just under £400. There is a discount registration deadline, which is at the end of March, and costs £300.

And that's just the cost of registering for the festival?

Yes, it's the cost of being in the festival programme and receiving all the support and information from the fringe office.

You could still choose to go up to Edinburgh if you miss this deadline, but you won't be in the fringe programme. Personally, I wouldn't do this, as I think you would struggle to get an audience without being in the programme. You could still give people flyers in the street, but nobody will be able to find you in the programme, which is the main way people choose what to see. In order to register in April you must have all the information that you need to make an entry into the fringe programme: you need to know your venue, your time slot and your ticket prices. If you have no existing relationship with a venue I would start contacting them promptly in the New Year; however, at that point they often say, 'We haven't opened our applications yet, but when we do you're welcome to submit one.' It's worth politely badgering a venue if you really want to perform there; often I have made four or five contacts before they will confirm a slot. Be careful not to nag, though – try to find positive ways of keeping in touch with them, such as asking for some advice on what information they will need when you apply. So it's not just a case of sending in your application and waiting, because the bigger venues will choose between hundreds of applications every year. The level of competition depends on the popularity of the time slot and the venue.

If you have enough money to pay for a top slot in a top venue your choices will be more open, but if you don't it really helps to be specific about the type of venue and the time slot you want before you search for your venue. For example, last year we knew that we wanted to be in a very student-friendly venue in the centre of town, in a late-night slot; and it had to be under a hundred seats because we couldn't afford a bigger venue and we didn't think we'd fill a larger space.

Is there a fringe website where you can find out about the different venues: their locations, sizes, hire prices and so on?

Yes, you go to www.edfringe.com which is the Edinburgh fringe website, and register as a participating company. You can then find all the information you need about each venue and download information packs on how to approach venues, on marketing, and other useful information.

How much did your venue cost last year?

There are three types of deal at the fringe. The usual deal is a box-office split with a guarantee. So, firstly you have to pay an upfront guarantee, or deposit: usually this is paid in instalments between April and July. The venue also specifies a percentage of the box office to which they are entitled. After the end of the fringe, they would take whichever amount was greater. So, for example, they may offer you a deal where the guarantee is £1,500, with a 60 per cent to 40 per cent split in your favour. You would have to pay £1,500 before the festival began, in instalments. At the end of the festival, the venue would calculate what a 40 per cent share of the box-office takings was, and keep the larger of the two amounts.

However, some venues may offer a straight split, in which case you don't need to put down a guarantee – they just agree to take a percentage. Others may ask for a flat fee paid upfront, which is more expensive and risky. We've been in flat-fee venues in the past where we didn't have good experiences because they didn't have any incentive to sell tickets. I would be extremely wary about going into a flat-fee arrangement unless you know the venue well. The Bedlam Theatre, where we went last year, was a flat-fee deal: it was more expensive initially but it was the right venue for the show. It does mean that you then take all of the box-office takings, minus any additional charges. We felt that since we knew the venue well and trusted them it wasn't unwise.

Have you signed a contract with the venue, prior to the deadline, in order to be in the fringe programme?

Yes. The contract would be signed and sealed, although it often happens quite close to the deadline, as the venues and companies wrangle and settle the deals. In fact, if you don't have a lot of money and you're willing to sail close to the wind, you can wait until quite close to the April deadline and hope to bag a last-minute slot where another deal has fallen through. This can happen because some companies will get two or three offers from venues and try to haggle to bring the prices down; inevitably venues can find there's an empty slot – in 2009 we got a very good deal that way (around half the normal guarantee for the slot, and a 70 per cent to 30 per cent split), but you have to be flexible about the venue and time slot – and realise you may end up without a venue at all!

It depends what your objective is: if you just want to get a show on to get it seen by critics and audiences and your costs are low, or you don't need to fill the venue, being flexible about the venue and time slot might be fine; if you have to make a certain amount of money to cover your costs, and so need to maximise your audience, you need to be more careful about the venue and the slot.

Once you're in the programme is there much to do apart from preparing the production?

If, like many people, you send your information in to the programme close to the deadline, you soon get sent proofs to check, quickly followed by many publicity requests from your venue and from the fringe office itself, so there's quite a lot of administration. June and July will be busy, because as well as making and rehearsing the production you may have to organise accommodation and travel for the cast and crew; book transport for the set; arrange the design and printing of your own publicity material; and then send it to the right places to be distributed. In addition, you may wish to have some previews of the show, perhaps in mid-July, not only to try it out in front of an audience, but also to make sure you have thought through the show organisationally and technically, particularly if it is your first fringe visit. So there is a fairly constant amount of work and planning, and all of these elements will have to be paid for in advance of you taking any money, so budgeting and cashflow are really important.

Are there particular shows that suit certain venues and time slots?

Time is the really important thing in Edinburgh, and the day is very much split up into different times for different types of work. It is difficult – but not impossible – to buck the trend.

It is hard to sell tickets for a show until noon unless it's children's theatre. There are a lot of children at the fringe and families are a massive part of the market – good-quality family shows can be quite profitable, unlike most types of show! Particularly well attended are adaptations of well-known children's books or writers.

From noon until about four o'clock tends to be quite a cheap time slot, so if you don't have much money or it is your first time at the fringe, this can be a good time. It tends to be an older audience who are looking for shows to see at this time – since the comedy clubs are open until 4 a.m., the student crowd are still getting up at noon! This time is also the prime time for flyering on the Royal Mile, so other performers (who make up a lot of the fringe audience) are busy. If the play or the writer is well-known, or you get some great reviews, you can still get a good-sized crowd.

From about four till eight or eight thirty is prime theatre time. Obviously, traditional theatre starts at seven, seven thirty or eight o'clock and so those slots are very expensive.

Past that time, the slots are suited for sketch comedy, stand-up, music, cabaret, or something that's attention-grabbing and robust – be prepared to play to a crowd who have had a drink or two. We looked for a very late slot for our show because it's a late-night kind of a show – it's very cheeky and it's very rude.

When you book your slot, how much time do you actually book, because you have to get your show in and out of the space each day?

Yes, you need to hire enough time to cover the length of your show plus however long you need for a get-in and a get-out. You negotiate that with the venue and it is included in the contract. Different venues have different policies: one venue only gives ten minutes to get in and ten minutes at the other end to get out, and that includes the audience entering and exiting the space. Fifteen minutes, including audience entering and exiting, is not unusual. For example, if you need to rig special lanterns in the lighting rig, or you need to do a sound check because you've got live music, you may have to pay more for your slot to extend it.

Does the venue give you storage space for your set?

Yes, but you need to discuss this carefully with the venue in advance so that you can plan how you build and store your set, props and other equipment. For example, last year the venue told us that we had a storage space of a metre square, but we could stack it as high as we liked: it just meant that we made sure that we brought lots of plastic boxes that would stack high. So the storage space has enormous implications in terms of your design.

Does the venue provide any in-house staff such as a sound and light operator or do you have to staff it yourself?

The venue's technical manager will usually oversee all the auditoria and the venue but you would be expected to bring your own operator – and there is usually a clause in the contract stipulating that the technical manager has to be happy that the operator is competent. Usually there's a standard lighting rig – a good fringe venue will ask for your tech plans in advance and they will design a general rig that covers all the shows, and then inform you if you need to rig any specials each time. It can be quite expensive finding a technical person for your show, and the venue will charge you extra if you need them to provide an operator, so if you know any friendly technical people you should charm them for the year before you go. We have always had one technical person on the show.

So does that mean that the actors are usually involved in actually getting the set up and getting the show in?

It may not always be the case, but in a typical fringe theatre set-up everyone takes responsibility for themselves, which means you don't need to have a stage manager responsible for the set, costumes and props. Usually, through practice, you can get the get-in down to below the fifteen minutes – when you've done it for three weeks you can do it in superhuman time.

Although there are set contracts for get-in and get-out times, you can enter into an informal negotiation with the company that's on before or after you, because it might be that while your company are still getting out of their costumes backstage they can be setting up on stage, so you can share the time to expand it.

What about front of house? Does the venue normally provide all front-of-house and box-office staff?

Yes, usually they would provide front-of-house staff. They may ask you to provide someone to tear tickets so it's important to check the contract.

Presumably once you sign up to a venue you get sent a contract, so you can then check all the conditions?

Yes. The key thing is to make sure that you and the venue are in agreement about the details, because the worst thing is turning up on the day of your get-in to find your set pieces won't fit in the storage area, or that you haven't got the right staff, and that is a dual responsibility. A lot of people wait for the venue to contact them to ask these questions, but that's risky.

Are there any clauses that you should particularly look for and question?

Yes, in particular there are two financial clauses that are worth checking. The first is what I call 'the mystery £500'. In addition to the festival programme, there is another big brochure, which goes into the *Scotsman* newspaper as a supplement at the start of the fringe. The cost of inclusion in this brochure is £500 plus VAT. Some venues demand that you are a part of it. This used to be limited to the biggest venues, but now a number of the smaller ones are also included. Given the choice, I would always enter it because it's a huge marketing tool and it does work, but unless you read the venue contract carefully you may not realise you are going to have to spend an additional sum.

The second financial point to check is how much the venue will charge you if you overrun your time slot. It's typical to be charged a really high rate for going over by more than five or ten minutes. Venues are very strict about it contractually, because they might have twenty shows every day running back to back; if one show goes over by even fifteen minutes, the audience could be leaving for one show after the audience are supposed to be arriving for the next. The penalties are high because people lose audiences and money through it – just make sure you know what the penalty will be, and manage your time carefully. If you are late getting into your slot because of the company before you, you need to inform the venue straight away, or you might be charged when you overrun your slot.

So apart from advertising in the official festival programme and the brochure in the Scotsman, *how do you get an audience? I associate the Edinburgh fringe with flyers – is that really the main way of getting an audience?*

Yes, flyering is handing out leaflets or bills on the street. It's one of the main ways that you can get your information into people's hands. I usually order somewhere between ten and fifteen thousand for the whole festival. Some of those will go in racks in your venue and other venues and festival offices. If you have a small cast you won't be able to hand that many out.

Do the cast go up to Edinburgh with the expectation of handing out flyers on a regular basis?

Yes. I think it's a major issue if people are not aware of it before they go because it's a lot of work. You do see a lot of companies, especially younger companies, who are very enthusiastic in the first week but less in evidence in the following weeks – it's very hard to keep motivated all the way through the festival. The producer and director have to manage the cast's expectations about their responsibility for flyering, and to set up fair rotas. Otherwise, you might give away all your flyers in the first week or burn out. You can also put on performances – often short extracts from the show – on the High Street (also called the Royal Mile or the Fringe Mile) but you need to book them in advance with the fringe office, and follow the guidelines they give you about what you can and cannot do.

And how do you get reviews?

Some people are unlucky and don't get many reviews, just because the show doesn't appeal to critics – it may not seem very original or exciting, or be at a venue which is off the beaten track, or at an awkward time of day.

So although you've paid £400 to be part of the festival and your £500 to be in the Scotsman *brochure, there's no guarantee that critics are going to come and review the show?*

If you've got the money the answer is very simple – get a press agent. But most people can't afford one: I was quoted £1,500 for a press agent last year. It's expensive because you're not just paying them for the four weeks of the festival, you're also paying them for all the work beforehand, which includes going to meet the press on your behalf and sending out targeted press releases. A list of press agents is available from the festival fringe office; as is a press list of the reviewers attending the festival, which the office will send you automatically when you register.

There's a paper called *ThreeWeeks* which is a fringe-specific publication. They have a commitment to reviewing everything at the festival, and some shows will only get a *ThreeWeeks* review. I love *ThreeWeeks*, but if you go north with an expectation of reviews from national papers, you could come home disappointed. You might get the *Guardian*, the *Scotsman* or the *Daily Mail*, and that can be brilliant – or it can destroy you. Assuming it's positive, if a review is pretty immediate and in a high-profile paper it can make an enormous difference to your audience numbers – that's why people work so hard to get reviewers in. The irritating thing is that a critic might see the show in its first week but they may have seen fifteen shows that week and your review only appears a week and a half later, which of course is near the end of the fringe. It's OK to phone them up, politely remind them that they had a press ticket and ask them when the review is coming out. They might choose not to publish at all, but asking politely when it will be out is usually OK.

Once you get a decent review you put it up outside your venue in massive letters! You should also print off quotes to staple them to your flyers; some people leave space on their flyers and then put the quotes on sticky labels and attach them. What you can't do is to get your flyers reprinted with the quotes because you want the review on the flyer quickly and cheaply.

Do you book accommodation for your cast and crew, or do you expect them to find it themselves?

This year I asked the cast to find their own accommodation, but that was quite a specific decision because the actors were in several shows: often, because it's expensive to go to Edinburgh, actors will take as many opportunities to perform and showcase themselves as they can. A number of the actors already had accommodation booked through another company. Normally I would try and find a big flat that would accommodate everyone through the letting agents in Edinburgh. There is a guide to letting agents and accommodation on the fringe website. As a guide price, we would budget between £300 and £350 for each person for the month; although we have brought that down substantially by sleeping on floors, on bay window ledges and by sharing beds – privacy is at a premium in Edinburgh.

What do you need to do after the festival?

Frequently people forget to book a van to get their set and props back; and it's very hard to hire a van in Edinburgh at the end of August. And the financial tying up can be quite complicated if you've offered a profit-share to the cast: it's not as simple as dividing the box-office income by the number of people who took part because the actual amount of ticket-office income, minus VAT and charges, has to be worked out. For example, a percentage cut is taken off any tickets sold through the fringe office as a processing fee. A good venue will be very clear on what you can expect to get back, but it takes a while to get the final information, and the money. The fringe office takes a month from the end of the festival to process everything, so it's important to be clear with the people on a profit-share that they're not just going to get their money on the last day of Edinburgh, and not to give an over-optimistic estimate of what the profit-share will be.

As somebody with your own company, do you think that the Edinburgh experience is a useful one in building up the work and profile of your company and your experience as a producer and director?

I think it's a very risky thing to go there, as a theatre director, and expect to be picked up and asked to direct a show at a producing theatre – that doesn't really happen. It can happen to actors – many agents and casting directors come to Edinburgh.

Potentially it can give you a clutch of positive reviews for your CV. You can show what you've achieved if you document it well, or even film it, but more importantly it can help you to ascertain exactly what you're trying to do as a director because you're stripped down to the basics: you may not have the scope or budget for a full collaboration with a designer, so you have to think as a designer; and you won't have a large production team, so it's a soul-searching mission about your work, your tastes and your aims. It's also a great place for networking, so although it might not put you on the career path that you want to be on tomorrow, it will help get you started.

You could hire a fringe venue in London and put a show on, but condensing the experience into four crazy weeks at the biggest arts festival on the planet gives you a lot of invaluable experience in the pragmatic arts of directing and producing a show.

It doesn't have to be incredibly expensive but there is a cost involved – the greatest of which is living for a month without pay in Edinburgh – but the actual production costs can be kept low. You can also take a show to what's called the Free Fringe or the Free Festival: these are places where you can enter into different types of deals which are not monetary, so you can circumvent financial barriers. The broad basis is that there are no venue costs, but you don't charge for tickets for the show. Usually you can shake a cup and ask the audience to give you a bit of money at the end, which can be surprisingly lucrative. The venues are usually a bit rough and ready – in or above pubs, sometimes with the bar still open in the background; you have to be prepared to compromise. It's not terribly good for highbrow theatre – you've got to be robust.

Forest Fringe is another free part of the festival, currently curated by Battersea Arts Centre (BAC), which also avoids monetary exchange, looking for new ways of producing work at the festival in a collective and collabo-rative way.

It's an incredible festival: I've been to other fringe festivals and Edinburgh is unique. It's full of rubbish theatre, it's full of appalling comedians – that's all true, but in addition there are amazing success stories, amazing plays to see as well. And it changes your opinion about what it is to make a piece of work. You quickly learn an awful lot about making theatre as a director or producer: you end up doing a bit of everything, and you get really excited about the show that you're selling, every day, by hand, with a flyer, because you have to – otherwise no one will come.

Practical exercises

Exercise one

This exercise is about seeing a production and contextualising and critiquing it in a manner that develops an empathethic understanding of how the production was made. Choose a production you have just seen or are about to see. Rather than reviewing the production itself consider the factors that either shaped the production, or led to its programming: focus on how it was made rather than its finished form. For example, questions about the production might be about casting choices – how might the whole production and relationships between certain characters have been different if another actor whose work you know had been playing that particular part? Run through the whole play, or pivotal scenes, imagining them played by another actor and assess the different qualities that the actual actor and your imagined actor bring to the part.

Questions about the programming of the production might involve looking at the whole year's repertoire of the theatre in past and current theatre brochures and trying to discover where that production sits in an overall artistic policy and what audience the theatre is trying to reach by programming that play: is it the only piece of new writing that year and is it only scheduled to run for two weeks rather than the usual four? Does the production marketing image reflect the production accurately and is the image and marketing directed at a specific demographic and was that the audience you sat next to – indeed, how full was the theatre?

Exercise two

Think of an actual theatre company you know well and imagine that you are pitching an idea for an existing play, or a new play or project, to that theatre. Imagine that you are pitching the idea verbally to the theatre's board. Although in practice you are far more likely to pitch an idea just to the artistic director, and hardly ever to a board, this exercise makes the task more difficult as you need to think about the whole context of the production, not just the production itself. The board will include the artistic director and chief executive, who will want to hear why you have chosen this project and how it excites you artistically, and how you see your production of it, rather than a description of the play; they will also want to know how you see it fitting in with and developing the theatre's current artistic policy. There may also be a head of continuing development, or a teacher who will want to know about the educational benefit of the production and to hear about your education plans to support the production. There will be a marketing person who will want to hear a three-sentence description of your production – not the play – that will go on the website; any ideas you might have for images; and the specific audience the production will appeal to. There might be an accountant, or the chief executive, who will want to know about the cast size and the resources needed for the production and whether it will fit the theatre's usual budgets and cast sizes. All of these factors, and others, will influence the programming of a project: can you find a piece that you are genuinely passionate about directing that will also excite the board and audiences of that particular theatre?

Exercise three

As was suggested earlier in the chapter, begin some form of database of the actors, directors, designers, lighting designers, sound designers, fight directors, choreographers and musical directors whose work you have seen, perhaps annotating each name with the production you saw and one or two sentences either describing their work or qualities of their work you admire. You could also divide the database, or annotate individual names, to indicate those whom you might conceivably work with in the next few years: a peer database. Every six months or every year you might review the database and choose, say, three designers whose work you have most admired over that period and make a note of why. If you keep it updated and regularly reviewed the database will not only be an invaluable reference source but also help you define your tastes and knowledge and see how these change over a period of time. It becomes not only a history of your theatregoing but also of your thinking.

Weblist

Arts Council England	www.artscouncil.org.uk
Arts Council of Northern Ireland	www.artscouncil-ni.org
Arts Council of Wales	www.artswales.org.uk
A Younger Theatre	www.ayoungertheatre.com
Bristol Old Vic	www.bristololdvic.org.uk
Bush Theatre	www.bushtheatre.co.uk
Conference of Drama Schools	www.drama.ac.uk
Creative Scotland	www.creativescotland.com
Department of Culture, Media and Sport	www.culture.gov.uk
Devoted and Disgruntled	devotedanddisgruntled.ning.com
Directors Guild of Great Britain	www.dggb.org
Edinburgh Festival Fringe	www.edfringe.com
Forest Fringe	www.forestfringe.co.uk
Gate Theatre	www.gatetheatre.co.uk
The Guardian	www.guardian.co.uk
HighTide Festival	www.hightide.org.uk
Latitude Festival	www.latitudefestival.co.uk
Lyric Hammersmith	www.lyric.co.uk
National Student Drama Festival	www.nsdf.org.uk
National Theatre	www.nationaltheatre.org.uk
The Official London Theatre Guide	www.officiallondontheatre.co.uk
The Old Vic	www.oldvictheatre.com
Royal Court Theatre	www.royalcourttheatre.com
Royal Exchange Theatre	www.royalexchangetheatre.org.uk
Royal Shakespeare Company	www.rsc.org.uk
The Scotsman	www.scotsman.com
The Stage	www.thestage.co.uk
Theatre Record	www.theatrerecord.org
ThreeWeeks	www.threeweeks.co.uk
UK Theatre Web	www.uktw.co.uk
Up The West End	www.upthewestend.com
West Yorkshire Playhouse	www.wyp.org.uk
Whatsonstage	www.whatsonstage.com
Young Vic Genesis Directors' Network	www.youngvic.org

Bibliography

Braun, Edward, *The Director and the Stage*. London: Methuen, 1982.

Delgado, Maria M., and Heritage, Paul, editors, *In Contact with the Gods?* Manchester: Manchester University Press, 1996.

Dromgoole, Dominic, *The Full Room*. London: Methuen, 2000.

Eyre, Richard, and Wright, Nicholas, *Changing Stages*. London: Bloomsbury, 2000.

Hartnoll, Phyllis, *The Theatre: A Concise History*. New York: Thames and Hudson, 1998.

Huxley, Michael, and Witts, Noel, editors, *The Twentieth Century Performance Reader*. London: Routledge, 1996.

Leach, Robert, *Makers of Modern Theatre*. London: Routledge, 2004.

Rea, Kenneth, *A Better Direction*. London: Calouste Gulbenkian Foundation, 1989.

Spotlight, *Contacts 2012*. London: Spotlight, 2011.

Wardle, Irving, *The Theatres of George Devine*. London: Jonathan Cape, 1978.

Wardle, Irving, *Theatre Criticism*. London, Routledge, 1992.

2 The director and the actor

This chapter explores the most complex of the director's relationships with other creative artists: the relationship with actors.

➢ What does an actor do?

➢ What is the job of the professional actor and where does the work of the actor end and that of the director begin?

➢ How does a director absorb, select and reject a range of different approaches to acting in order to develop a personal synthesised approach to directing; how do you then modify that approach in response to the particular demands of the play?

➢ How does a director combine having a rehearsal structure and guiding the whole process towards a common goal with being open and flexible, genuinely collaborating with actors?

The interview with Annie Tyson, head of acting at Drama Centre London for the past eight years, answers some of the questions about what actors actually do, and where the personal work of the actor ends and the work with the director begins. The interview with Sarah Esdaile discusses her directorial approach which she has synthesised from several acting methodologies and from observing other directors.

This chapter is divided into two sections: the first section provides an overview of actor training and some of the most commonly used acting methodologies; the second part discusses how you might synthesise your own directorial approaches, perhaps informed by some of the acting methodologies, and apply those approaches to different plays and rehearsal situations. It is advisable to read the first section in order to follow the discussion in detail in the second part.

Before considering the numerous acting methodologies which inform how actors work today, it is important to say that it is not necessary for a director to know all, or any, of these practitioners to work successfully with actors. There is no substitute for working with professional actors and learning and evolving by doing it, and watching how other directors work.

It may be simplistic, but it is helpful to bear in mind that however an actor is trained, whatever acting methodologies they are used to, and whatever directing approaches you may employ, at the root of all acting there are two fundamental questions an actor will wish to ask. First, what are the 'given circumstances' or 'non-negotiables' of a character's situation at any given moment in the play – the time, the place, the relationship with other characters in the scene, what has just happened, where is the character going? These are sometimes known as the 'Six Ws': *Whence, Where, What, Why, When, Whither?* Second, the actor needs to ask what is his/her character's objective (sometimes also called intention, task or motivation) in the moment, in the scene, and in the play? If an actor knows the character's situation in as much detail as possible, and can define as precisely as possible what the character wants, the actor can then respond truthfully and imaginatively and inhabit the world and world view of the character.

Actors respond imaginatively by being in possession of the facts – 'the whats'. The way in which actors work technically to transform themselves into their character, and the way in which their character expresses their individual responses to 'the whats', are 'the hows' of acting: and perhaps 'the whats' are primarily the area of work between the director and the actor and 'the hows' are primarily, but not exclusively, the work of the actor rather than the director.

If as a director you know nothing of the numerous acting methodologies discussed later but you bear in mind the actors' need pragmatically and methodically to answer those two questions, you have a method of communicating with actors which they will understand and an initial approach to the play to which actors will be able to respond. Although you may have ideas about the whole production of *Macbeth*, or believe that a particular scene has a particular dramatic function, actors cannot play concepts, dramaturgy or abstract ideas. As Annie Tyson says in her interview, it might be useful to discuss the function and ideas which underlie a particular scene, but although actors will find discussion of those ideas stimulating, in the end actors can only play objectives and actions. So, for example, the actor playing Lady Macbeth cannot play the quality or character trait of evil when she is questioning Macbeth's sudden decision not to kill Duncan, but she can play the objective 'to get my husband to change his mind' or 'to persuade Macbeth to kill the King': these are specific, achievable, actable objectives – 'the whats'. Lady Macbeth may appear to be evil in doing so, or she may appear quite reasonable, even admirable, but that is a 'how' – a by-product of the objective and action the actor has chosen for the character: many directors direct using verbs, not adjectives, and as the director and writer David Mamet remarks in his book *True and False*, an actor's action or objective should be no more complicated than opening a window.

While it is perfectly possible to work productively with actors by just bearing the above in mind, it is important for any director to have what many directors call their toolkit. The toolkit may include individual games or exercises and it may include whole patterns of structuring rehearsals based on reading about the work of directors such as Mike Alfreds or Katie Mitchell (both discussed later in this chapter), but the idea of the toolkit implies that no single methodology is solely employed to the exclusion of all others, and that the use of Anne Bogart's viewpoints, or of actioning, are strategies that can be called upon to solve a particular problem and returned to the toolkit once they have done their jobs.

It is also useful to have a broad understanding of how actors are trained and of the acting methodologies used in actor training to develop a better shared working language with actors.

Actor training

In the UK today the training of professional actors takes place in twenty-two drama schools across the country, although most are based in London. Those drama schools that offer professionally recognised actor training are members of the Conference of Drama Schools (CDS), and detailed information about member schools, issues around actor training and individual acting courses can be found on their website, listed at the end of this chapter.

The standards of each school are also overseen by the National Council for Drama Training (NCDT), which is a body made up of representatives from theatre managers, TV and film companies, the actors' union Equity, and the drama schools. Each drama school is regularly re-accredited to ensure it continues to train actors to professionally recognised levels. The NCDT also has a website about accredited programmes and information and advice for aspiring actors and stage managers about professionally recognised training and routes into the theatre.

Most actor training programmes are for three years full-time, although there are a growing number of postgraduate one-year programmes at drama schools. Over a three-year programme an actor will have a minimum of 900 hours in classes led by experienced professionals, and with final-year productions and optional classes, an actor's training may exceed 1,000 contact hours. By any standards these are intensive courses and this is partly because actors have to learn a range of skills in addition to acting, voice and movement, such as singing, dancing, fighting, acting for camera and radio, and accent and dialect work; but a stronger reason is that actors have to learn the key skills of breathing, speaking, movement and acting to a level where those skills become muscle memory, not something one has to think about while playing Hamlet. It is analogous to a driver not having to think about clutch control when pulling away from a set of lights – the driver's conscious thoughts need to focus on the traffic, not finding biting point: Hamlet needs to think about his objectives and to respond to Ophelia in the moment, not to think about diaphragmatic breathing, voice control and body alignment.

Actors in training often feel that the acting skills and creativity that they have when they begin training are unpicked and dissected to a point where midway through their training they feel that they can no longer act, but what they do in the first year is to analyse how they breathe, how they speak, how they move, so that they have a much greater awareness of how their bodies work and much greater control of their bodies. Through constant repetition of exercises on breath, voice and movement they not only become immensely fitter but they can be heard at the back of a large auditorium, such as the Olivier at the National Theatre, night after night without losing their voice, or repeat an exact sequence of actions take after take for film or TV.

Actor training not only teaches a physical muscle memory that can be used without having consciously to think about it, but also an imaginative muscle memory. An actor's ability to draw on past personal experiences and access fundamental emotions with ease and to envisage the world of the play beyond what the set looks like are just two examples of a much broader development of an actor's imaginative and creative resources that are developed over three years. This is why, as Annie Tyson mentions in her interview, it is not always necessary for a director to know, or have to intervene in, how an actor 'gets there' – the 'how' of acting.

Training will also develop the actor's sense of stagecraft: a sense of the dynamics of space and an awareness of the overall stage picture and how these physically and spatially relate to other actors. Many directors, quite rightly, do not want to direct by telling actors where to move – 'blocking' the actors and the scene – but a more fluid and creative process of enabling actors to choose their own moves and spatial relationships is made much easier when they have an innate awareness of stagecraft built up through training.

As John Gielgud once remarked, style is knowing what type of play you are in, and trained actors have also developed a level of playcraft – knowing the differences between a play by Noël Coward and a play by Harold Pinter and the different demands of different types of writing; and all will have some experience of verse speaking, particularly speaking Shakespearean verse. These are the core skills that a director can expect a trained actor to have, and these core skills mean that a director's rehearsal can focus on the particular demands of a play and take certain approaches to acting as a given.

To this extent all accredited drama school courses are the same. There are some university drama departments that offer courses that equip actors to have successful professional careers, and some actors come through universities rather than drama schools, but it is only those courses run by CDS schools and accredited by the NCDT that are widely recognised by the theatre profession because there is an agreed number of contact hours and range of skills and knowledge imparted by these schools to actors in training. It is true that not all actors have trained, or trained on an accredited course, but the vast majority have, so the language taught at drama schools tends to be the default common language of the rehearsal room.

The interview with Annie Tyson describes the evolution of one drama school – Drama Centre London – and its influence on the teaching at several other drama schools over the past thirty years, and many of the approaches pioneered at Drama Centre have become commonplace at other drama schools; but every drama school is different from others through its history, mix of acting approaches, and strengths of its current staff.

East 15 Acting School was born out of Joan Littlewood's Theatre Workshop and traditionally its actors have a high level of skill with new plays and with improvisation. Arts Educational has in recent years significantly developed its training for acting for camera and many of its graduates have thriving careers in TV. Guildford and Mountview are known for their training of musical theatre actors as well as 'straight' actors, and Rose Bruford has an innovative course for actor-musicians. Unsurprisingly schools such as RADA, LAMDA, Guildhall and Bristol Old Vic still have reputations for training actors for the classical repertoire, but all also offer some experience of TV and radio acting and work in a broad repertoire of plays. The differences between the schools tend to be differences of emphasis rather than fundamental training: all these schools spend the majority of the three years of training on imparting core skills that may be used in any medium, on any text, and on non-text-based work.

The methodologies used to impart these core skills also vary in emphasis from school to school, but the majority teach a broadly Stanislavskian approach to acting with elements and exercises from a number of other practitioners such as Michael Chekhov, Uta Hagen, Anne Bogart, Sanford Meisner, Jacques Lecoq and Rudolf Laban put into the mix. In addition to employing combinations of these existing methodologies many of the teachers of acting, movement and voice have synthesised their own approaches and often the exact nature and tone of acting teaching is particular to the current staff of a drama school, and so changes over time. Because actors are being trained to act rather than study acting it is not necessarily made explicit to actors in training that a particular exercise comes from Meisner or Bogart, or even Stanislavski, so as a director working with actors it can be counter-productive to say, 'Right, let's try an Anne Bogart Viewpoints exercise here' – first, because actors might feel that they are about to have to learn a complex new methodology (and not get on with the play); second, because it might make actors feel that they somehow should know this exercise but don't; and third, because they may well know the exercise from their training and would have happily just done it without Anne Bogart's name being mentioned.

Having auditioned many actors over many years I have found that it is possible to tell, for example, a recently trained LAMDA actor from a recently trained Drama Centre actor without seeing their CV, but, for the most part, the differences are subtle and quickly disappear in a rehearsal room once a common approach to the play has been established. Directors do have their favourite drama schools, and particularly when casting actors in their early twenties, who are still heavily reliant on the skills and approaches learnt on training, many directors will favour graduates of one school over graduates from another.

It is worthwhile going to see the third-year final productions at drama schools not only to build up a personal view of the qualities of the actors from each school, but also to build up lists of actors you may wish to work with in the future. All the drama schools have details of their current productions on their websites, which are open to the public, and tickets are usually cheaper than even most fringe venues.

Acting methodologies

A detailed examination of all the acting methodologies used by actors and directors would itself be a book on directing, so what follows is a brief description of the approaches most commonly used by emerging theatre directors today.

It has become apparent from the discussion of drama schools that the most influential figure in acting methodologies is Konstantin Stanislavski. Nearly all the other figures who have developed acting methodologies since Stanislavski's work in the early twentieth century have either based their work on his, or reacted against his work in developing their own methods. For this reason, and because Stanislavski's methods have greatly informed the common language of the rehearsal room, the description of Stanislavski's work is much more detailed than the description of other methodologies.

In considering each methodology as a possible component of your directing approach there are several factors about these methodologies it is worth bearing in mind. First, some of these approaches really require an actor or director to attend workshops led by an expert to appreciate them before they can be used with full understanding; however with such practitioners it is possible to extract single ideas and exercises which can be used independently of the whole methodology. For example, Michael Chekhov's work represents a complete practical philosophy that requires months if not years of physical immersion in the process to fully realise, but in her interview Sarah Esdaile says that she often employs Chekhov's methods to explore character in a four-week rehearsal period which also draws on other approaches; but you would be advised to fully understand the approach before using it piecemeal. By being an acting methodology magpie there is a danger of employing knowledge without understanding, but the judicious use of these approaches in a toolkit fashion is what comes from practical trial and error in a workshop environment rather than simply imitating them in a making or rehearsal situation.

Second, some of these approaches are intended to be actor training tools rather than approaches to be used in a production, and it is useful to distinguish one kind from the other; that is not to say that you can never use an exercise primarily designed to train actors in a rehearsal room, but it is helpful to be aware of the context and intention behind it.

Konstantin Stanislavski (1863–1938)

Stanislavski's work can be broadly divided into two parts: the *Method of Physical Action*, which is the process for working on a text in rehearsal, and the *System*, which is the process for actor training.

The *Method of Physical Action*

Stanislavski believed that an actor had to transform from being a person, the 'Real I', into a character, the 'Dramatic I', and that this is achieved through the actor knowing the situation and demands of the situation and then by reacting truthfully to those demands, which releases his or her creative energies and results in an organic conscious and subconscious response.

In order to achieve this the actor has to ask 'what if . . .' these events were true? The first step is to establish all the facts of the situation, which include the backstory or given circumstances at the beginning of the play, and then at each point of action to access the six Ws referred to earlier – *Whence, Where, What, Why, When, Whither* – then to fill in the missing times and events between scenes and so establish the facts that inform the beginning of the next scene, and then to establish the facts after the play has ended. The actor also decides on a provisional super-objective or super-task – the overriding goal of the character: perhaps 'to avenge my father's death' might be Hamlet's super-objective. With subsequent work through the play, the super-objective may change.

In order to identify the points of action at which to ask the six Ws, the play is first broken down into episodes or units, which might be as long as an act, or a section between the entrance and exit of characters, or major changes of action or intention, and then to break down each episode or unit into facts, events or beats, which can be single sentences or lines, or longer, but which represent one thought which is also one objective and one action. So, for example, by saying 'Shall we go for a walk?' the character has the objective of 'staying in this person's company' and the action to achieve that might be 'to entice you' or 'to tempt you', but it might just as easily be 'to threaten you'. The action is always a transitive verb which has an intended effect on the other character and their actions in order to achieve the character's objective.

In their introduction to *Actions: The Actors' Thesaurus*, Marina Caldarone and Maggie Lloyd-Williams posit the actioning mantra: 'One thought. One sentence. One breath. One action.' Katie Mitchell prefers the word 'intention' to 'objective' and the word 'tactic' to 'action', and Stanislavski's terms for breaking down scenes differ from director to director, drama school to drama school and actor to actor, but essentially they all refer to the same process and principle – that each scene or act is broken down into units, between major events, then into beats which have one objective and action, and every time there is a new beat the actor asks the six Ws so that the whole of a character's journey through the play is a string of objectives and actions, which itself is called the 'through action'.

In parallel to this process, which is to do with the spoken words and actions – the external life of the character – the actor is also establishing the 'through emotion': at the same points of action the actor is also asking the six Ws in relation to the inner life of the character, referred to as the 'subtext', which comprises his or her inner monologue – the unspoken words which link the spoken words – and the mental images and emotional memories which are associated with the spoken and unspoken words. So, at the end of working through the play the actor has two parallel strings – of outer objectives and actions and of inner subtexts. In this context the word subtext has a more precise meaning than it usually has when referred to as simply the thoughts which are underneath, and sometimes in variance with, the spoken words.

In Stanislavski's method, the actors improvise the dialogue rather than speaking their lines when first working through the play to establish the through actions and through emotions; it's only once these have been established that the focus becomes the text and work begins on the place and period of the play, analysis of the language of the play, the age and physique of the character and the interplay of the physical world and the inner life of the character. In the light of these discoveries the actors might reassess their through actions and through emotions and their super-objective. The final stage of work is to establish the rhythm and pace of individual scenes and the play itself, and to settle on the moves, and again to reassess the through actions and emotions and super-objective.

The *System*

The *System* trains the actor in the technical skills to create and communicate the 'Dramatic I'. As with the *Method of Physical Action*, the *System* divides the work into work on the outer (the actor's physicality and communication skills) and the inner (the actor's mental skills and imagination). As with the *Method of Physical Action*, the *System* also approaches the work by breaking down action and thought into its smallest component parts to build up a complete working process. Many of the physical exercises developed by Stanislavski raise an actor's awareness of their actions and body through detailed observation, analysis and monitoring of the smallest movement involved in producing a larger movement: for example, noting the exact muscle movement required to pick up a chair.

Actions are also differentiated as automatic actions which do not have to be thought about, such as lifting an arm to pick up a chair; organic actions, which require a sequence of logical actions to complete a task, such as moving the chair to sit at a table; and psychologically complex actions, such as moving the chair to arrange a meal for your family. All of the exercises not only increase the actor's awareness of their chosen actions but also train the actor to align and balance their bodies and to monitor and release tensions in their body, alike during an exercise and under performance conditions.

There are similar mental exercises designed to increase an actor's concentration, focus and powers of observation, such as 'circles of concentration' exercises that increase the ability to switch focus from objects and circumstances which are very near to those at medium distance or far away, and back again, and to have an awareness of all the factors and circumstances which may affect a character's behaviour. These mental exercises also include increasing the actor's ability to access mental images and emotional memory, as referred to in the description of the *Method of Physical Action*.

The best brief introduction to Stanislavski's work is Jean Benedetti's *Stanislavski and the Actor*. It sets out his whole work in a clear manner with illustrative exercises enabling a director quickly to understand and use the approaches. Stanislavski's work has come to the West in a tortuous, piece-meal and often confusing array of versions and translations of his key works. The best comprehensive account of his work is in translations by Benedetti in two volumes, *An Actor's Work* and *My Life in Art*.

The overview provided by a book like *Stanislavski and the Actor* gives a director a knowledge of the everyday language of drama schools, a number of exercises that are familiar to actors, and an understanding of the methodological framework upon which many subsequent practitioners founded their own approaches, or against which they reacted.

Bertolt Brecht (1898–1956)

In Chapter One, the German director Walter Meierjohann described his training in Berlin as a combination of Stanislavski and Brecht, which would seem to be a combination of polar opposites. He discusses the differences he has observed between English and German actors: that English actors are far more immersed in their roles and have a greater ability to move him, but that German actors have a greater ability to view their character from the outside and a greater awareness of their audience.

In Brecht's eyes the Stanislavskian character with a through action and super-objective appears to be on a linear, unalterable path, driven forward by inner thoughts and psychological impulses, so that we, the audience, are invited to identify and empathise with the character, but have no effect on his or her fate. Brecht's characters face decisions which demonstrate the ability of characters to shape their own destinies, driven forward by their reaction to their social and economic circumstances, while we, the audience, are invited to retain an emotional distance from the characters and to question the reasons why the characters make the choices they do. Brecht does not ask actors to transform themselves from the Real I to the Dramatic I but always to co-exist as actor and character, the actors demonstrating the decisions and actions of their characters, constantly reminding the audience that they are watching a piece of performance rather than suspending their disbelief and immersing themselves in the world of the play.

Brecht's approaches to acting are obviously applicable to his plays, although not all of his acting methodologies are universally applicable to all his works. But what can we take from his acting theories for work on plays not by Brecht? The theatre of Joan Littlewood, and many of the theatre companies of the 1960s and 1970s with politically inspired artistic missions, such as Red Ladder and 7:84, were hugely influenced by Brecht, and more recently, documentary or verbatim theatre, in which actors represent real people, draw on Brecht's notion of the actor as the character's tribune and often engage the audience with direct address, inviting them to question the course of events.

There are also elements of Brecht's work that can be applied to any play, whether new or devised, including entirely naturalistic plays. First is the idea of actors sharing the play with the audience. Having spent many years working in a 600-seat theatre in the round in which the actors have to communicate with the audience members in front of them and with those who are in the gods fifty metres behind their heads, I've observed that there is a palpable difference between those actors whose focus is entirely on their fellow actor two metres away from them, and those who subliminally acknowledge and embrace the act of communication with the audience.

Allied to this, is Brecht's notion of the 'not . . . but': 'My character chose *not* to do that, *but* chose to do this.' In the moment of decision before the eventual action is taken the actor and character demonstrate that there were alternative courses of action and that the one taken was not inevitable. Again, this is applicable to any play, and is particularly useful in the latter stages of rehearsal when you and the actors know the play and the character's journey well and can forget what is new and momentous to that character at that point; it can reinvigorate the stakes of a moment or scene to ask the actor to explore the alternatives to the chosen course of action and prevent a sense of predictability in the scene and character.

Third is the idea that the character's focus and motive need not necessarily come from internal psychological impulses but from the character's need to affect the external world, or to relate to an object: for example, when Lopakhin returns to the ball, having bought the estate, in Chekhov's *The Cherry Orchard*, Varya, the housekeeper, throws down her bunch of keys. In Lopakhin's speech in which he celebrates his new ownership he might pick them up and give as much focus to the keys, which symbolise his control of the estate, as to actioning his lines to have an effect on the characters surrounding him. This external physicalisation of an inner psychological state and the representation of the social and economic circumstances that affect a character is what Brecht called *gestus*, which can be translated as 'attitude', but which conveys more about the situation and character's relationship with the world than the word 'attitude' might suggest. The actor's relationship to the object is also a focus of Declan Donnellan's and Anne Bogart's work, which is discussed later.

The most comprehensive accounts of Brecht's work can be found in two books, one by John Willett, *The Theatre of Bertolt Brecht*. The second is by Brecht, translated and edited by Willett: *Brecht on Theatre*. Chapters in *Twentieth Century Actor Training*, edited by Alison Hodge, and in Shomit Mitter's *Systems of Rehearsal* offer focused discussions of Brecht's work with actors in the rehearsal room.

Michael Chekhov (1891–1955)

Michael Chekhov is one of the most influential and revered 'descendants' of Stanislavski, and actually the nephew of Anton Chekhov, but Michael Chekhov's view of actors and acting differs significantly from Stanislavski's. If Stanislavski's method is characterised as being a detailed, logical exploration of the text in which the actor responds to the demands of the text in order to immerse the actor in the character, then Chekhov's approach could be characterised as being led by the imagination of the actor, acknowledging the individuality of the actor, the differences between the actor and the character, and a conscious 'standing apart' of the actor from the character, so that, in Chekhov's words, the actor is 'not only a creator of the character but also its spectator'. Chekhov's actors, through this 'standing apart', also have a proactive relationship with the audience.

In order for actors fully to access and realise their imaginative powers they need to develop their physical sensitivity to external and psychological stimuli and to fine tune a balance between the physical and the psychological. Chekhov says that the '*strength* of the movement stirs our will power in general; the *kind* of movement awakens in us a definite corresponding *desire*, and the quality of the same movement conjures up our *feelings*'. And so, 'Through the gesture you penetrate and stimulate the depths of your own psychology.'

The notion of 'psychological gesture' is the part of Chekhov's work which is best known to those with only a passing knowledge of his whole work. Rather than building up a sense of character through logical progression as in the Stanislavskian method, Chekhov posited that the whole character could be expressed and encapsulated in one gesture, phrase or moment. Once an actor had gained an imaginatively generated physicalisation of that moment, then the actor had access to the essence of the whole character, which would then inform his or her whole performance.

Chekhov also devised his own method of breaking down the text into units, but his method differs from Stanislavski's not only in its terminology and how units are defined and subdivided, but also in his belief that every play has three main climaxes, which '(if they are found correctly, by artistic intuition rather than by reasoning) give you the key to the main idea and to the basic dynamic of the play. Each climax expresses the essence of that unit which it represents.' From this viewpoint Chekhov suggests that you do not work through a play narratively from page one to the end, but begin work on the moments of climax and work on the other scenes in the light of their relationship to those climaxes.

The prime source of information about Chekhov's work and ideas can be found in *To the Actor* by Michael Chekhov, with an eloquent introduction by Simon Callow, who makes the case that Chekhov's work re-affirms the actor as a creative artist, or artist-poet, rather than a simple imitator of life. But as Chekhov says in a memo to the reader in the book, the exercises he has devised to realise his methodologies really need to be practised in order to be fully understood. Reading *To the Actor* is inspiring and can offer individual tools for the director to go away and try, but really to experience Chekhov's work it is worth looking out for classes led by experienced Chekhov teachers. There are details of a UK Chekhov website at the end of the chapter.

The Group Theatre and 'The Method'

The history and competing versions of what became known as 'The Method' is a complex subject, but it is worth knowing a little of the genesis of the different versions of 'Method Acting' in order to understand its relationship to Stanislavski and to appreciate the different philosophies of acting that underlie the various approaches, and how it in turn has influenced other practitioners, and continues to do so.

A brief history. In 1931 three people who had studied at the Theatre Guild School of Acting – Harold Clurman, Lee Strasberg and Cheryl Crawford – established the Group Theatre in New York. It was an ensemble of twenty-eight actors, directors and writers, including Stella Adler and Sanford Meisner, Clifford Odets and Elia Kazan. It was called the Group Theatre as its emphasis was on creating a permanent ensemble of artists who would work collaboratively, rather than there being 'stars' in the company. Several of the members of the Group Theatre, including Strasberg, Clurman and Adler, had studied at the American Laboratory Theatre under Richard Boleslavski and Maria Ouspenskaya, two Russian actors from the Moscow Art Theatre who had studied with Stanislavski, and Stanislavski's methods became the most influential used by the Group Theatre.

Lee Strasberg, whose ideas were the dominant ones in the early years of the Group Theatre, believed: 'Re-living a specific or joyful emotional experience is the way to access a sequence of behaviour and express emotions when certain scenes are particularly demanding. The emotional memory is the actor's weapon to create a complete reality on stage' (*The Lee Strasberg Notes*, edited by Lola Cohen).

In 1934 Stella Adler and Harold Clurman went to Paris and studied with Stanislavski for several weeks. When they returned to New York Stella Adler gave a talk to the Group Theatre which greatly diminished the importance of emotional, or affective, memory, propounded by Strasberg, and placed much greater emphasis on the 'given circumstances', the analysis of the text and the use of the actor's imagination rather than personal memory. This difference of emphasis split the Group and resulted in Strasberg leaving it soon afterwards. Stella Adler later said of sense memory work, 'The emphasis was a sick one. You couldn't be on the stage thinking of your own personal life. It was just schizophrenic.' In 1949 Adler founded her own acting school, where her most illustrious student was Marlon Brando; other pupils included Robert De Niro, Warren Beatty and Harvey Keitel.

In 1947 Elia Kazan, Cheryl Crawford and others established the Actors Studio, and in 1951 Lee Strasberg became its director until his death in 1982, having also established the Lee Strasberg Theatre and Film Institute in New York and Los Angeles. Some of the many actors who studied with Strasberg were Paul Newman, Dustin Hoffman, Jane Fonda and Dennis Hopper.

Some theatre critics and writers consider method acting as the most important actor training system in history. Its critics claim that the actor's absorption in accessing personal memories and emotions prevents actors from being in the moment and leads to them dragging behind the moment of reaction. It cannot be denied that, in its many forms and distillations, it has been the most influential acting methodology in the US in the late twentieth century, and just as Stanislavski's work has informed subsequent generations of actors and teachers of acting, method acting continues to influence the development of acting, not least through Sanford Meisner and Uta Hagen, whose work is discussed below.

The Lee Strasberg Notes, edited by Lola Cohen, is a very thorough account of Strasberg's work, including clear and detailed descriptions of key exercises. *The Technique of Acting* is a comprehensive account of her work written by Stella Adler, and *Stella Adler: The Art of Acting* is a compilation of Adler's class notes and scene studies edited by Howard Kissel.

Sanford Meisner (1905–97)

As mentioned above, Sanford Meisner was one of the founding members of the Group Theatre, and if the chief criticism of actors trained by 'The Method' is that they are not in the moment, then Meisner's work is a direct reaction to this and is all about being in the moment.

Meisner said, 'I decided I wanted an exercise for actors where there is no intellectuality. I wanted to eliminate all that "head" work, to take away all the mental manipulation and to get where the impulses come from. And I began with the premise that if I repeat what I hear you saying, my head is not working. I'm listening and there is an absolute elimination of the brain. If you say, "Your glasses are dirty," and I say, "My glasses are dirty," and you say, "Yes, your glasses are dirty," there is no intellectuality in that.'

The best known of Meisner's exercises is the word repetition game, which Meisner describes as being like ping-pong, where two actors face each other and repeat what they have just said with no emotional or intellectual investment in what they are saying, and wait for a genuine impulse from outside, including their partner, to force them to change what they are saying: in other words, to bring nothing from inside them-selves to the moment but just to react immediately and spontaneously to that moment. For work on a scene Meisner asks actors to prepare them-selves before coming into the scene by imaginatively exploring all their given circumstances in order to enter the scene with an inner life, rather than being empty of history or impulse, but once in the scene only to react moment by moment to what has just immediately happened. To paraphrase Meisner, the text is a canoe which is carried forward by the flow of emotion, or the river.

Meisner's techniques are actor training techniques rather than production techniques, and he estimated it would take about five years to train properly under his system, but many directors have taken the ping-pong exercise and other Meisner exercises to explore communication between actors and to really investigate the visceral rather than intellectual impulses that provoke the character's next line. He also advocated the learning of lines in a completely neutral way before beginning work on a play.

There are frequent Meisner classes in the UK and many emerging directors use some of his techniques in their own work. The two most useful books on him are *Sanford Meisner on Acting*, by Meisener and Dennis Longwell, and *The Actor's Art and Craft: William Esper Teaches the Meisner Technique*, by William Esper and Damon DiMarco.

Uta Hagen (1919–2004)

Uta Hagen pursued simultaneous careers as an actor and teacher of acting throughout her life. Early in her career she was directed by Harold Clurman and later created the role of Martha in Edward Albee's *Who's Afraid of Virginia Woolf?*. She taught at the HB Studio from 1947 and was its leader from 1957 until her death in 2004, teaching many generations of actors.

Uta Hagen focused on how the actor moves from the 'Real I' to the 'Dramatic I' and believed that all actors should begin with their own lives as the basis for creating characters. She created her own variation on Stanislavski's 'Six Ws', which she called 'The Six Steps', and also the 'Ten Object Exercises'. She believed that actors should note the similarities and differences between their own lives and the life of their character and 'substitute' analogous experiences in their own lives for events in their character's life which they had not experienced: if their character's mother commits suicide but this is not in the experience of the actor, the actor finds a situation in their own life which might have the same emotional triggers as the suicide in the character's life. Allied with this idea is the idea that every object and element of the stage should be chosen with absolute precision, because objects can be endowed with a meaning and resonance for the life of the character and have the ability to be used as powerful emotional triggers for the actor and the character.

Many of her exercises are used in drama schools, particularly the exercise in which a student re-creates their own room from home in a studio and goes through routine actions they may go through in the privacy of their room in the studio. This exercise is often referred to as a 'private moment' exercise and promotes the idea of acting as if unobserved while being aware of the audience. Many of her Object Exercises have been widely adopted and adapted by directors for use in production.

Uta Hagen wrote two widely available books about her work: *Respect for Acting*, with Haskel Frankel, and *A Challenge for the Actor*. Although *A Challenge for the Actor* develops many of the ideas and exercises in *Respect for Acting*, *Respect for Acting* remains the more widely read of the two books.

Anne Bogart (b. 1951)

The choreographer Mary Overlie invented the 'Six Viewpoints of Dance' on which Anne Bogart has based her own Viewpoints system of training. Bogart met the director Tadashi Suzuki in Japan, and together they established the Saratoga International Theater Institute (SITI) in 1992. Viewpoints was further developed with Tina Landau, and in 2005 *The Viewpoints Book: A Practical Guide to Viewpoints and Composition*, by Bogart and Tina Landau, was published. Anne Bogart has also written *A Director Prepares: Seven Essays on Art and Theatre*, and *And Then, You Act: Making Art in an Unpredictable World*.

Viewpoints draws on ideas from the theatre but also from dance, painting, architecture, music and film, in order to draw on and reflect a wide cultural heritage. It works with the principles of movement, time and space to train performers, to create movement for the stage, and to build an ensemble. It is intended to be a collaborative and non-hierarchical system of training and rehearsal. There are nine physical viewpoints – tempo, duration, kinesthetic response, repetition, shape, gesture, architecture, spatial relationship and topography – and five vocal viewpoints: pitch, dynamic, acceleration/deceleration, silence and timbre. By describing movement in time and space through the frame of the nine viewpoints, Bogart has invented a language for analysing and creating movement, providing the actor and director with a means for greater awareness of the possibilities and effects of movement on time and space. The 'Composition' part of *The Viewpoints Book* also offers methods of creating new work from compositional principles from outside theatre practice to also create new forms as well as new work.

Although Anne Bogart and Tina Landau warn against 'lazy or undigested ways of teaching Viewpoints' and that 'Viewpoints is an open process, not a rigid technique', many directors have found inspiration from it and incorporate some its principles and exercises in their own work alongside other methodologies.

Rudolf Laban (1879–1958)

Rudolf Laban was a dancer, director, architect and mathematician who devised a system for notating dance movement, known as Labanotation or Kinetography Laban. Labanotation uses symbols to define: the direction of movement; the part of the body doing the movement; the level of the movement; and the length of time it takes to do the movement.

In the theatre, the aspect of Laban's work that is most widely used is the 'Eight Efforts'. Efforts, or Effort Actions, are comprised of three 'Effort Elements': Weight, Space and Time; so, for example, an effort which is strong, direct and sudden is Thrust, an effort which is light, flexible (or indirect) and sustained is Float: all eight efforts are different combinations of the three elements of weight, space and time.

What makes this system so applicable to theatre is not just that it provides a language for describing an actor's relationship with space and other actors, but also that it has a psychological dimension: outward expression is a sign of an inner psychological state, so that the efforts not only denote a physical movement but also the internal impulse that creates that movement. Laban's efforts provide a language for visceral and expressive choices which may be applied to whole characters or the reading of one line. In her interview in this chapter, Annie Tyson refers to Laban's work as a cornerstone of the movement psychology developed at Drama Centre, and now used widely in other drama schools; a number of theatre companies, including the RSC, regularly use Laban's methods in their work.

The most comprehensive and useful book on Laban's work is *Laban for Actors and Dancers: Putting Laban's Movement Theory into Practice*, by Jean Newlove.

Contemporary UK directors

Mike Alfreds

Mike Alfreds has been a director for over fifty years and founded the celebrated theatre company Shared Experience in the 1970s. His book about his work is entitled *Different Every Night*. It is subtitled *Freeing the*

Actor and it does what it says on the cover. This is an inspirational book which asks questions about how and why we make theatre, as well as giving a highly detailed account of Mike Alfreds's own pre-production and rehearsal processes. Nearly half the book describes his preparation for a production – a model of forensic examination of the text to release hidden knowledge and meaning, and a valuable tool for any director. Mike Alfreds also uses actioning, but his method of actioning is physically active rather than sedentary, encouraging embodied rather than just cerebral reactions to the moment to decide upon an action. His methods also include patterns to break up the working rehearsal day into hour blocks of contrasting activities, referred to later in the chapter and in the interview with Sarah Esdaile. His painstaking methods of interrogating the world of the play and the characters are intended to give the actors so much information and understanding of the character and the scene that moments and movements never need to be fixed, freeing the actors to be different every night.

Declan Donnellan

In 1981 Declan Donnellan co-founded the theatre company Cheek by Jowl with designer Nick Ormerod. Cheek by Jowl's manifesto is to be an international touring company reinvigorating the classics, putting the actor and the ensemble at the centre of the work and evolving the design through the rehearsal process.

Like Mike Alfreds, Declan Donnellan seeks to free the actor and eschews imposing fixed moments or movements, so that each performance feels invented in the moment. He has been quoted as saying, 'I am more interested in training the actor than in imposing specific interpretations on the play.'

The essence of his approach, described in his book *The Actor and the Target*, is that good acting is always specific and that rehearsals are about removing blocks for the actor by the actor focusing on an external object, or person, which needs to be changed by the character – the target. 'You can never know what you are doing until you first know what you are doing it to. For the actor, all "doing" has to be done to something. The actor can do nothing without the target.' The six rules of the target are: there is always a target; the target exists outside and at a measurable distance; the target exists before you need it; the target is always specific; the target is always transforming; and, the target is always active. So, instead of *wanting* a cup of tea, you see a cup of tea that *needs* to be drunk: the focus is not on an internal impulse but on what the external target is forcing the actor and character to do, so all action is a reaction to what the target is doing, and there are always stakes in responding to the target, there is always something to be won and lost in different courses of action.

By taking the actor's attention away from their internal world and thinking in terms of needs provoked by the outside world rather than wants generated by intentions, to many actors and critics Donnellan has created productions in which actors can *be* rather than demonstrate.

Katie Mitchell

Katie Mitchell has directed many celebrated productions for the National Theatre, the RSC, and other leading theatre and opera companies in the UK and Europe.

Like Mike Alfreds's book, Katie Mitchell's *The Director's Craft: A Handbook for the Theatre* does what it says on the cover, and like his, might be deemed a methodology for directors more than actors; but it has so much to offer in terms of rigorous practical craft, as well as insight and inspiration, about the director's work with actors, that, with Mike Alfreds's book, it has quickly become one of the most influential works for emerging directors in the UK over the past few years. Based on her own work, and particularly her production of Chekhov's *The Seagull* at the National Theatre in 2007, Katie Mitchell's book offers an extremely detailed guide to approaching a production at every stage, from first reading the script to the last night, which can be applied by any director to any production without prescribing an aesthetic or directorial taste. Like many of her productions, the devil, and the craft, is in the detail, but the overall effect is inspirational to other directors.

Max Stafford-Clark and Actioning

I have already referred to *Actions: The Actors' Thesaurus*, by Marina Caldarone and Maggie Lloyd-Williams, as offering a useful introduction to 'actioning' and 'unit-ing', and how to apply these methods practically in a rehearsal room, and it is a valuable book, not only for its economic introduction, but also as a ready reference tool – a thesaurus – for expanding an actor's and director's actioning vocabulary. The book also acknowledges that the leading exponent of actioning in the UK in the past few decades has been the former artistic director of the Royal Court Theatre,

Max Stafford-Clark. Also recommended is his book *Letters to George* – an insightful account of a director trying to communicate with a long-deceased playwright, George Farquhar – especially for the chapter on the director and the author, in which Max Stafford-Clark offers detailed descriptions of how he uses actioning in his rehearsal process and how this informs subsequent rehearsals and the production. Actioning does have its critics – that it can be too cerebral, that it relies on the linguistic rather than imaginative acuity of actors, and that it can restrict the adaptation of early decisions as the production develops – but it is a tool commonly taught to actors at drama school, and is therefore part of their acting language, and it can be a very useful tool to use on occasion, even if you do not wish to action the whole play as Max Stafford-Clark does.

Other acting methodologies

The above account of practitioners who have developed distinctive acting and directing methodologies is not by any means exhaustive, but it does, first, give a broad picture of the main methodologies that have developed since the late nineteenth century, and also reflects the range of practitioners who are key influences for emerging directors currently in the UK, based on the interests and reactions of directors in training over the past few years. Twenty years earlier such a descriptive list would have certainly included Peter Brook, Jerzy Grotowski and Joan Littlewood, and although these directors remain as inspirational figures theirs are not currently the distinctive methodologies on which many emerging directors seem to wish directly to draw in developing their own practice. To the extent that my descriptive list is drawn upon my own experience of working with emerging directors it is a personal one, and there are many other directors and other practitioners of whom it is useful to have a knowledge, even if it is initially a brief one, so that you can then decide if you wish to pursue your interest in them.

There are several books which offer chapters on a range of practitioners not covered in detail here. Firstly, *Twentieth Century Actor Training*, edited by Alison Hodge, offers useful chapters on Joan Littlewood, Jerzy Grotowski, Vsevolod Meyerhold, Wlodzimierz Staniewski, Peter Brook, Jacques Copeau, Eugenio Barba and others mentioned in this chapter. *In Contact with the Gods?*, edited by Maria M. Delgado and Paul Heritage, includes short interviews with, and biographical and bibliographical details of, several important figures, including Augusto Boal, Lev Dodin, Ariane

Mnouchkine and Peter Stein. Shomit Mitter's *Systems of Rehearsal* is a very interesting appraisal of the methods in practice of Stanislavski, Bertolt Brecht and Jerzy Grotowski, viewed through their influence on the work of Peter Brook. It is a book of analysis that is founded on many detailed and interesting observations of workshops and rehearsals.

Even these books do not contain chapters or sections on such important figures as Jacques Lecoq, Pina Bausch and Philippe Gaulier, all of whom have been extremely influential in actor training and on the work of many directors.

And, finally, there is David Mamet, the great iconoclast of acting methodologies, who describes actor training as 'institutionalised ancestor worship'. In his entertaining bombast against acting gurus, *True and False*, he remarks: 'That they managed, in spite of their human frailty, to assert their view sufficiently to found a school and attract followers might inspire us – but instead of inspiring us to worship in their shades, it might inspire us to found our own schools.'

Off we go then.

Developing your own approach

Personalising the gurus

As I stressed earlier, it is not necessary to know any of these methodologies in order to communicate successfully and work with actors: some directors will feel the need to train as a director and absorb some of these approaches before making work; others will try to combine reading some of the books mentioned here with seeking out practical workshops led by peer directors and experts on these practitioners to devise their own form of training; others will try to combine this with assisting peer directors; and others will be far more gung-ho and decide the only way of developing as a director is by doing it. An alternative strategy is to read some of the practitioners mentioned above, to decide on one or two with whom you connect intuitively as well as intellectually, to find a free space, to inveigle some actors, or friends who can act, or supportive directors, and to try out some of their approaches in workshops. It is much better to try these approaches out in an environment in which the purpose is experimentation with the techniques, rather than trying to use them for the first time in a rehearsal situation, where the focus is the production.

The other reason for trying the exercises in workshops is to fully own them yourself. One cannot simply replicate a Meisner exercise or a Mike Alfreds rehearsal method without trying it, evaluating it and probably adapting it so that it feels natural in your hands and becomes part of your personal synthesised approach, rather than your approach being an acting methodology mega-mix.

Very often the approaches or individual exercises feel strangely alien in your hands the first time you try them, or they may not simply unfold in the way you expected from reading about them: how many times do you have to try a recipe before the meal is edible for friends? You don't want still to be at the stage of slavishly following the instructions on the packet, or the quantities in the recipe book when you are cooking against the clock to feed six people; neither do you want to be following an exercise by rote when you are trying to get on a production in three weeks.

As I said earlier, it may be unhelpful to announce that you are going to use an Anne Bogart 'Viewpoints' exercise in a rehearsal room before doing so; it will be more helpful if you have tried the Viewpoints in workshops, evaluated how it actually worked and how long it took; what it actually achieved; what elements of it you might personalise; and for what specific play, or for what situation or moment in rehearsals, it might be useful to you and the actors. And at the risk of being accused of plagiarism, I don't think directors should let any other directors into their rehearsal room – not Sanford Meisner, Mike Alfreds, not even Konstantin Stanislavski. If you use their exercises or approaches in a rehearsal room ideally they will have already been tried and personalised by you and become part of your approach or toolkit.

Personal skills

Over the past eight years applicants for a place on the Master of Fine Arts in Theatre Directing at Birkbeck, University of London, have been asked to lead a forty-five-minute workshop on a chosen section of text with two professional actors. As programme director I have watched over 200 such workshops led by emerging directors, and have often been delighted and surprised by the creativity and originality of the directors' work. However, over the years certain approaches have been repeated on which it might be useful to make some observations.

We all like to feel that we have achieved something at the end of a workshop, even if a modest goal has been set, so planning a workshop or rehearsal session should not only have a definite achievable goal, which it might be useful to set out, however roughly, at the beginning, but the amount of material covered and the work involved should not be longer than forty minutes in a forty-five-minute workshop. It is really easy to try to cover too much, which results either in the workshop being cut off rather than brought to a natural end, or skimping on the detail and thoroughness of the work because you are constantly under time pressure. Planning a workshop or rehearsal session of forty-five minutes which covers the material well and reaches a natural conclusion in just that time is a fundamental directing skill which it takes time, and a will, to acquire.

Regardless of how brilliant and stimulating your rehearsals might be, actors will lose motivation and get quite grumpy if you often overrun calls and keep them waiting half an hour after you've called them to rehearse their scene, or if you cut off the work on a scene because of time, without getting to a good stage to leave the scene until the next time. If you can't plan and manage time, it can undermine the actors' confidence in you and the production. If you do choose to run workshops to try out a text or some exercises, it is worth consciously making goal-planning and time-management part of your agenda.

The highly respected and experienced director Peter Gill has commented that he never, or very rarely, goes into a rehearsal room with a script. He knows the play he is directing, he has done his research and planning for that rehearsal, so why does he need the script? Many emerging directors, and many not-so-emerging directors, set up the work for a scene, then, as soon as the actors begin to work, their eyes go to their script. This is understandable, but it can mean two things: first, that the director is just not watching the actors and what is happening between them and what they are bringing to the scene; and second, that, subconsciously, by hearing what the actors are saying while reading the script the director is seeing whether the actors' responses to the text match their own response, rather than focusing on the actors' response and taking that as the point from which to build ideas and work on the scene.

This can lead to a directorial approach which is quite fixed in its agenda and closed to working collaboratively with the actors: the comments that often follow the scene may be notes about variations from a director's pre-formed ideas of how the scene should work. It may begin as an unconscious mannerism from not feeling as on top of the text as you would like to be, but it can become an ingrained habit that is not conducive either to collaboration or to enjoying watching actors work – which is a shame for any director.

Although I suggested earlier that a workshop should have a goal, the word 'goal' is not necessarily the same as 'result'. Sometimes a director will go into a rehearsal or workshop with a fixed idea of what the scene should look like; it might be better to go in with a structure of work and an area and level of exploration, which is a goal for the amount of work covered and a good place to get to by the end of the workshop, rather than a picture of the scene that you have envisaged before the workshop, which would be a 'result'. Many directors spend a lot of time working with actors over the first few years of their career developing strategies whereby the workshop or rehearsal is structured and productive, but how you all 'get there' is left flexible and open to genuine creative work, which will engender unprescribed and spontaneous results.

As Annie Tyson suggests in her interview, it might be helpful to think of your work with the actors in the following way: first as being a facilitator who helps to establish the given circumstances and world and ideas of the play; second, as being someone who allows the actors to explore their responses to that situation and to find their own physical, emotional and intellectual response to the play; and only then being someone who helps shape those responses in terms of the tempo, rhythms, climaxes and visual and spatial needs of the production: you build from the responses of the actors.

You may have collected enormous amounts of information on the writer, the world of the play and the language of the play, and you may choose to assemble an 'actor pack' with information about the play for actors, but how you really integrate this research into the practical work requires sensitive thinking. It is not necessary to feel you know all the answers on day one of rehearsals, and it is not necessary to demonstrate the depths of your research to the actors: you may overwhelm them with information in the early stages of rehearsals, making the first day seem like a seminar rather than a rehearsal. Sometimes directors spend a lot of time on the background and research at the beginning of rehearsals and then, assuming that 'that's done', don't refer back to and integrate the research in a practical and applicable way when working through the play. It might be better to decide what is useful information for the company to have at the beginning, but to be sparing, and then to introduce other research at the point that it becomes practically useful. It might be helpful to think of bringing the world of the play to the actors, rather than bringing the actors to the world of the play.

Finally, actors are generous, open and brave people who are usually up for trying anything they think will help the production and their work; however, it is important to say briefly why you are proposing to try something and how you think it might help them and the production. Sometimes directors think that by not saying why they are launching into a particular exercise and hoping that its meaning and relevance will become evident at the end, it will make the exercise more stimulating: this is a high-risk strategy that will often leave actors thinking not how exciting it is, but, 'Why am I doing this?' Actors relish going on a journey, but will commit to it much more if they know there's a map and a purpose, so saying a few words to frame exercises or different stages of work is important: it gives a sense of the specific serving the whole and avoids actors thinking that you are trying to teach rather than direct the production.

Preparation for a production and auditioning

Because the whole process of casting and auditioning has to fit in with the time line of other preparations for a production, casting and auditioning are discussed in Chapter Six, 'The Director and the Production', as is some of the preparation that you will wish to do in the months and weeks before you begin rehearsals. As the focus here is on the actor–director relationship we will concentrate on how your knowledge of acting and directing approaches can be translated into decisions about how best to plan and structure a rehearsal period.

There is also the question of what, if anything, you ask actors to do in preparation before rehearsals begin, and how that might affect your rehearsal planning. As is discussed in the interview with Sarah Esdaile, you may ask the actors to do some work on the play before rehearsals begin, such as preparing the four lists – 'What do I say about myself?' 'What do other characters say about me?' 'What do I say about other characters?' 'What does the author say about me?' – or to do other background work on the play. Sir Peter Hall said recently, 'In the last five years, I've made another radical change. I now ask the actors to learn the part before we start rehearsals. Some argue that, if you do that, the actor won't develop. Absolute bunk. What it gives you, in effect, is an extra two weeks' rehearsal.'

There are practical and contractual questions about asking actors to do preparation before they are actually being paid, but increasingly, particularly with shorter rehearsal times, actors are being asked to do such preparation, and this can effectively give you and the actors more working time – but it is important to mention these expectations at the audition, and, dare one say it, before the actor accepts the job.

Rehearsal patterns

As Sarah Esdaile mentions in her interview, part of her preparation for rehearsals is to look at three factors and to choose which method, or combination of methods, is going to work best for each production.

The first factor is the nature of the play. For example, as she suggests, the methods she uses, inspired by Mike Alfreds and Michael Chekhov, are particularly suited to plays such as Arthur Miller's, with a great deal of historic, social and personal information embedded in them, which leads to a dense psychological realism requiring thorough analysis; these methods might be less suitable for a Shakespeare play which, though psychologically complex, has the subtext in the text rather than underneath it. As Sarah Esdaile also mentions, she will rummage in her toolbox for the best methods and leave some in the toolbox.

The second factor is the time available. In planning a rehearsal period it is often helpful to work backwards. Most actors and directors will want to end the rehearsal period with at least two run-throughs of the play before leaving the rehearsal room, and if it is a full-length play each run may take a whole session – or half a day – and you will also want time to give notes and work through certain sections after each run, so that could mean that the final two days of the rehearsal period are devoted to runs and subsequent notes and work, so you will have to aim to have worked through the whole play, in whatever pattern you choose, by the middle of the final week.

You may wish to begin the first week with a read-through, a discussion about the design, and one or two sessions about the research and background to the play, which might include a field trip or inviting in a guest or expert on an aspect of the play. So the first two days of the rehearsal period might not be spent on actually working through the play. Suddenly your actual work-through time might be a week shorter than you thought, and if there is a fight director, musical director, choreographer or dialect coach, and it is not practical to have simultaneous rehearsals, you will have to factor in the time these sessions will take and also deduct them from your work-through time.

It may seem mechanical, but as part of your pre-rehearsal preparations it is worth making a chart of the rehearsal period, session by session, marking all the sessions which are not work-through time and then calculating the number of hours you have to work through the play. If you plan, say, three full sequential work-throughs of the play, you may then take the number of pages in the play, multiply them by three and from that you can work out how many pages an hour you would have to work through to get three work-throughs in the time available: can you really work at six pages an hour? You may decide to spend most time on the first work-through and less time on the second, and an even shorter time on the third; or you may decide to scrap the visit to the zoo or try to hire a second rehearsal room to have simultaneous rehearsals. This may sound reductive, but it is really worth doing the maths on the pages-per-hour rate you will have to observe before becoming too emotionally attached to your pre-work-through sessions or having four runs in the final week.

The third factor is the cast. You may have discussed your proposed working methods with actors at the auditions, but if actors are unfamiliar with a working method they might be nervous about it, or resistant to it, or completely open to it: from your audition process you should have a fairly good instinctive understanding of how appropriate your working methods will be for your cast, or how much you may have to explain your chosen approaches before beginning the work. If you are going to use a very distinctive approach which is not within the broad Stanislavskian tradition, or going to use approaches which might not be expected from the nature and requirements of the play, it is worth being open about this at the auditions or meetings. This not only prepares the actors before they accept the job, but in discussion you may also get a sense of how an actor might respond to your proposed method of working, and get the opportunity to explain why you have chosen this approach, giving the actor a better understanding of the production and the opportunity to bear this in mind in their pre-rehearsal preparation – and whether or not to accept the job. How to plan a making period for a devised piece of work is discussed in the interview with Simon Pittman in Chapter Three, 'The Director and the Author'.

Overall patterns

There are an infinite number of ways of working through a play, but whatever approaches you use it might be helpful initially to consider three broadly different patterns and then to create variations on these template approaches: walking and talking; tablework followed by physical work-throughs; and daily multi-focus before physical work-throughs.

There is a fundamental tension between wanting to establish the facts of a scene, and therefore discussing it, and wanting to 'get it on its feet', and therefore exploring the play physically and viscerally as well as intellectually. No perfect balance is possible, and actors have differing preferences: it is a huge but true generalisation that many more experienced actors want to move the play rather than spending a lot of time on discussion, and some actors relish research and debate and others have very little to say and want to be allowed to make their own connections with the play by doing it. You simply have to take into account the three factors above, make a judgement, and then be adaptable and responsive if your plans are not working out as you thought they would; but maintain an overall plan for working through the play in the time available.

The term 'tablework' has been increasingly used over the past few years to describe the work done at the beginning of rehearsals spent sitting round a table before physically working through the play. This might include unit-ing the play, going through the play scene by scene and establishing the facts of each scene; clarifying the meaning of words or phrases; integrating the research; asking questions about the intentions of characters; and possibly making provisional decisions about facts which are not in the play but have to be deduced from the text. An example would be whether Lady Macbeth's 'I have given suck' implies that the Macbeths have children, even though Macduff says, 'He has no children,' which may, or may not, refer to Macbeth. Or, as in Max Stafford Clark's rehearsals, it might include actioning every line before moving the play, or in actioning specific lines or sections.

Many directors use the tablework approach because it means that once you do begin to move the play all or most of the facts and questions have been addressed, so that everyone can focus on the physical world of the play, make instinctive decisions that are solidly based on the facts rather than conjecture, and actors can better connect with each other. The down side is that tablework time consumes physical work-through time and if the discussions are not focused and productive they can become time-consuming, so that actors not only go off the boil but become frustrated, and increasingly worried that they are not working through the play; others argue that well directed and timetabled tablework saves an awful lot of time later. Usually, but not always, tablework is conducted with the full company present throughout, which does mean that everyone, whatever size their part, shares in the knowledge of the world of the play and the decisions that are being made; the down side is that actors can get very frustrated if there are several days of tablework between their scenes.

The walking and talking approach is perhaps the most conventional. After the read-through you begin working through the play in sequence, moving the scene and asking questions and discussing it at the same time. To many, this has the advantage that all aspects of the world of the play and the actors' work are being addressed, so that connections between, say, the newly discovered meaning of a line can be physically expressed at the moment of discovery and shared, physically, with the other actors, rather than remembered and only expressed a week later. At worst it can mean that everyone's focus is in so many directions at the same time that the work becomes unfocused and that important information is undigested before it is expressed. It can also mean that discussions, such as the one about Macbeth's progeny, can take longer than anticipated and either throw out your rehearsal call or remain unresolved until you next come to that scene. This pattern of working does usually mean calling the actors scene by scene and not sharing the discoveries and decisions with the rest of the cast at the time, so you have to find a mechanism for keeping actors not in the scene up to speed with decisions that may affect them.

To have my cake and eat it, I have combined tablework with walking and talking – often calling actors scene by scene and allocating tablework time for that scene; then physically working through it; then doing the same with the following scene, remembering to keep 'new' actors informed of decisions and newly discovered facts that affect them.

The third method is described in the interview with Sarah Esdaile and described in great detail in Mike Alfreds's book *Different Every Night*. This is a multi-focus approach to the first period of rehearsals in which each day is broken up into deliberately different forms of activity, such as an hour on the world of the play, which may include assimilating research on its society and culture; watching a film, or learning a period dance, or skill; an hour on one person's character, which may include going through one person's four lists, hotseating a character, or other improvisations about that character; an hour on unit-ing or actioning or establishing the facts of a scene and asking questions about events and facts and the relationships in that scene. This three-hour pattern of a different activity every hour might be repeated morning and afternoon in a six-hour day, or some sessions might take an hour and a half, with fewer different sessions.

In a four-week rehearsal period Sarah Esdaile allows seven to ten days for this process before beginning the first draft or work-through of the play from page one. In her interview she is very clear about the benefits of this approach for creating a genuine ensemble of actors, for the level of detail this brings to the work, and for the knowledge and confidence it gives the actors when it comes to beginning the first work-through. Although it may have taken the best part of a third of the whole rehearsal time, it pays dividends of time when you do come to work through the play. It also means that not all of every day is spent in discussion, or around a table, and that all the actors are engaged in the work on a regular basis throughout the day. This multi-focus approach does not have to be limited to the activities described above but can be adapted to the requirements of the play; it is the notion that the play can be approached from several different and complementary angles simultaneously during the course of a day before beginning a sequential work-through that is distinctive.

Indeed, all three of these template approaches can be adapted in terms of their patterning, and each can incorporate specific exercises or methods: tablework might include unit-ing, actioning, close reading of the text or incorporating research and character work; walking and talking might include improvisations, physical exercises, Meisner, Chekhov or Bogart exercises as well as conventional rehearsing. In describing these patterns I am not implying that there is no scope for including a variety of different approaches within them, or that you should have a pattern on day one which you rigidly stick to; but planning an overall pattern for the full rehearsal period allows you to have a sense of the whole chosen process when immersed in the detail and to check in with yourself that you are making the expected progress, whether in terms of the stages you wish to get to at different points, or how many pages you have worked through. The purpose of detailed rehearsal planning is not to manage the actors or the creative process but to manage time in order to choose the best creative process for the time available and to know that you are maximising your and the actors' productivity.

Whatever pattern and methodologies you choose, if you accept that the broad task of the director is first to introduce the world of the play and the text to the actors, then to allow the actors to respond to it, then finally to help shape those responses, that would imply three work-throughs:

an establishing work-through so that the actors can be in full possession of the facts, physicality, intentions and ideas of the scene and go away and think about them, and then in a second work-through to explore practically a variety of responses and ideas and to communicate with the other actors without the encumbrance of a script; and then a third work-through to further explore, refine and shape those responses. Each of these will vary in content and length depending on the work done previously and the point you wish to get to in your work on a scene before moving on; there is no rule that says you must work through a play sequentially, or that you must have three work-throughs, but it is a template approach that is helpful to actors, allowing them to work on a scene in the room, go away and think about it and absorb the work; to come back to it and explore it again without having to commit to certain decisions, and to go away again and reflect on the possibilities and choices in the scene; then, in the third work-through, to reach a shared understanding with you and the other actors in the scene that this is an agreed shape with which they are comfortable, providing a firm foundation on which they can build in later run-throughs and ultimately performances.

As mentioned earlier, by the time you are in the second half of the last week of rehearsals, you and the actors will want to run the play several times and will only have time to work on individual moments or small sections, so the goal of the last work-through is reaching a broad consensus about the shape of a scene which will enable actors to develop it together without much further discussion or experimentation.

A common language

Hopefully, before the first day of rehearsals you will have chosen your methods of work on the play and a rehearsal pattern and time plan, and those choices will have been based on your previous experience, your research on the play, the time available and your knowledge of the cast and your assimilated toolkit. Referring back to the suggestion that you do not let any other director into your rehearsal room, either on day one or as you work through the play, it is worth briefly setting out your overall plan for working through the play and its rationale, and acknowledging that as all the actors in the room come from different backgrounds you need to take a few moments to agree some basic terminology. For example, if you are going to unit the play, you might say that for the purposes of our work, let us agree that a unit means *this*, an action means *this*, and an intention means *this*. It need not be a seminar, but most actors know and agree that many commonly used terms can mean different things to different people, so it is simply an agreed clarification, not a lecture on Stanislavski. Not only does this clarify, but it also brings actors from different backgrounds to a common language and hopefully a sense that you have a common ownership of your collective work process over the next few weeks. It also establishes a language out of which your discussions during the work-throughs and your notes after run-throughs will naturally develop and be understood by all.

How to use runs

I have worked with many actors who fear the 'R word': having been able to work in a secure environment for three or four weeks in which experimentation and the opportunity to try choices that may not be right has been the working atmosphere, suddenly you are running the whole act or the whole play for the first time and, very often, the stage manager, lighting designer and sound designer, who hitherto have only been in the room occasionally, as well as the rest of the company, are now sitting there to watch the run. It can be a very unnerving moment for you and the actors, and general calls to arms by the director like, 'Oh, just relax and enjoy it!' do nothing to help the situation.

It is often more helpful to suggest some specific, but overall, objectives for runs. For example, for a first run, during which actors might still be clinging to lines and trying to remember what comes next as it is the first time the play has been worked through in real time, you might ask them not to worry about pace but concentrate on listening to each other and making connections with each other in the moment. For a second run you might choose one or more points of concentration, such as bearing in mind how cold it is in act two, or that it is three in the morning in act three, or just to be aware of your place in the family and your connection to other family members during that run. Whether the focus is about the playing of the run or a point of concentration, a specific overall objective which can be focused upon alongside the actual acting of each scene can take the fear out of the first few runs, and prevent them being generalised, fearful attempts on an unattainable summit, while bringing useful dimensions to the playing which will be left as watermarks in the production after the point of concentration has been left behind. The same applies to dress rehearsals and previews: by focusing on something specific one can reduce the fear of the general – and the generalised fear.

Notes

Although you will have undoubtedly made comments and observations during the rehearsal process, 'notes' often refers specifically to the observations a director makes after a run-through, dress rehearsal, preview or performance. A notes session is often led by the director with the whole company and stage manager present, although some of the notes might be for individuals. Hopefully, through your particular working methods you and the actors will have a shared vocabulary and the notes you give will be couched in that vocabulary and be a natural extension of your working methods, so by the time you come to run a whole act, or the whole play, you and the actors will have a fundamental confidence in the work you have created. In that case your notes might fall into one of four categories.

The first type of note might be about fine-tuning choices and intentions in a particular scene within an agreed framework for that scene. These notes might be to do with questioning or affirming decisions about actions, agreed shapes or objectives in scenes, the level of stakes in a moment or decision, the relative status of characters or the relative levels of intensity of intention at moments in a scene. Perhaps something like, 'I think the intention behind that moment is spot on, but it could just be a slightly bigger decision – can you up the ante on that?' or, 'I think the status distance between you has become a little close – can you play the difference in status a bit more?' As with all four categories of notes, a note does not have to be an instruction – it may even be retraction of an earlier idea or note, or it may be a suggestion for development from something that happened for the first time in the last run, or it may be an affirmation of a recent choice or change. Many notes are about decision housekeeping – clarifying what has most recently been collectively agreed – as much as being about (constructive) criticism.

The second type might be global notes about the whole play, such as about how one scene follows another or about the pacing of scenes or sections in the light of the tempo of the whole play. These notes might include 'storytelling' notes. In the fourth week of rehearsals it is often very difficult to remember what first struck you as the climaxes and revelations of the play and it is sometimes useful to remind yourself and the actors what is new and thought-changing at a given moment; what the characters do and do not know; and not to play the end of a scene or act at the start of the scene or act, but to remember the full journey of the play and characters as they first experienced it. This type of note might be one of very few notes before rather than after a run: 'Just let your character have a really surprising journey, just for this run concentrate on what is new information, or a real shock to them at every stage: let the play hit them and rather than concentrating on being active – be reactive.'

The third type might be 'technical' notes about fine-tuning entrances and exits and other pieces of physical action. You may not have 'blocked' the play and there might be stage shapes or sequences of movement where your and eventually the audience's attention needs to be drawn or focused – or there might be too many focuses at one point. There might be notes about the timing of entrances and the change between one scene and the next to tighten up the pace of the whole production. An example might be asking an actor to enter a scene as late as possible as their entrance is distracting from a really important moment. However, sometimes one can get too hung up on these details in the rehearsal room, only to find that the tech and the set change stage shapes and timings, so many of these notes, unless they are internal to the scene and action, are probably best left until after the first dress rehearsal.

The fourth type of note might be a clarification note: you and two actors may have agreed on a decision which then isn't acted upon in a run – it may have just been forgotten, or the actor may have had second thoughts about it. The clarification note can be a disguised reinforcement note, asking an actor to commit more to an earlier note or to make sure that an agreed decision will not be unpicked in the future. An example might be: 'Do you remember we changed that moment, as we thought it would be better if "x" happened? Are you still OK with that?'

Whatever the vocabulary you have established there are some general observations about notes which might be useful. Particularly after a first run-through, dress rehearsal or preview, but after any run, it is important to emphasise the positive aspects of the run and what has been learnt. Many actors don't find it useful for you to draw attention to one particular line or moment, even if the note is a positive one, as it can spring into the actor's mind the next time they perform the line, and can jolt them out of the moment – praise is probably the only type of note which can be helpful if it is generalised. Be as precise and specific as you can: if a note is to be helpful to an actor, it needs to be clear and playable, and you need to be certain that the actor is not left with a vague note which they won't know how to play and which may make the moment worse.

It is probably unwise to give a note if you know that there is a problem, but don't know what the solution is: notes should be constructive suggestions of alternative choices rather than criticisms which don't assist the actor. It might be that you don't know the answer but feel confident that the actor does, in which case you might simply ask the actor to go away and have a think about the moment – something like, 'It's fine, but you might be able to investigate it more, or consider other choices', but you need to know the actor well enough to feel that they will find it helpful rather than confusing. Such notes are usually notes about the development of a moment which is already working but could be explored further.

It is often said that the art of note-giving is not just about the note, but when to give a note, or even not giving a note at all. As has been remarked earlier, directors need to understand the actor's processes and to allow them the time and space to discover and develop their work themselves. There might be moments in a run that are not realised as they were in rehearsal simply because it is the first time an actor has reached that moment in that way; it might be an actor trying something new, or they might have been thrown by a new prop or something that happened three lines earlier – it might be a one-off. See the moment again in another run, and then if there is a problem, mention it.

There are times to give many detailed notes, usually when there is opportunity to actually discuss and work them before the next run or performance, and there are times, such as between a dress rehearsal and first performance, when it is best if the notes are kept to the most important acting notes, to technical issues, such as lighting cues, quick changes and any issues of safety, and really positive points.

Notes are usually given with the whole company and the deputy stage manager present because a note to any one individual might affect someone else, but sometimes if a note is particularly complicated, or delicate, and applies to only one or two people, give it privately.

It is important, particularly during the previews and performances, that notes from the actors are heard, discussed and, if necessary, worked on. Very often notes sessions after a tech, dress or opening are there to sort out unresolved confusions or changes that have arisen during the tech period, which actors are trying to deal with individually but for which they need a collective solution.

Finally, be precise, be constructive, and don't forget to mention the positives as well as the work still to be done: we all need praise and reassurance to continue the work and have faith.

Directors are people too

Acting methodologies do not a director make. Of course, all the acting and directing approaches discussed in this chapter will help inform your developing practice as a director, but ultimately they will only inform your personal approach, which will also be influenced by your previous experience in workshops, in rehearsal rooms, either as a director or assistant, by what theatre you see and your personal taste and practical philosophy about the work you wish to make. Your directorial approach will also be influenced by your life experiences and your personality, and although as a director you will have a very clear professional relationship with actors and other collaborators you cannot leave your personality at the rehearsal room door. Whether it is conscious or unconscious, how you personally interact with people and how you lead the rehearsal process will affect the 'creative temperature' of the room and have an influence on the whole working process and production. Some directors say that they believe in collaboration and the ensemble but allow actors with smaller parts to feel peripheral to the larger project, or dismiss suggestions from actors which do not fit in with their vision of the production. Others do not acknowledge how terrifying it is to lead the first day of rehearsals or to direct hugely experienced actors, but it may well show through.

Directing actors is as much about personal skills as it is about directorial skills, and developing those personal skills can begin with an honesty with yourself about your strengths and weaknesses as a communicator and leader of a process as well as your preoccupations or mental blocks about a scene or character, or how you are going to solve a problem. Many directors feel a huge sense of relief when they realise that they do not have to know all the answers in a rehearsal room, since feeling the pressure to know all the answers is much more blocking and debilitating than admitting you do not know something. It can be daunting to direct extremely experienced actors, but it is worth remembering that if you have met or auditioned the actor, they will have met and auditioned you, and that they want to be there.

Actors and directors all have to start afresh on every project, and as long as you have confidence in your approaches, and can communicate that confidence, you will maintain the actors' confidence by structuring the work in ways that feel germane, purposeful, and enjoyable for the production you are working on. It might be helpful to consider that the play is the unknown quantity for you both, and you will be helpful to an actor of whatever experience if you both focus on the particular needs of the production: you are not there to demonstrate your directing skills in general, you are to address the specific demands of your shared project. To plagiarise and paraphrase Declan Donnellan, the target is not the wants of the experienced actor, it is the demands or needs of the project.

One of the most concise and pithy quotes about setting the creative temperature of the rehearsal room came from the director Phyllida Lloyd, when she said: 'I like to make the rehearsal room a safe space in which dangerous things can occur.' This implies that the director has organised an approach and a rehearsal plan in which everyone has confidence but that, as Sarah Esdaile says in her interview, no question is too stupid, and that no one is going to be judgemental when actors, or the director, take risks without knowing the outcome. It is the job of the director to create this environment from day one.

Even the most experienced directors are nervous about beginning a new project and leading a company of actors, but the better you are prepared – and the more confident that your chosen methods will enable actors to creatively engage with the play and each other, and result in work in progress that can be taken further by the actors in performance by the time you leave the rehearsal room – the easier it is to watch the actors rather than your script and to engender a shared working process that can be genuinely responsive and collaborative. Removing the fear by planning allows you actually to enjoy and to be joyful in the room and to immerse yourself fully in being a creative and responsive artist, because the organiser and planner in you has done their job. This attitude too will communicate itself to the actors and others in the production. Being 'in the moment' is as valuable to directors as it is to actors. Enjoy.

Interviews

Interview with Annie Tyson

From 2002 until August 2010 Annie Tyson was Course Director for the BA Honours Acting Course at Drama Centre, where she taught acting and directed across all years in the school. Her final-year productions have included Schiller's Mary Stuart, Wild Oats *by John O'Keefe,* A Laughing Matter *by April de Angelis,* All's Well That Ends Well, Love's Labour's Lost, Richard II, The Second Mrs Tanqueray *and most recently* A Winter's Tale *and* A Cure for a Cuckold.

She studied Drama and Theatre Arts at Birmingham University before training at Drama Centre London, and has worked extensively as an actor in regional theatre, TV and radio and in London, where work included new plays on the fringe and founding two new writing companies, one of which, Direct Current, was set up to produce new music theatre and work at the Old Vic and the Young Vic.

Annie has worked in many major drama schools as well as abroad in Paris and Portugal as one of the founder tutors of the Pieta Project which created a young company of actors from the UK, France, Portugal, Italy and Romania. She was a visiting lecturer and tutor at the Carnegie Mellon School of Drama in Pittsburg, USA. She continues to work at Drama Centre and for the MFA in Directing at Birkbeck College, as well as now pursuing her freelance acting and directing career. I first asked her: 'What do actors actually do?'

To put it as simply as possible, in the most fundamental way, what actors do is to make themselves into other people. It sounds absurdly simple, really, but that's what actors do. They take on the personalities, the thoughts and the life of somebody other. Now that somebody other may be completely different to themselves, or that other may be a personality that is rather close to their own. And by transforming themselves into somebody other they make relationships, they tell stories, and out of those stories they create some sort of meaning.

I think the process of doing this is straightforward to articulate but rather complex in execution. One of the questions that one asks potential acting students in their audition is, 'What do you think you need from your training?' Quite often people say, 'Well, I need to train my voice, I need to train my body.' Fewer people say, 'I need to train my imagination' or 'I need to actually get hold of my imagination because I have it but I don't know quite how to use it.' And I think that a good, serious training is going to do that for you, as well as training the instrument, training the voice to be flexible and open and capable of taking on different colours, and training the body to be able to do what you want it to do so that you are truly expressive. It will also give you the skills that are essential: the ability to analyse a text in terms of action; to sight-read with confidence and skill; a sense of musicality; an ability to sing; to dance; to do stage combat; to be at ease in front of a camera and in front of a microphone.

There are many strategies and skills that make up your toolkit, but the most fundamental thing that an actor does is to turn him/herself into somebody else and the process is a business of turning yourself inside out in order to be able to do that – to be able to connect to things that allow this process of change to take root in you. Something that I've become more and more obsessed by is what actually creates change in oneself. A question that one asks increasingly is: 'What is this play actually about, what is this scene about, what is this moment about, so what is the idea under it?' Now you can't play an idea – if you ask an actor to play an idea they'll look at you and maybe nod sagely, but inside they will probably think that you're mad, or at the least somewhat pretentious, and be asking how do I actually do that? But it's the idea that gives you the kind of vital connection to the thing that's inside you that is the capacity to change.

What do you mean by the idea?

If you take a scene between two people and you improvise it, or you play it out, and you say to the actors, 'Well, what is it about?' they'll say, 'Well, it's about the fact that he tells her he's leaving her and she's making a fuss about it.' But then you say to them, 'Well, yes, I know that's what's happening, but why's it written, why's it there? Why did Shakespeare or Chekhov or Pinter or Beckett or whoever, why did they write that? Why is it necessary? What are they trying to say? What is it that they're trying to offer as a piece of meaning to the audience?' And so you try to refine it down to what I would call the guiding idea of the scene, which may be as simple as betrayal, or unrequited love, or belief in a cause, or something big like that. What's the guiding idea of the play or the scene? If you can get hold of it in a way that excites you, there's something about its meaning that grabs you and makes you think, 'I have to do this now, I have to do it for this audience on this night' – or indeed in front of the camera, at this moment. It's your ability to connect on a very personal level, and it's where that idea hits you, where it hits your imagination, where it hits your gut, it hits your heart. So it's not something you understand intellectually, although that comes into it, but something that you experience through the whole of you that's utterly meaningful. And that gives you the capacity to change. And I think that training an actor is helping people to make those connections. In the end, how you do it is entirely your own affair, it's nobody's business but yours. Certainly the director on the film set, or the director in the rehearsal room with only three weeks' rehearsal, isn't going to have the time to interrogate how you get there, that's entirely your affair.

From the point of view of a director who's never worked with trained actors, where do actors see the dividing line between their work and the director's work? Actors presumably expect to have to access their own emotional memory, for example.

Yes, I think that pragmatically you know that's going to be your work. From my own point of view as an actor, my slightly arrogant attitude is, 'Actually, it's none of your business how I get there, I just know that I have to get there and I have to do whatever it takes.' To unpick it too much and to talk about it might make 'it', whatever it is, go dead! Now it may be in certain rehearsal situations there is enough space and time and trust for a director to help facilitate that, and there are many ways that directors can help. Certainly, in a recent acting job, I was helped a great deal by the director asking probing questions at the right moment. I think it depends on all kinds of things: it depends how much time you've got; it depends on the nature of the relationship with the director; it depends on the style of the director. I know actors who absolutely like to be left alone and to get on with it and do it, and what they need is to have a very clear idea of what the overall vision of the play is, and how they're going to contribute to that. There comes a point where directors can interfere too much, and you have to be very sensitive as a director as to when an actor just needs to be allowed simply to do it and explore it and swim about a bit. You can only play one thing at any one time, you can't play six things at once, and I think a director's got to be very sensitive as to when an actor needs input and information and stimulus and ideas, and when you feel, 'Actually I need to let them run with whatever's going on.'

Presumably, in the first instance what an actor is looking for is what some people call the 'non-negotiables' or the 'given circumstances' or an agreed environment in which they can then make their own decisions.

Yes, I think so. In my experience an actor feels comfortable if you get a smell of the vision of the play. You think, 'OK, right, I'm in that world. We think it means this.' A skilful director will then allow and facilitate the possibility of play in rehearsal and allow the vision to be realised by the actors, if they believe that they have got the intelligence, imagination, and sheer capacity to play and invent. Also, a skilful director will have the flexibility to think, 'Oh, we don't need to do it like that, which is the way that I thought we'd do it – actually they're coming up with something that is much more from them, and it's actually a damn sight more exciting than the thing I thought of.' And then there's going to come a point where you have to make decisions. You have to say, 'OK, having done all that work, this is how I think the scene should go. These are the rhythms of it, these are the climaxes of it, this is the musicality of it.' But hopefully that will come from a smelling out of what the actors have got to offer.

Could you talk about the ethos of Drama Centre? Every drama school is different, and changes from time to time, but I think it's true to say that many drama schools in the UK have teachers and heads of courses who came from Drama Centre over the last thirty or forty years?

It's been hugely influential. It was founded almost fifty years ago, as a result of a very profound disagreement between various interested parties at the Central School of Speech and Drama – a very well-thought-of school. There were many factors, but the most important was the revolution in the theatre in the 1950s: there was a new, gutsy, vibrant, for want of a better word working-class voice. Plays were being written that were to do with issues and tensions within society, there was a huge amount of new writing coming out of the Royal Court, and a lot of very exciting voices, including regional voices. And there were other exciting developments: the growth of theatre for young people; the growth of community theatres; and a moving away from a sort of West Endy, London-centric ethos. There was a fundamental schism at Central, and one of the major tutors, John Blatchley, decided that it wasn't really an environment in which he wanted to continue working, and he decided to leave; and a couple of other tutors, Yat Malmgren and Christopher Fettes, decided to leave as well, because they were much more concerned with how you were to train for this emerging and developing theatre rather than for the old stuff that they felt was being regurgitated. There was at that time a group of very feisty, forward-thinking students who decided that it was the training and ideas being pursued by those particular tutors they wanted to engage with. So there was a kind of student revolution, and they said, 'We want to finish our training with you, and if we find premises will you train us?' So the great myth is that they got on their mopeds and they rode around north London and they found this old Methodist church in Chalk Farm – and the rest is history.

Not always an easy history, not always a comfortable history. But the philosophy as I see it – and I was a student at the school in its first decade of life – was that the making of meaning through theatre, and the making of art through theatre, was something that was absolutely crucial to the health and well-being of society, and that it made a difference, and that the process of acting, the art of acting, was something to be taken seriously. There was a very strong sense of handing down tradition not as something ossified and antiquated but to be reinvestigated and reinvented. It was a philosophy that set itself up to be shot down in certain quarters. But it was, and still is, an extraordinarily demanding, challenging and exciting place to be. Its intensity didn't suit everyone – and we could get very up ourselves at times – but there was passion in abundance.

Yat Malmgren always used to say that your talent is your talent: it may be a very small talent that will earn you an awful lot of money, or it may be a very versatile and huge talent that might fox people. Your talent is your talent – but you can be taught how to work. I think it's fair to say that it was the first school that absolutely believed in a methodological approach to acting. Now that is not the same as 'The Method', and people get really confused about this. They think that Drama Centre is a Method school – it's absolutely not the case. It's a school that takes a methodological approach to the serious interrogation of the art of the actor, and indeed, as developed, the art of the director as well, but fundamentally the art of the actor. It took itself very seriously, and it had a politic, which was the thing I found extraordinarily exciting when I went there. It believed that the art of the theatre, the art of the actor and the art of telling stories to the world, was a political act. We were made to relate the work that we did on the great classical plays to a contemporary setting; it wasn't that you updated them, but you were constantly asked: 'What does this mean to us today, why would we bother to do these plays by these dead authors today?' And it was very thrilling – you were in a place where there was a kind of philosophy of art and an intellectual ferocity, which sounds academic but it absolutely wasn't, and you were made really to think about what you were doing, and to take that thought into physical, sensuous action on stage. You did feel that you were on the barricades.

The school was founded on four cornerstones, and no one thing was more important than the other, which is what I found so gripping. The first cornerstone was the Stanislavskian approach, coupled with that of Uta Hagen – much less Strasberg, much more the work of Uta Hagen. The Stanislavskian approach provided a methodological approach to acting: a way of unlocking the doors to the subconscious, and unlocking the doors to your instinct and intuition, because sometimes those things could be very fickle and they could leave you quite often, so you needed to have things at your disposal which enabled those things to be released.

Then there was the approach of John Blatchley, which was very Eurocentric and very much based on the work of Michel Saint-Denis, and that was the other side of the coin to the work on the inner life and the inner world of the character. John's work was glorious in terms of its highly extrovert, highly physical storytelling, using playfulness, fast comedy, Brecht and mask work. His work had an extraordinarily disciplined anarchy to it.

The third pillar was the intellectual ferocity of the course, which was headed up by Christopher Fettes in his Analysis classes, in which we were encouraged to contemplate the whole arc of Western theatre in its political, social and cultural context. That was a very exciting and practical interrogation into the great movements of Western theatre: where they sprung from and what the universal truths were in those works. They were fairly terrifying classes because you had really to get to grips with ideas and give flesh to those ideas in terms of rehearsed readings of plays, and put things up on their feet. It was a chance for you to get to grips in a practical sense with what makes a play by John Ford a play by John Ford, or what makes Molière Molière, what is the essential nature of, say, German Romantic drama?

And the final influence was the influence of Yat Malgmren, which I think many people would believe is the heart of Drama Centre, but actually really doesn't work without the other three elements. Yat was a great expressionist dancer, and his work comes from the world of dance. He created this extraordinary synthesis of physical typology from the physical work of Rudolf Laban, and the work of a man called William Carpenter, and connected it to the Jungian archetypes. He developed it into an extraordinary physical system of sensation, which is to do with how character manifests itself in physical tempi, and it is remarkable work. It creates an extraordinary language which absolutely works. The danger of it is that, until you really smell it practically and feel it physically, it can become a series of labels and a rather intellectual construct, but it isn't in practice.

The great strength of the training at its most vibrant was that those four pillars worked both in harmony and in abrasion with one another: so you'd be working with the inspiring Doreen Cannon on action playing and previous circumstances and all the Stanislavskian stuff, and you'd be very concerned with your inner life, and the impulse and the truth of the moment; and then you'd go into John Blatchley's class and he'd say, 'No no no no no, we're not bothering about that, we're going to put on this mask and tell the story in this way, I'm not interested in your inner life – do this.' And if you absorbed all of this and took from it all, you were going to find your own way: a methodological approach that gave you a way of working, and at its very best it offered you a degree of flexibility and openness, and it could absorb many other strategies; at its worst, if you took it as a kind of mantra, it meant that people closed themselves off and thought that there's only this way of working.

What was exciting about it, if you look down the years, much of what it espoused and what the school did is now *de rigueur* in most major drama schools, so I think its legacy is that those ideas and thoughts are at the heart of a lot of training today. That just might be a controversial notion but I think it's true.

Interview with Sarah Esdaile

Sarah Esdaile has directed The Deep Sea Blue, Crash, Death of a Salesman *and* The Grouch *all at the West Yorkshire Playhouse. She also co-directed* Philip Pullman's His Dark Materials *with Rachel Kavanaugh (West Yorkshire Playhouse, Birmingham Rep and Tour). Other work includes* The Lady in the Van *(Hull Truck and Number One Tour),* Cling to Me Like Ivy *(Birmingham Rep and Tour),* Life X 3 *(The Watermill),* The Horse Marines *(Drum Theatre, Plymouth),* Drowning on Dry Land *(Salisbury Playhouse),* Kafka's Dick *(Watford Palace),* James and the Giant Peach *(Octagon, Bolton; M.E.N Award, Best Family Show 2007),* Crocodile Seeking Refuge *(Tour),* Lysistrata *(Arcola Theatre),* Pictures of Clay *(Royal Exchange Manchester),* Young People's Taming of the Shrew *(RSC),* Compact Failure *(Clean Break, Arcola Theatre and Tour),* Coyote on a Fence *(Royal Exchange Manchester/ Duchess Theatre, West End; M.E.N Award Best Fringe Production 2004),* The Maiden's Prayer *(Bush Theatre),* See How Beautiful I am *(Bush Theatre/ Pleasance, Edinburgh),* Bill and Esme *(Chelsea Theatre),* The Woolgatherer *(Battersea Arts Centre),* The Boys Next Door *(Latchmere),* Downtown Paradise *(Finborough Theatre/Chapter Arts Centre, Cardiff),* Flip *(Hen and Chickens),* Resistance *(Old Red Lion) and* Loot *(Thorndike Theatre, Leatherhead). Her work as Assistant Director includes* Troilus and Cressida *and* A Month in the Country *for the RSC, and* Henry V, The Merchant of Venice *and* A Chaste Mind in Cheapside *for Shakespeare's Globe. Sarah was also an Associate Director at the RSC on Michael Boyd's Olivier-Award-winning productions of* Henry VI Parts I, II and III *and* Richard III.

I first asked her whom she would you cite as main influences in terms of acting methodologies or directors' work she'd admired and employed in her own work.

I would have to say, in a generic sense, it's everything I've ever seen and everyone I've ever assisted. I really admire the detail in Mike Bradwell's work. The broad-brushstroke, Russian-trained, methodology of Michael Boyd has been a massive influence on me because I was his associate on the tetralogy of *Henry VI Parts I, II* and *III* and *Richard III* as well as assisting him on *Troilus and Cressida*. I'm very interested in Katie Mitchell's process. Mike Alfreds's and Michael Chekhov's work has been the most direct influence on my process. I think one takes on aspects of the methodologies of the people one assists and customises that to play to one's own strengths as a director. And as you do more and more work you evolve your own methodology, which is a sort of magpie accumulation of everyone you've ever worked with, with the backbone being where your instincts lie and where you've achieved the best results in the past. It all has to be siphoned through your own self-awareness and processes.

At the beginning of each project I evaluate which method or approach I'll use. To use the analogy of a toolbox, I look through my tools and I select some, according to the nature of the play; the time scale that I have; and the nature of the actors that I've cast. I'll say to myself, 'I'm going to utilise this and this and I'm going to leave that,' because my instinct tells me that it's not going to work well with these people, in this time frame, on this project.

A lot of my directing students rock up to rehearsals with Mike Alfreds's or Katie Mitchell's book under their arm and that's very worrying sometimes. I'll give them a note like, 'You know he's standing with his back to the audience?' and they'll say, 'Mike Alfreds says you mustn't do blocking, you know,' and I think it's a road to nowhere, to make yourself into some sort of little mini-me.

Are there any approaches that you use more often than not?

The Mike Alfreds and Michael Chekhov-influenced character work is something that I inevitably miss when I don't use it.

Could you describe what that is?

It's the most brilliant representation of what I believe the creative process to be, which is to forge a marriage between mining a text like a detective and the extraordinary creative process of an actor. One of the things it does for me is to create a genuine ensemble. Most actors do the work that I do in some form on their own, but what I'm interested in is the sharing of that work. For example, I've just directed Arthur Miller's *Death of a Salesman* at West Yorkshire Playhouse. It would be ludicrous to equate the size of part and workload of the actor playing Willy Loman with the actor playing Stanley. But what the Mike Alfreds and Michael Chekhov work does is to even the playing field at the start of the creative process: so we take Willy Loman through his character work and we also take Stanley through his, and while we are hotseating Stanley he has absolutely equal weight and importance in the process, and that for me has proven invaluable.

Do you ask the actors to do background work before rehearsals?

Yes, I set the parameters of that research for the actors and then use it in the first week to ten days of rehearsals. So, firstly, I ask actors to prepare the four lists: everything you say about yourself, everything you say about others, everything others say about you, and everything the author says about you, including stage directions.

Then I ask for the character's animal. Actors have the caveat of saying, 'I don't know what it is yet' and I'm very clear about not imposing it – I don't want someone to say, 'Oh yes, I'm a chipmunk,' just to humour me. Then their physical centre, colour and then their music, which could either be, 'This makes me think of my character,' or 'This is what my character listens to.' Then pictures, which could be several pictures or photographs. Then their object, and finally I ask the actors to think of a secret that they can share with the rest of the group, and one that they can't share.

Once the actors have shared all that work I ask each of them to do hot-seating, which involves all the actors, as actors – not in character – asking questions of one actor, who is in character. The actors can do that very subjectively; so if somebody was playing Richard III the actor who was playing Lady Anne could quiz him very rigorously about that relationship in a way that was useful for her. And then at the end of that process I do something where, for example, the actor playing Willy Loman will put on his music and watch while the rest of the company plays at being Willy Loman, which can be anything from very literally re-enacting a typical day in his life to something profoundly expressionistic. And the larger the company, and the more playful and open the group of actors, the more extraordinary, emotive and rewarding that work is for the actor who has to go on and play that character. Particularly if an actor has a very small part, or a non-speaking part, it's fantastic for that one moment to have everybody focused on that individual, before they retreat into the inevitable focus of what their own character says and does.

How long a rehearsal period did you have for Salesman, *and what rehearsal pattern did you use?*

We had four weeks in the rehearsal room. I started off by talking a bit about Miller and the play. I set up a kind of library of resources in the room that everybody could access – movies, books, and other research – and guided the company through which things might be useful for which people. I also set up a model showing and a read-through. I think it's as good a way as any of saying, 'This is the top of the mountain that we're trying to climb.' I tend to keep first days quite short because they can be quite emotionally overwhelming.

And then for the ensuing week to ten days, depending on how big the company is and how big the play is, I'll start off by unit-ing it. With a piece like *Salesman* that text work was absolutely vital because the structure of the play is so fluid, and deconstructing it is massively important in terms of beginning to approach it: we needed to delineate at the very least where and when scenes were taking place. So with the whole company we read the play and unit-ed it and named those units; we kept the names very non-judgemental and objective so that we all knew immediately where and what a certain unit was. I tend to be really pragmatic about unit-ing in terms of dividing the play into logical, manageable chunks. That might be when a radical action happens or it might be more literally when someone leaves or enters, or, as in *Salesman*, it might be when the sequence moves into a different timeline.

I find that with an eight-hour day of unit-ing around the table people will lose concentration, so I'll break it up with beginning character work: so you'll have two hours' unit-ing and then you'll have the treat of some-body's character work for the next hour and a half; or by doing other practical things, such as some voice or dialect work, or watching a movie for research. I'll quite self-consciously break the day up so there's not too much time doing any one thing. Therefore, by the time you get up on your feet to look at act one, scene one, page one, the play is not this intimidating sprawl any more: you have a definitive structure of several units to work through, people have an absolute sense of who they are and, perhaps more importantly, who everyone else is, and how they relate to them.

By that time everybody's raring to get up on their feet and get going, but I believe if you try to do it on day one or day two there's a kind of reluctance, a kind of fear: 'How dare I have the audacity to walk in and be Willy Loman? I have no sense of this.' With my process there's a back-pack of homework and knowledge and confidence that comes from it, and what the work does is to shortcut that process of doing a first draft: all those questions that you would normally be discussing have come up, either in the text discussion or through the character work, so that there's an element of the play unravelling itself a little bit in that first draft work.

Obviously it's been very successful on Salesman, *but are there any plays that you think it's been less successful on?*

Miller writes with great richness and great detail. In a more fragile new play that kind of work may not stand up so strongly, because it depends on the strength and depth of the writing. I don't think it works with Shakespeare, for example, because the plays are not rich in subtext. They're psychologically rich, but the substance is expressed through the language. The work is most successful with a very skilled writer whose strengths lie in psychological detail and subtext – Rattigan, for example.

Do you get any reluctance or concern about working that way with actors? And a supplementary question to that – are you explicit about how you're going to work when you meet people to cast them?

Yes, if I'm meeting leading actors that I'm just having a coffee and chat with, rather than auditioning, I'll absolutely bring it up because there's a certain amount of pre-rehearsal preparation that's required and I firmly believe you have to do that work with great integrity, with a certain amount of belief in it and very thoroughly; and it just doesn't work if you don't write down every repetition. If you say, 'My character says he's tired about ten times but I haven't written down the specifics,' that's not OK. As I do it more and more, and I believe in it more and more, I think my profound passion for it and belief in it is sort of infectious. In a company of, say, eight to ten, I can guarantee that for a percentage of those actors it will be instrumental in transforming their performances, and if they haven't experienced it before as a group activity they'll find it really rewarding and inspiring and moving and exciting. When I was younger I worked with older male actors, particularly, who thought that it might be slightly studenty, or unnecessary and faddy, but as I believe in it more and more I have less trouble selling it.

And you can see the work in the performances?

I very self-consciously use the phrase 'shared experience', but the shared experience of the work bleeds through into the performance. So if a waiter passes somebody in the scene, they know intimate details about him and there's a kind of truth and a detail, and a life force, that comes from that and I haven't found a way to achieve that through any other method.

Often productions are let down by the weakness of people who have less to do: I'll see a great show with great performances and someone will come on and say, 'Your coat, My Lord,' and I think, 'I don't believe you. I think you've just been texting in the wings and you've come on and said your line and gone off again and I don't have any sense of your life beyond this moment.' And that for me often makes or breaks productions.

Practical exercises

Exercise one

This exercise follows on from the comments about planning a forty-five-minute workshop which lasts for that time and covers the intended work to the point where you and the actors have a sense that you have achieved even a modest goal and reached a good point to leave the work; and from the comments about responding genuinely to the work the actors create.

Take either a series of exercises, or a short piece of text, that you know well, and set yourself and the actors a very specific task or point of enquiry. For example, take three different status exercises to explore their relative strengths and weaknesses, or take the post-murder scene from *Macbeth* and explore the options for pauses and rapid exchanges. The intention is to use something with which you are familiar with a modest goal, so that you can concentrate on the actual construction and running of the workshop. You then have a template to approach structuring any workshop which you no longer have to negotiate when exploring new and unpredictable material.

You may wish to adapt Annie Tyson's three-stage framework for working with actors as a model: first introducing the actors to the material and setting out a rough goal for the workshop; then choosing a number of strategies and exercises that allow the actors to explore imaginatively the material, which will be the main part of the workshop; and then responding to the work that the actors have created and pulling it together into an overall shape and taking an overview of what has been learnt and achieved. This practical overview might be followed by two or three minutes in which to evaluate verbally the workshop and what has been learnt.

Initially you may even wish to write yourself a 'script' or series of bullet points to refer back to during the workshop to check where you are, clearly identifying the points at which you need to set up or lead the activity and the points at which you need to see what is being created, to respond to it, and perhaps have two or three exercises or strategies for developing that work. It is often useful to have many more exercises or strategies than you will actually need and then to choose the one or two in the workshop that seem most appropriate to the developed work; or you may abandon all of them and respond in the moment to what is happening. Having a 'script' or structure which you can then go back to gives you more confidence to go 'off-script' knowing that there is an overall plan you can slip back into at a later point to give the workshop an overall sense of direction while allowing you to be responsive.

Once you have a 'template' workshop structure that you are comfortable working with, you can then adapt it to suit new material. You may then wish to read about Sanford Meisner's, Michael Chekhov's or Anne Bogart's work, or actioning or unit-ing, and then try out some of these approaches in workshops that help you to synthesise your own ways of employing these approaches. You may wish to take the same two or three short pieces of contrasting texts for each workshop and try out different techniques and approaches, so that you may more easily compare their relative merits.

Exercise two

Taking together all the discussions about rehearsal patterns in this chapter, including the interviews, choose a play you know well and devise three different rehearsal patterns: one which begins with a period of tablework, followed by practical work-throughs; one which has no tablework but only work-throughs; and one which employs the multi-focused approach outlined in the interview with Sarah Esdaile, before the work-throughs. To make this exercise as practice-based as possible, you may wish to take a framework of a four- or three-week rehearsal period, with each actor allowed to work a maximum of forty-three hours, and to factor in time for a read-through, model-showing, research visits or film watching, and estimates for the time you may have to devote to combat, choreography, dialect work or other skills work. You may even take the number of pages in the play and, having worked out how much pure work-through time you have, see how many pages an hour you would have to work at to cover the play in several work-throughs. Evaluate the different patterns of working and then consider if one pattern better suits a particular type of play.

Weblist

Conference of Drama Schools	www.drama.ac.uk
Drama Centre London	courses.csm.arts.ac.uk/drama
Michael Chekhov Centre UK	www.michaelchekhov.org.uk
National Council for Drama Training	www.ncdt.co.uk

Bibliography

Adler, Stella, *The Technique of Acting*. Ontario: Bantam Books, 1988.

Alfreds, Mike, *Different Every Night*. London: Nick Hern Books, 2007.

Benedetti, Jean, *Stanislavski and the Actor*. London: Methuen, 1998.

Bogart, Anne, *A Director Prepares: Seven Essays on Art and Theatre*. London: Routledge, 2001.

Bogart, Anne, *And Then, You Act: Making Art in an Unpredictable World*. London: Routledge, 2007.

Bogart, Anne, and Landau, Tina, *The Viewpoints Book: A Practical Guide to Viewpoints and Composition*. New York: Theatre Communications Group, 2005.

Brecht, Bertolt, edited and translated by Willett, John, *Brecht on Theatre: The Development of an Aesthetic*. London: Methuen, 1964.

Caldarone, Marina, and Lloyd-Williams, Maggie, *Actions: The Actors' Thesaurus*. London: Nick Hern Books, 2004.

Chekhov, Michael, *To the Actor*. London: Routledge, 2002.

Cohen, Lola, editor, *The Lee Strasberg Notes*. New York: Routledge, 2010.

Delgado, Maria M., and Heritage, Paul, editors, *In Contact with the Gods?* Manchester: Manchester University Press, 1996.

Donnellan, Declan, *The Actor and the Target*. London: Nick Hern Books, 2002.

Esper, William, and DiMarco, Damon, *The Actor's Art and Craft: William Esper Teaches the Meisner Technique*. New York: Anchor Books, 2008.

Hagen, Uta, *A Challenge for the Actor*. New York: Scribner, 1991.

Hagen, Uta with Frankel, Haskel, *Respect for Acting*. New York: Wiley Publishing, 1973.

Hodge, Alison, editor, *Twentieth Century Actor Training*. London: Routledge, 2000.

Kissel, Howard, editor, *Stella Adler: The Art of Acting*. New York: Applause Books, 2000.

Mamet, David, *True and False*. London: Faber and Faber, 1998.

Meisner, Sanford, and Longwell, Dennis, *Sanford Meisner on Acting*. New York: Vintage Books, 1987.

Mitchell, Katie, *The Director's Craft: A Handbook for the Theatre*. London: Routledge, 2009.

Mitter, Shomit, *Systems of Rehearsal*. London: Routledge, 1992.

Newlove, Jean, *Laban for Actors and Dancers: Putting Laban's Movement Theory into Practice*. London: Nick Hern Books, 1993.

Stafford-Clark, Max, *Letters to George*. London: Nick Hern Books, 1989.

Stanislavski, Konstantin, edited by Benedetti, Jean, *An Actor's Work*. London: Routledge, 2008.

Stanislavski, Konstantin, *My Life in Art*. London: Routledge, 2008.

Willett, John, *The Theatre of Bertolt Brecht*. London: Methuen, 1959.

3 The director and the author

This chapter explores the director's many kinds of relationship with the author rather than the text – a relationship with another collaborator rather than a medium. The author might be a single individual who is not the director, an individual who is the director, or a group of people who are creating the text with or without a playwright.

The reason for not using the word 'text' is that its interpretation has become so variable. Traditionally, 'text' suggests a pre-existing set of words, but the director has analogous relationships with written plays, new plays in development, plays which do not yet exist but are to be devised, and plays in which the text can be physical or visual rather than verbal, or in which words are not the dominant medium. It is important to acknowledge that in some areas of theatre-making, text does not necessarily mean written words, but for the sake of our discussion here of existing plays, it will be assumed to mean written words.

As with the exploration of other relationships with collaborators, this chapter will outline key considerations and principles and suggest books which deal in detail with each area under consideration. The approaches outlined here are framed within the premise that you have been asked to direct a play and you are formulating your approach to the production: it is about approaching a play not through literary criticism but as a living entity with which the director has a creative, two-way, relationship.

The director's relationship with the author is viewed in four different ways: with the classic author, such as Shakespeare, where the only, or main, reliable information is the text; with the historic author, such as Chekhov, where there are also contemporary accounts, (auto)biographies, critical works and a canon of work to reference; with the living writer, both as a non-present author of an existing play, and as a present author of a new work; and the processes of devising, with or without a playwright.

This way of looking at the relationship with the author has been chosen as a means of isolating key elements in that relationship and discussing them with reference to examples. In practice, many of the principles and approaches discussed in the director's relationship with the classic author might be applied to the relationship with the living, present author, and vice versa. In discussing the director's relationship with the actor there was a clearly identifiable range of methodologies devoted to acting, which provide a common language for actors and directors. There is not a similar range of dramaturgical theories to refer to in discussing the director's relationship with the author, although there are some excellent books on particular aspects of working on plays as texts, which will be referenced. What follows is a series of 'template' approaches based on the methods of a number of directors, which raise the issues you may wish to consider when approaching a text, and a number of strategies for exploring a text you are about to direct. Ultimately, as with the director's relationship with actors, every director will synthesise these approaches and develop their own personal way of working, but considering these approaches might be a useful starting point for finding that personalised approach.

The director and the classic author

Before sitting down to read the classic play you are about to direct it is worth considering that you are entering three worlds simultaneously: the world in which the play was written, the world in which the play is set, and the world in which the play will be presented. It may also be useful to acknowledge three assumptions.

First, you are directing, say, Shakespeare's *Macbeth*, and not a version of *Macbeth*. When is *Macbeth* not *Macbeth*? Verdi's *Otello* is clearly an opera based on Shakespeare's *Othello*, but that is not to say it is Shakespeare's *Othello* with some songs. Recently Denis Kelly translated Heinrich von Kleist's *The Prince of Homburg*, produced at the Donmar Warehouse. The publicity clearly stated that it was 'in a new version by Denis Kelly', and

Denis Kelly had changed the ending, but even acknowledging that this was a new version rather than a faithful translation did not stop some critics objecting to the changes that Denis Kelly had made to von Kleist's original text. Factory Theatre regularly stage productions of Shakespeare's and Chekhov's plays with the casting being decided at the beginning of each performance and the involvement of the audience – who even provide the props – but the critics don't object because they know from the company's reputation and publicity the type of production they are about to see, although it must be acknowledged that Factory Theatre do use Shakespeare's text and investigate it thoroughly. Perhaps the critics just didn't read the Donmar's publicity carefully enough.

It is unfortunate, but when you direct a classic play you are dealing with the critics' and audiences' preconceptions about what they have come to see. Without trying to define when *Macbeth* is not *Macbeth* in literary terms, it might be better to ask what are the expectations of the audience about your production, and if it is not an interpretation of Shakespeare's original words but a version of *Macbeth* based on Shakespeare's words, then be absolutely clear about it in all the information about the show. There is nothing wrong with using out-of-copyright plays as the basis for new plays or new versions of existing plays (as we know, Shakespeare 'borrowed' many of his best plots from existing plays and stories), but to 'scape the critic's tongue, do what it says on the tin. The assumption here is that you are directing the classic author's play, not a version of it.

Second, most classic plays are rich and complex in their plots, characters and themes, and as a director rather than a literary critic you are going to have to make choices about which themes and situations resonate with you, and you will need to acknowledge that you will foreground some and background others. There is no right or objective view of *Macbeth*, but a set of complex interrelated choices and options which have to be considered on their own and in relation to other elements of the play. The casting of Macbeth and Lady Macbeth will be the result of much thinking about the whole production, but the eventual choices, even just in terms of their relative ages, will have an enormous impact on the whole play.

Third, and related to these choices, is the fact that you cannot escape yourself and the world you live in. This is not to say that you have to impose a reading on the play to make it 'relevant' or impose twentieth-century concepts on Shakespeare, but rather that you should acknowledge that you and your audience will bring your current world view to the play. Some directors claim to be making a play 'relevant to a modern audience' in their production: this implies that they have to manipulate the play in some way to make it accessible to an audience. It might be better to consider that classic plays we still wish to direct will always be 'relevant' – that is their brilliance. Our job is to make choices from the multiplicity of possible interpretations that release their inherent relevance to us today, rather than straitjacketing them into one overriding 'meaning'.

The director Jonathan Miller once remarked that directing a classic or historic play is like shaking hands with the past: that implies a meeting of two equals who are ready to enter into a dialogue and a mutually respectful exchange of ideas. It also implies that the director is not a slavish servant to a notion of the independent truth of the text, and that the director is not going to impose his or her ideas on the play without listening to what it has to say. What follows is a detailed, and therefore highly prescriptive, method of reading a classic play and having an open dialogue with it. For the purposes of discussion I have chosen to use *Macbeth*, on the grounds that it is one of Shakespeare's most widely known plays, but the discussion could equally apply to any classic play where the text is the prime source of information as to the author's intentions.

First reading

The first reading of a play is a special occasion which can never be repeated. If someone shows you a picture of a house without telling you anything about it, you will observe details about it which have the most meaning to you. If that person then tells you that's where they grew up, or it's where a murder took place, you will not be able to look at that picture again without those associations, and your relationship with it will never again be your unmediated response.

Even if you know a play from previously reading it or seeing it, as a director you are trying to come to it afresh. So reading the play should come before any thoughts about how to direct it, or any research or questions. Sit down, without pen or paper, and read the play straight through without interruption, stopping or making notes. The notes you make after reading straight through might be the most significant notes you make. Reading the play straight through gives you a sense of its arc in 'real time' and gives you a sense of the scenes which seem pivotal, the scenes that set up or follow on from those scenes; scenes which may seem too long, or may not appear essential to you; and the same applies to the journeys of the characters. Reading the play before doing any research or thinking about it will be the closest experience you will have to an audience's reception of the play: the audience may not have read the Arden notes, but they may come to it with your world view and sensibilities.

Many directors then make two sets of notes which will inform all future work on the play: an instinctive or imaginative response to the play; and a factual or intellectual response. The imaginative response is subjective, impressionistic and possibly global; the intellectual might be a series of questions about whole themes in the play or specific moments, and might include a work plan of the areas for future research.

Imaginative research

Sadly, initially directors usually work alone on a project, so it is helpful to have your own set of questions to ignite an internal dialogue about your visceral and intellectual response to a play. Here are some questions and exercises which might open up your imaginative response to the play.

If you had to give the play one 'action' that it intends to have on the audience, what might it be? What might its Laban effort be? Make drawings of five or six key moments in the play as you saw them in your head when you were reading. Take a magazine and cut out colours and images that – impressionistically, not literally – give you a sense of the whole play. Make graphs of the play: they might be graphs of its several plots and when they come together and separate out, or the emotional intensity, or the intensity of physical action. The factual research might include precise plot, scene and character journey graphs, but these are quick and impressionistic. Say what the play is about in two sentences: one is the story or plot, the second is the subject matter or overriding theme. Why do it? Not for a factual or external reason, such as 'because it's a neglected classic and deserves to be done', but an internal and personal question with a response such as 'because it speaks to me about the consequences of breaking your own moral code'. Why you? What will you bring of yourself to the production and what is your fundamental connection to the piece – not what the play says to you, but what you say to the play.

An exercise you may wish to repeat after each reading of the play is to record yourself telling the story of the play: listening back to it might alert you to what you consider are important events and themes of which you weren't aware. What are the dangers in the piece for you: what might you become preoccupied about, to the exclusion of other themes or elements?

What most challenges your experience and knowledge as a director? What moments are you most excited about directing? Key moments can encapsulate your underlying connection with the play, and release a wide range of thematic and visual ideas, or, for good or bad, can be moments around which you base the whole design and production. Do the moments of danger and excitement loom too large in your mind?

Sometimes you can be seduced into directing a play because of one scene, moment or character, making you less analytical of possible problems or shortcomings elsewhere. Are there sections of the play or characters with which you do not have a connection, or of which you need to develop a greater understanding?

Factual research

The obvious place to begin is the text itself, but, particularly with a play by Shakespeare, this can be a forbidding task. Many directors of Shakespeare will want to read the First Folio and the quartos, if any, to note differences in the versions, and to have them in the rehearsal room for reference, to make informed choices about what final version of a given word or line to use. Editions of Shakespeare, such as the Arden, provide comprehensive notes on the meanings of words and phrases and often refer to alternative versions in the notes. At this stage you probably don't want to make final choices or to consider cuts, but simply familiarise yourself with the different versions and options available to you.

Although the task of choosing one version of the final script is particularly relevant to Shakespeare, it can often apply to other classic and historic plays, and many new plays, particularly where the script has been printed before the play has opened, and the printed version is not the final one. With authors who are alive, or who have been dead for less than seventy years, the play will still be in copyright, but that doesn't mean that it is not worth checking with the author's agent whether there are alternative versions to the published play that you might be permitted to use.

Particularly with classics there is also a need to become familiar with the form in which the play is written, whether that be verse, blank verse or prose, and to connect with the words on a visceral and aural as well as as an intellectual level. There are three books by masters of their craft which are essential reading for any director wanting fully to appreciate the richness of Shakespeare's language. The first is *Playing Shakespeare* by John Barton, a transcript of a series of televised workshops he led in the 1970s, and the DVD of those workshops is also available. There are countless scholarly books and articles on Shakespeare's verse and language, but John Barton's workshops explore Shakespeare's language in a way that gives you enough technical knowledge of, and sensitivity to, the possibilities of the verse and language to enable you to explore it practically with actors.

The second book is Sir Peter Hall's *Shakespeare's Advice to the Players*, which has sold thousands of copies and has recently been re-edited and republished by Oberon Books. As the title suggests, Hall's book examines the amount of 'hidden' direction that is embedded in Shakespeare's verse, and his advice about how to uncover and 'read' that direction in the form of the lines is extremely valuable and practical. Hall describes himself as an 'iambic fundamentalist', and the book is also partly a memoir of productions and very entertaining.

The third book is *From Word to Play* by Cicely Berry, who has written many valuable books on voice, particularly for actors. But this one is written for directors, and makes the essential connection between the body, the breath, the voice, the sound of words, and the meaning of words conveyed through their sounds. This appreciation of the power of the sounds of words is then related to character and dramatic structure and a richer appreciation of the whole play. All three of these books heighten a director's awareness of the power of the spoken word and much that is contained in them is extremely valuable for work on any play.

The next area of research might be the world and time in which the play was written. How much research do you need to do? Some directors take the view that you only need to know enough about the original circumstances of the play in order to make it intelligible to a modern audience, so that knowing that at the time of writing *Macbeth*, James I had just come to the throne and Shakespeare was keen to secure his patronage through writing about one of his obsessions, witchcraft, is not going to have a bearing on the audience's appreciation of the play. Remarkably, Donald Rumsfeld, the former United States Secretary of Defense, can be of help in deciding how much research to undertake and where to focus it. His notion of 'known unknowns' and 'unknown unknowns' is useful in a scoping exercise of where there might be profitable areas of research. It may not be pertinent to your production to know in detail about original staging practices at the Globe or the Rose, but to not know about them at all might leave a useful source of knowledge or insight unexplored. Actually making as comprehensive a checklist as possible of all the potential areas of research does not mean you have to research all of them, but later you may come back to sources of research you didn't initially think would be of benefit. Then at least the 'unknown unknowns' become 'known unknowns'.

Many editions of Shakespeare provide well-researched introductions which give useful information about the key contexts of the play: at what point in Shakespeare's life it was written, and the plays that precede and follow it; other plays that are related to it, either in terms of locations or themes; stories or plays that Shakespeare borrowed from for the play; the recent events that might have informed the play or are referenced in it; possible reasons for Shakespeare writing it; and how and where it might have been staged. This is not an exhaustive checklist of research areas but it offers a quick overview of the world of the play and possible future research.

The second reading of the play

The second reading might be much more leisurely and staggered than the first, folding in to your engagement with the play the factual and imaginative research you have done so far – even if it is a scoping exercise, and not all the research you intend to do. It will undoubtedly prompt more questions and avenues of research and at the same time it might change or reinforce your initial responses to the key themes and incidents. From your second reading and research, are the themes that you thought were the dominant and most interesting ones as prominent as Shakespeare's themes, and are they supported by the play? For example, an objective reading of *Macbeth* might suggest that the themes of free will and fate, the morality of murder, and the divine right of kings are three of Shakespeare's main themes, but you might have been excited by the collision of Christian and non-Christian worlds and belief systems: how does that connect with other themes in the play? Does the text support that reading as a dominant theme, and does it illuminate the play in an interesting way?

The word 'concept' is often used pejoratively about productions which attempt to impose a reading of the play which is not supported by the text or structure of the play, and has the effect of dominating and flattening out other themes and aspects. Many classic plays are wonderfully complex, layered, multifaceted pieces of dramatic fiction, and although in some ways they are robust and can take very didactic readings and still 'work', they are also delicate, and any single decision about where to focus your attention on the play is going to have repercussions on other parts of the play and its potential to speak about interrelated subjects.

At this point it might be helpful to make some provisional decisions about your key responses and choices and to begin to test them against the play and consider what effects they will have on other themes and aspects: it is a process of dialogue and checking back between your ideas and the play. If these choices seem to illuminate the play and you wish to pursue them, you may have a new agenda for further imaginative and factual research. Perhaps the imaginative research might include finding music and films that have a resonance with the play for you – pieces of music and images that express your connection with the play rather than those you might use for the production itself.

At the same time you may wish to do more factual research on the context of the play and its world. This might include becoming better aware of what might be called the internal architecture of the play. For example, 'How far is't called to Forres?' What are the distances between the battlefields, Forres and Dunsinane? Might Shakespeare have known this and does it matter? What might matter is that Macbeth can get from the battlefields, to meeting the witches, then meeting Duncan and back to his castle, Dunsinane, some time before that night's feast. If this is taken together with the relatively small number of named Scottish noblemen, it suggests that although the whole future of Scotland has been at stake during the battle, Shakespeare is deliberately portraying Scottish nobility as a small close-knit society, which has implications for how well each of the characters knows the others. Or is this not Shakespeare's intention, and is he less concerned with the geographical landscape, and more with the dramatic structure of the first few scenes, so that, having had an epic opening, he wants to reduce the landscape to the domestic and the key protagonists, and move the action on quickly?

It is said that the time scale in *Othello* cannot be worked out logically, but it might be worth trying it out to find where the anomalies lie. Many of Shakespeare's plays depend on miscommunication, as, in *Romeo and Juliet*, with Romeo's suicide stemming from him not receiving Friar Laurence's note, sent to him in hiding in Mantua, which tells him that Juliet is not dead. If the play has a contemporary setting the audience might ask why the Friar didn't use his mobile phone to contact Romeo. Is your developing conception of the world of the play supported by or at odds with the internal architecture of the play?

At this stage it might be useful to differentiate between two different types of approach to the play: those that have a direct influence on its chosen location and visual world, and those that are thematic and do not directly influence the visual world. For example, a director might take the view that Lady Macbeth is not a malevolent manipulator of Macbeth but that what Macbeth and Lady Macbeth do is out of love for each other. This approach could equally exist in a dystopian futuristic world, or a vision of ninth-century Scotland. That approach may have huge casting implications, but not design implications at this stage. Although, finally, every element will affect every other element, it is worth considering which aspects of the final production each choice or approach has most effect on, in order to be aware of the ripples and implications of each decision.

The third reading and onwards

Hopefully the third reading will bring the text, the structure and internal architecture of the play into a closer dialogue with your responses, and your research will have deepened your understanding of the world of the play. From single ideas, facts and responses, the different approaches will begin to mesh together and you will be able to evaluate the effect of single decisions on the whole play. It might be a reading of pleasant surprises in which you make new connections between elements, and the global view of the play informs and illuminates individual moments in new ways.

The world of your production and the play is becoming more detailed and richer with every subsequent reading. This might be the point at which you wish to share your ideas with a designer, before the world of the play becomes too rigidly conceived, which would limit your collaborative relationship. It might also be the point at which you consider the resources at your disposal. Although you might know from the moment you begin reading the play that you have a cast of nine and it will be on a thrust stage, there is an argument for allowing yourself first to have an entirely free relationship before considering how the results of that relationship might be realised within your resources, rather than allowing the resources to determine your vision of the production from the start.

This might also be the point to reconsider your intended audience and whether your production will speak to them as it does to you. You may also wish to go back to your two-sentence description and your subjective reasons for wanting to do the play. This is not to say that they should not have changed – they probably will have – but this might be when you need to begin articulating your ideas to other collaborators and to the theatre, and even the marketing department. This suggested process does not imply that you should know every fact about the play and production before you meet a designer or work with actors, but it might be the point at which you know enough about the production – the production as well as the play – to talk about it clearly.

To reiterate, this is a template approach, and it is simply a way of having a dialogue with the author through the play. It might not be as simple and straightforward as this suggests and there may have to be major U-turns in your thinking. But as with other collaborative relationships, it is a way of having a process and a dialogue rather than being results-driven, and so closing down possibilities that the play offers. And many of the approaches outlined here may be equally applicable to a play by a historic author or a new play.

A wonderfully honest and insightful account of a director's attempt to communicate with a classic author can be found in Max Stafford-Clark's *Letters to George*, written in the form of a diary of his simultaneous work on his revival of George Farquar's *The Recruiting Officer* and on the first production of a new play, *Our Country's Good* by Timberlake Wertenbaker. It is a fascinating account of working with a classic author and the living, present writer on a new play, and underscores the Royal Court's maxim of directing classic plays as if they are new plays and new plays as if they are classics.

The director and the historic author

The term 'historic author' refers to an author who is no longer living, and who therefore cannot be consulted, but about whom we have a body of reliable information that we do not have about the classic author. This may include autobiographies and biographies, letters to and from the author, reviews of the first production, a body of critical work, and, often, a larger canon of work through which the author's voice can be discerned.

It is also different from the relationship with the classic author in that the only reliable method of gleaning the classic author's intentions was through the text. Here begins the triangular relationship of the director, the text and the author, and sometimes the comments or avowed intentions of the author may seem to be at variance with what the text is saying. Many directors are still bemused by Chekhov's description of *The Cherry Orchard* as 'A comedy in Three Acts'. Most directors would argue for the primacy of the text over the author's views, but many would feel that all information is useful and may shed light on the play, although this information does not tie a director to a reverential revival. As with the classic play, the possible areas of research can deepen a director's connection with and understanding of the play, but it is, once again, an informed dialogue, even if it is now three-way rather than two.

So what might be useful research? It seems logical to begin with the play and the world of the play you are directing; then to look at other work by the author; the life of the author and possible genesis of the play; contemporary reviews and reactions; critical commentaries on the play and the author in the intervening years; and possibly (although this has dangers as well as merits) reviews of recent revivals.

Many of the approaches to the classic text might be applied to the historic text, particularly the first unmediated reading of the play before any research begins. Mike Alfreds often cites *The Cherry Orchard* as an example play in the book I have recommended, *Different Every Night,* and Mike Alfreds's methods of creating lists of facts about not only the characters but the world of the play are particularly useful when applied to historic plays, particularly those set in their own time and place, such as Chekhov's and Ibsen's. Equally helpful is Katie Mitchell's book *The Director's Craft,* which also draws upon a number of her productions of work by Chekhov and other classic and historic authors. Starting with a thorough analysis of the world of the play – the facts – as described and referred to in the text can focus other research on the place and time of the play and prevent your historical research becoming generalised, time-consuming and not that productive.

Dissecting the play in the numerous ways suggested by Mike Alfreds and Katie Mitchell reveals its internal architecture and brings you to a much closer connection with it. Examples of such lists, which are only drawn up from references in the play itself, might include: all the events which happened before the play – both public, world events and private events; what happens between each scene; the number of times God or money is mentioned; characters who are referred to but not seen, both living and dead; foreign towns and countries, etc. These approaches not only bring the world of the play into real focus for you (and the actors, if you choose to share these exercises in the rehearsal process), but they also produce a clear picture of the world view, and world size, of the characters.

In the early 1990s, six months before I directed *The Cherry Orchard*, I was lucky enough to spend a month in Russia just after the end of the Soviet era. One Russian woman said to me that if I wanted to understand the Russian character I should think of Russians as melancholic Italians. A Russian theatre director told me that in newly post-Soviet Russia *The Cherry Orchard* would not be performed because it was too political and too painful: the cutting down of the cherry orchard, for him, symbolised the cutting down of Russian culture during the Soviet era. The first comment gave me a greater understanding of why Chekhov might have called *The Cherry Orchard* a comedy: the evident ability of Russians to go from tears to laughter in an instant and a much readier disposition for displaying emotion than we are used to in Britain. The second comment opened my eyes to a symbolic and metaphorical world of the play which I might have otherwise ignored in solely concentrating on the naturalism of the play. I would have gained neither of these insights from simply reading research material. Modern Russia is, of course, very different to the Russia of 1905, but there is often no substitute for actually doing your own research and experiencing first hand, as fully as possible, the geography, society and culture in which a play is situated.

The next area of research might be other plays by the same author. The first benefit of this reading is to be able to identify common themes, preoccupations and devices in the author's canon: Arthur Miller's use of the structure of Greek tragedy for example, which might not be evident from the reading of a single play. But on a more subliminal level it also familiarises you with the world that the author's imagination occupies and the author's voice in the structure, vocabulary and cadences of the dialogue. The writing of Harold Pinter is a prime example of this: every character has his or her own voice, but there are shared characteristics across Pinter's plays in the shape of lines and in what is said and left unsaid; and as Pinter was famously unforthcoming about the background, backstory and motives of his characters, this is a particularly valuable resource. Pinter would say all the information is in the dialogue, and that includes his voice.

Arthur Miller once wrote: 'The plays are my autobiography. I can't write plays that don't sum up where I am. I'm in all of them. I don't know how else to go about writing.' In the mid-fifties he worked on a screenplay called *The Hook*, about a New York longshoreman, or docker, which he sent to his friend and colleague, the director, Elia Kazan. It was the time of the McCarthy hearings and Elia Kazan was called as a witness to the

House of Un-American Activities Committee. Kazan named Miller as a communist sympathiser, and so ended their friendship. In Kazan's hands *The Hook* was reworked and provided much of the story of the film *On the Waterfront*. In Arthur Miller's hands it became *A View from the Bridge*, in which longshoreman Eddie Carbone betrays his family and close friends, but rather than Miller using the play to vilify the betrayer he uses it as an opportunity to explore the motives, circumstances and psychology that lead a person to do this. This says a lot about Miller's attitudes to his writing and offers a brilliant insight into the character of Eddie Carbone for the director and actor. It also tells you that *On the Waterfront* is a valuable period, geographic and visual reference point for *A View from the Bridge*.

Some authors reveal very little about themselves but most have written or talked about the inspiration for their plays, and although one doesn't have to take everything an author says at face value, such comments can be very illuminating. It is also worth reading about an author's life to discover the social and cultural world they moved in and whom they may have been influenced by – and not just other playwrights: knowing that Strindberg was a painter and part of the expressionist movement can be a valuable source of research, particularly for design ideas.

Contemporary reviews and commentaries on the first production of a play can also be helpful: it would be very limiting to approach a production of Ibsen's *A Doll's House* without knowing the effect that Nora's slamming of the door and choosing to leave her husband and family had on its shocked first audiences; or the scandal caused by the first production of *Ghosts*. Knowing that Chekhov's three-act plays were first presented with long breaks between each act also tells us a lot about why he structured the plays in the way that he did, and his expectations of an audience's concentration levels, and might caution us against putting a single interval in the middle of act two.

Even with the work of recently deceased authors such as Harold Pinter and Sarah Kane, there is a wealth of critical analysis of their work, and much more on, say, Chekhov and Ibsen. This information can also be useful, but it can be more in the vein of literary criticism than the type of analysis that is immediately useful to a director, and while it might offer perspective and objective judgement, it is not immersing you further in the voice of the play or the author.

Some directors have written very interestingly and enlighteningly about their relationships with writers and their first productions of plays, and while there is a danger of thinking, 'Peter Hall directed *The Homecoming* in this way – I must take note about what he said about the furniture and the shape of the room,' there can be real benefits in learning from the experiences of other directors: ideally perhaps one should read the comments of a director working on another play by the same author so that one can learn by analogy without risking imitation.

The same risks may apply to reading reviews of recent revivals. It is one of those things directors don't like to talk about, but with plays by writers from Shakespeare to Kane you cannot help but acknowledge the weight of expectation placed on you by productions of the past: hence the idea of trying to have a fresh relationship with the play from the beginning. The irony is that if you have seen, or heard of, a really brilliant way of staging a scene it is then the last way you would do it, even if it might have been the most natural way for you to do it: so rather than plagiarism, avoidance of the obvious becomes the curse, as well as the weight of expectation. On the other hand, knowing how a relatively recent audience has received a play can give you an insight into how a modern audience's sensibilities will connect with a historic play.

Copyright and agents

Under European law a writer's work remains in copyright until seventy years after their death. This means that for anyone who has died more than seventy years ago you do not have to seek permission to produce the play, and you are free to make changes and adaptations to a work which may not be permitted with a writer whose work is still in copyright.

For writers whose work is still in copyright you have to find out who is the agent of the writer, make initial contact by phone, and then email the agent with the place, or places, and dates of the proposed production. The agent will usually let you know fairly quickly if the rights are not available, or if they are, in principle, before then sending you a contract to confirm you have the rights. If you are given the rights to produce a play you will be sent a contract with a number of conditions in it, including the condition that you present the approved edition or version of the play, and that you, the director or producer, guarantee that there will be no changes to the text without the agent's permission, and if there are unauthorised changes, you may have the rights withdrawn and possibly face legal action. Some writers also have surviving relatives who take a keen interest in every production of a writer's work: the enforced early closure of a female version of Beckett's *Waiting for Godot* springs to mind. As mentioned earlier, there may be more than one version of a play in existence, but the agent will have to approve which is to be used, and you may not create your own version from existing versions.

The same copyright laws apply to translations and adaptations, so although Chekhov died in 1904, Michael Frayn's translations are still in copyright, so you will have to contact his agent to get the rights. The same applies to adaptations of novels and other works of fiction: you will probably have to first contact the agent of the adaptor, who will have been given the rights for the stage adaptation by the original writer. Getting the rights may take longer if the adaptor's agent has to check for permission with the original writer's agent. If you wish to write or commission the adaptation of the original work you will have to discover the agent of the original writer. If a stage adaptation of the work already exists you may have to use that version; if not, be prepared to supply a great deal of information about you, the playwright and the proposed production to secure the rights, which may only last for a fixed period, after which, if you have not produced the adaptation, you may forfeit the rights.

Translations

For most of the well-known European historic authors there are several translations to choose from; there might be only one authorised translation for a living author, which you may have to use. Because any two languages will not have entirely equivalent words or phrases, and simply because the subtleties of any language will contain an enormous amount of information about meaning, tone, subtext and character in any one line, dramatic translation is an art as well as a craft, and it is extraordinary how much translations of the same line can vary, producing quite different effects on the play.

It is worth finding out all the different translations that are available. There are some translations of Chekhov, for example, that are themselves out of copyright, and so they are free and without conditions, but be aware that translations can date very quickly: even translations which are only twenty years old may contain idiomatic phrases that now seem dated. Many translators of plays are playwrights themselves, and this obviously gives them a great understanding of the dramatic form, but it sometimes means that their work can be more of a version than a translation. As mentioned, Denis Kelly's translation of von Kleist's *The Prince of Homburg* was clearly called a 'version', because he had changed the ending, but another playwright may, intentionally or not, draw on their own dramatic voice as much as the original playwright's, and still call the play a translation. Another factor to take into account is that not all translators speak or read the original language, and they, or the theatre, may have commissioned a 'literal translation' by someone who is not a writer but a fluent or native speaker of that language, and the playwright will have re-written the literal translation into their own English dialogue. Some of these translations are as good as those by a playwright who is translating from the original language; they may just have different qualities.

If a writer has been dead for more than seventy years there is nothing to stop you commissioning or writing your own translation of a play, or adapting a novel or other work of fiction. A full translation or adaptation from a professional writer might set you back about £5,000; but you might be able to get a native speaker 'to do a literal' for £100.

Stage directions

The agent's attitude towards the interpretation of an author's stage directions is entirely different from the attitude towards the dialogue, and Arthur Miller's agent would not expect a director and designer to follow Miller's detailed description of the set for each scene in the design of *A View from the Bridge*. Although each rights contract will have different conditions, it is fair to say that the author's stage directions can be taken as guidance, which you can choose to take or not, rather than instructions.

In some published plays it is clear that the author's voice is in the stage directions, and you may wish to consider them as useful pieces of advice, but often the stage directions are taken from the deputy stage manager's prompt script and simply record what happened in the first production. Most directors loathe stage directions – particularly those in the dialogue such as 'moves down left and picks up a glass' or 'taken aback' before a line – and go to the bother of either striking them out or having the whole play typed up without them before sending out scripts. The research on the author's life and other work might give you a sense of the value of his or her own stage directions, and just how much these are an integral part of the play and the writer's vision: you may take quite a different attitude to Brecht's, Beckett's and Pinter's stage directions than some other authors who have different styles of writing and relationships with the worlds of their plays.

The director and the living author

If you are about to direct an existing play by a living writer treat them as if they were dead. That is to say, all the approaches and research for the classic and historic author are equally valid for a play by a living writer: analysing and researching the world of the play, finding out as much as possible about other work by the writer and their life and influences; reading reviews and critical commentaries on their work. Once you have done some of that work and immersed yourself in the play it might be worth contacting their agent – who would have granted you the rights – and asking if you might email, phone or meet the writer to ask some questions about the play. All the writers I know are delighted that a director has taken an interest in their work and will be glad to be of help to you, albeit perhaps over one or two emails, phone calls or meetings, depending on their availability.

While there is no obligation for a director to contact a writer, it can be extremely useful, but it is much more valuable if you have a good knowledge of the play and are ready with questions rather than hoping the writer will simply talk. There are no guidelines about such a conversation, but it might be better to consider questions about specifics, which might naturally lead on to a more general discussion, than asking global questions to begin with. The situation might be different if the writer wishes to rewrite certain sections of the play, and the writer may wish to attend rehearsals and be more involved in the production. Depending on where the writer is in their career path may determine how much contact you have; most established writers are heavily involved in the first production of the play, but do not have the time to become involved in subsequent productions.

The director and the author of a new play

Although there are a few playwriting programmes, the ways of meeting new writers with a view to working with them are much less clear and structured than for actors and designers, who are trained formally and have productions and showcases at the end of their training through which directors can get to know them and their work.

The fundamental situation is that writers who have written a play want to see it produced, and this is far more likely if they send their play to a theatre which specialises in new writing than trying to find an individual director for it. The Royal Court, the main developer of new writers and the leading new writing theatre, receives approximately 3,000 unsolicited scripts a year, and the National Theatre approximately 1,500. Both these theatres, and other new writing theatres, have sophisticated systems for reading these plays, with teams of readers who report to other readers, and then to the literary manager, and ultimately the artistic director, and there are a number of responses to the play and the playwright. The first might be an outright rejection. The second might be that the writer has an interesting voice but the play has fundamental flaws, in which case someone from the literary department might meet the writer, offer advice and perhaps suggest applying to go on one of the writing programmes for playwrights at one of the new writing theatres, and ask the playwright to send their next play to them. The third response might be that the theatre is interested in helping the playwright develop the play, and the literary manager or another dramaturg in the theatre might suggest some changes and encourage further drafts, or arrange a rehearsed reading to help the writer develop the play.

The fourth but least likely outcome is that the play might be produced by the theatre, or, if the theatre thinks the play is good but cannot programme it, they may suggest another theatre which might be able to do so, possibly with their recommendation. In any version of the fourth scenario, a director chosen by the theatre will be asked to direct the play. In other words, many interesting new writers and new plays are, quite rightly, supported and developed by specialist theatres, and the opportunities for emerging directors to work with many exciting new playwrights might be quite limited. There is sense in pairing an experienced director who specialises in new writing with a new writer rather than an emerging director. However, this is only the scenario at the heart of the new writing ecology in Britain, and there are many interesting playwrights who follow other paths and with whom it is possible to meet and build a relationship.

Many playwrights begin writing at university, where their plays are directed by them or their friends. They might then become aware of theatres and places where playwrights network, and there are a number of venues in London which have evenings of short plays by new writers, such as theatre503, Soho Theatre, the Tristan Bates Theatre, Start Nights and Daring Pairings at Hampstead Theatre, Future Perfect run by Paines Plough, Rogue Writers at the Canal Café Theatre, and at Goldsmiths, University of London, where writers from the MA in Writing for Performance put on their work. An increasing number of regional producing theatres either have similar regular events or produce seasons of short new plays by writers who have sent in scripts or have been taking part in their playwriting workshops. It is worth checking the new writing programmes and events that are on at theatres near you and going to see the work. Most of the playwrights whose work is being showcased will be there, and if you really like the work of a writer simply go and talk to them and perhaps ask if they have something you can read.

Other theatres provide ways to find out about new writers who are looking to meet directors, and have information about emerging play-wrights on their websites. The Bush Theatre recently launched Bushgreen, a social networking and information website to put writers with plays in touch with other writers, producers and directors. The Old Vic's New Voices programme supports directors, playwrights, actors and producers, usually under twenty-six, and has information about playwrights and a regular message board about playwrights looking for directors and producers. The websites of some are at the end of the chapter. You can subscribe to bulletins and e-newsletters from most of these new writing theatres and they will let you know about workshops, rehearsed readings, scratch nights and one-off showings of new work on a regular basis.

Entering into a relationship with a writer

So, you've been to a ten-minute showing, liked one piece, met the writer and got on well, and the writer has sent you a full-length, unproduced play of theirs. How do you proceed?

With caution and honesty. As a director it is easy to seize on oppor-tunity, and when that comes in the form of an enthusiastic producer, or an undiscovered writer with a new play, it is tempting to become over-enthusiastic and proprietorial. As with the reading of a classic play, the first reading of a play by a new writer needs to be completely open-minded, empathetic and objectively critical at the same time. Some directors can be over-enthusiastic about a new play, particularly to the writer, because they don't want the writer to give the play to anyone else. It is as impor-tant to try to remain as dispassionate and open about a new play as it is about a classic play and to ask the same questions about what the play says to you and what you can bring to the play, only with even more honesty and precision, as it may affect the career of the writer.

Taking into account the scenario outlined above, with new writing theatres steering writers in their development, and the production of their plays being directed by directors they have chosen, attaching your name to a play as the suggested director when it is sent to theatres may actually reduce the chances of the play being produced. If you are at an early stage in your directing career, and the writer in an early stage of theirs, you may have to be willing to find the means to produce the play yourself – and not make exaggerated promises about the chances of a production.

In Britain the playwright is commonly viewed as the primary artist, and in what is often called 'the Royal Court tradition', for a first production of a new play the prime motive is to serve the writer's vision: you, as the director, are a secondary artist, and although you may suggest changes, new drafts and cuts, the moral prerogative (if not the actual, in some cases, depending on the relative perceived status of the director and the writer) is with the writer; and the reviews will all be about the writer and the new play and the director might be lucky to get a mention – which is why so many emerging directors choose neglected classics to make their critical mark.

Reading and discussing a new play with the writer

Although many of the approaches outlined above can be used to read and analyse a new play by a writer, there are other dramaturgical tools which might be particularly useful for a play in development, and there are principles and professional expectations that are worth considering before meeting the writer to discuss the play.

In terms of dramaturgical tools, in addition to the books already mentioned for directors, there some books which are primarily for playwrights that can be useful. The playwright David Edgar's *How Plays Work* examines the structure of plays in terms of plot, character development, structure and genre, drawing on examples from across dramatic literature, so it is as useful for analysing the structure of classic and historic plays, but it is mentioned here because looking at the construction of plays as if they were clocks – intricate working mechanisms – and from the point of view of a writer rather than a director, might be useful ways to frame your responses to the new play and the playwright. Like many other books referenced in this book, Edgar's is written by a practitioner, so it suggests a range of practical strategies rather than a more academic analysis of dramatic writing, as offered by some other books on the subject; it was also written recently.

Some emerging directors go to workshops for playwrights to develop a set of dramaturgical skills which are shared by playwrights, and to participate in writing exercises to get a better understanding of playwriting skills and the challenges of writing a play. The playwright Simon Stephens has pointed out that the word 'playwright' is not spelt 'playwrite': the word-wright, as with the wheelwright and shipwright, denotes a craft, and playwriting is a craft with a set of skills that can be passed on and learnt.

There are some principles that might guide your work with playwrights in line with generally accepted professional practice. If they have sent you an unperformed script for you to read and you have read it and are interested in it, it is worth arranging a first meeting to discuss the play without giving any promises or expectations as to your possible future commitment, but simply to ask the writer some questions about the play. Not every play you read and admire is necessarily going to end up on a stage, so it is important to be clear with the writer exactly what your and their commitments are to working together on the project at every stage.

It might be that you consider that the play is perfect and can be produced without one word being altered, which is great but unlikely. Even if that were so, you and the writer are going to collaborate on casting, design and other production elements which will need joint decisions, so it is worth first establishing that you have both read the same play.

For example, it might be that the writer considers that the play will have *this* effect on the audience and is about *that*, whereas you thought the play's effect would be entirely different and is clearly about something else, so it might be worthwhile simply asking the questions, 'What is the play about?' and 'What do you want the audience to feel?' fairly near the beginning of the meeting. Sometimes the play that is in the writer's head is not the play on the page; sometimes, as discussed with the classic play, a director can alight on one scene or theme that has created a skewed view of the whole play. Although the writer may not be familiar with Stanislavskian or Laban terminology, it is worth asking, in other terms, what might be the action or super-objective or effort of the play. It might also be worth asking what the writer considers to be the main dramatic spring or trigger of the play and what is the pivotal scene. If yours and the writer's responses to these questions are widely different it could signal a difficult working relationship, and it might be important to ask yourself if you have misinterpreted the play, or, in your view, the writer has not written the play they think they have. If your responses are similar you might have a good working relationship even if you jointly decide that the play needs a good deal of work before it is ready to be produced.

At this point it might also be useful to bear three other considerations in mind. The first is that although there will undoubtedly be many personal experiences of the writer in the play this is a meeting about the play, not the playwright. Keeping focused on the play can prevent the meeting and the relationship becoming about each other rather than the objective facts of what is and is not in the text. If there are differences of opinion, the final arbiter is what is in the play, and what will make the play work better, not your different tastes or attitudes.

The second, related consideration, which might seem to be in contradiction of the first, is that the play is the work and voice of the author. There is a tendency on the part of some directors to think that they can 'fix' a writer's work, and that assumes that they have a vision for a play which is not yet this play, but with certain changes it could be. It is not the job of directors to impose their own tastes and value judgements on a play and try to get the writer to write the play they want. Rather, it is the job of the director to ask questions about the play which might clarify the objectives and mechanics of the play for the director and writer, better to serve the play that the play wants be. It is an empathetic relationship with the play, trying to get inside its world view to understand that world view better, and to help it be expressed as clearly as possible, but it is also as dispassionate as a mechanic working on an engine, clearly analysing the dramaturgical properties of the play and accurately diagnosing problems and identifying ways of unblocking them.

Third, although different directors, literary managers and dramaturgs get involved in the rewriting and redrafting of the play to different degrees, it is ultimately the job of the writer to find the solutions to problems and to make rewrites. Although the relative experience of the writer and director and the personal relationship between the two may alter this scenario, as an emerging director it might be helpful to consider that the job of the director is to ask questions of the play which might provoke the playwright to have new thoughts about it, rather than the director providing the questions and the solutions. Some directors or dramaturgs confine their notes to writers to either the small and factual – such as

'Leeds is in West Yorkshire, not North Yorkshire', or the very broad – such as, 'Have you considered the number of locations you have used and does the play need all of them?' – and leave the writer to go away and do the thinking and the work.

By the end of the first meeting you should have a good idea whether you and the writer have a shared view of the play, a possible future working relationship, and a broad idea of what the next stage of work might be. Assuming that you and the writer are not under contract to a theatre and being paid for your work, there might be the prospect of a lot of unpaid work ahead for you both. So either at the end of this meeting, or shortly afterwards, having had a few days to think about it, it might be the time for you and the writer to clarify what your respective commitments are. If you have doubts about the play or your ability to work productively with the writer, this is the time gracefully to withdraw. It might be that the play has been given to other directors who are interested in it, so it is important to ask the writer to clarify who else has been shown the play and, if you are to put a lot of work into it, what might be your future involvement. There are no guarantees that the play won't be picked up by a theatre that offers a commission and chooses its own director, but it is worth asking the questions.

If, after reading the play and meeting the writer, you don't passionately want to direct the play that the writer either has written or wants to write, then walk away from it: either wanting to 'fix it' yourself or seeing it as a career opportunity more than a passion will end in tears: you have to be honest with the writer and with yourself, for there is a lot of collaborative hard work ahead.

Workshops and rehearsed readings

Assuming you have committed to each other and working on the play there are several ways of making practical progress. The first is for you to have another meeting, or series of meetings, and for the writer to go away and do anything from redrafting the whole play to making minor changes to individual scenes. Two other ways involve other people and space to work in. It might be beneficial to do a workshop on the play or aspects of the play. Workshops can be really useful if you have specific questions which cannot be answered by discussion, but might be by actors putting scenes on their feet. Broadly speaking, workshops are good for four different situations. First, where there is a problem with a scene or scenes which you and the writer can't quite identify – why is that scene not working? Second, if you have identified the problem but there are several possible solutions – which is the best solution? Third, to try out cuts or additional scenes. Within a given scene it might be that an actor needs fewer lines to convey the scene than are there at the moment – what can be acted and shown rather than spoken and told? Within the play there might be a case for scenes between existing scenes or backstory scenes which would help plot or character development: the scenes can be improvised in different ways before choosing which scenes the writer will develop. Fourth, to give exercises to the actors and ask questions (assuming they have read the play before the workshop and are familiar with it) to get their perspective on a character and how he or she might react in given situations. Workshops are always time-pressured and the more clearly you set out the objectives, the agenda and the schedule the more likely you are to come out with concrete and usable results.

The second practical method is a rehearsed reading. A rehearsed reading of the play is usually a script-in-hand reading with actors, often seated rather than moving, often to an invited or public audience, which has been preceded by a few hours' or few days' work on the play by you, the writer and the actors. The danger with rehearsed readings is that they are often an unproductive mixture of workshop and performance, and it is important to ask what exactly can be learnt from a workshop and what from a rehearsed reading. Often less can be learnt from a reading than a workshop, and a reading is more a marketing than a dramaturgical opportunity; if you are combining both in one period or process it will be helpful to separate out when the workshop ends and the preparation for the reading begins.

If there is an invited or public audience, perhaps with potential producers, there will be a number of considerations about how best to present the reading to work through. How much of is it seated or partly moved? Where do the actors sit in relation to each other? How much of the stage directions are needed to convey the play and who reads them? Is any basic music, sound or lighting needed? Because rehearsed readings involve actors with scripts and very little to create the world of the play, they need to be thought of as offering distinctive staging and presentational choices which are different from those for a production. If there are only a few hours or a day followed by an evening reading, there might be no time to do anything apart from read the play through twice to establish the facts and answer any questions from the actors, so that they can make sense of it, and to offer some very broad observations and notes. If there is more time, it will be possible to explore scenes and characters with the actors, but it is again really beneficial to make it clear to the actors what they are being asked to contribute to the workshop, and when the workshop ends and the preparation for the reading begins.

Even if the prime motive for the reading is to invite producers and other possible collaborators, it is still useful for you and the writer to have an agenda of points to learn from to inform the next stage of writing; although hearing the whole play read aloud in front of an audience for the first time is a great occasion, the nature of the occasion can mean that it is a wasted discovery opportunity. A reading just for you and the writer will be very different from a reading for an invited audience of potential producers, so it is useful to be clear with the actors and writer who the reading is for.

There will come a point where further development might feel like development for its own sake, and when it is time to try to get the play a production rather than doing yet more work on it. Some directors and literary managers feel that there is a growing tendency in the UK to over-dramaturg plays and to lose focus on actually giving the play a production. It might be difficult to find the resources yourself, or to get a producer on board, or find an interested theatre, but there comes a point where there is little more to be learnt about the play until it is in the crucible of a production. As Peter Gill has pointed out, new plays still need to be directed, and there is an awful lot of directing work to be done on a new play which cannot be substituted by dramaturgy, and over-dramaturged plays can lose their essential voice and spontaneity.

Assuming that you do manage to secure a production of the play, there will still be a continuing relationship with the writer and work to be done on the play. Many writers will want to be fully involved in the casting process and some in the design process, and even some issues around marketing. In most writers' contracts it states that the writer has the right to be at rehearsals and to make comments and changes.

In many cases the writer might come to the first few days of rehearsal when the play is being explored and then return after a few days or a week to see how work is progressing. There might be further work and changes that come from your experience with working with actors and the real production resources that you will want to discuss with the writer, and the writer might want to make their own changes. In the early stage of rehearsals the writer can be a very valuable 'research resource' for you and the actors – a point of further information about the background and backstory of the play, and of unwritten but important facts about characters. You may still wish to do some of the background research that you would do for a classic or historic play and share that with the actors, or undertake some of the play dissecting exercises referred to elsewhere, but there is nothing like having a playwright who is willing and able to talk about the play in the room.

There are a complex set of relationships and communication channels to be managed by the director, and although the overall objective is to serve the vision of the primary artist – the playwright – it is the task of the director to lead the collaborative process in the rehearsal room, and the writer–director relationship is now no longer one on one, but one of many collaborative relationships which the director must facilitate. It may sound over-prescriptive, but there is an argument for setting up a situation where the playwright is invited to contribute as part of the process with the actors within the working ethos established by the director, and it might be worth establishing that the writer discusses the play with the actors with, or through, the director to prevent there being contradictory leading voices in the room. It is really worthwhile discussing the writer's role in the rehearsal room before rehearsals begin, to establish a verbal contract about the verbal contract so that the process is clearly led. Colin Teevan mentions more on this in his interview.

Every situation is different, but some productions have had increasingly unproductive rehearsal processes because there are too many competing reference points in the rehearsal room. Particularly in the final week of rehearsals, when time is short and there are runs of the play followed by targeted notes sessions, it is often better if the writer and director meet separately and share notes that the director then gives to the acting company and whomever else they may affect. This is not to exclude the writer from the production process, but efficiently to incorporate their views into a production process which is, by now, almost the same as the production process for any play. As was discussed in Chapter Two, 'The Director and the Actor', decisions about which notes to give, when to give them, and how to work through them should be part of the craft of the director, complementary to, but distinct from, the craft of the playwright.

There are formal agreements setting out the rights and expectations of writers working on new plays. The agreements between the Writers' Guild of Great Britain and the Theatrical Management Association (TMA) and the Independent Theatre Council (ITC) can be downloaded from the Writers' Guild website and they provide good guidance concerning a director's and producer's formal relationship with a writer which can be used as models of good working relations even if you are not working for a TMA or ITC company. You may also view the current commissioning rates for new plays: the commissioning fee for a new full-length play with an ITC company is £7,328.50 and £5,810 for a new play produced by a small subsidised rep.

Interviews

Interview with Colin Teevan

Colin Teevan is a playwright, translator and adaptor of plays in ancient Greek, French and Italian. He also writes for TV and radio. His stage plays have been produced by the Abbey Theatre, Dublin; the National Theatre of Scotland; the National Theatre, the Young Vic, Soho Theatre, the Gate Theatre and the Tricycle Theatres in London; West Yorkshire Playhouse and other regional theatres in Ireland and the UK. His plays have been performed at the Ancient Theatre Epidaurus, the Pentagon, the Bouffes du Nord, Paris, the Barbican and in the West End, and they have toured internationally. They include: Kafka's Monkey with Kathryn Hunter at the Young Vic; Peer Gynt for the National Theatre of Scotland; How Many Miles to Basra? for West Yorkshire Playhouse, The Bee and The Diver, both with Hideki Noda and starring Kathryn Hunter at the Soho Theatre and Setagaya Tokyo; Euripides' Bacchae directed by Sir Peter Hall at the National Theatre and Epidaurus; and The Lion of Kabul, part of The Great Game, a series of plays about Afghanistan at the Tricycle Theatre. I asked him how most of his plays came into existence.

Have you written them and then sent them to theatres or have most been commissions? And depending on which of those routes has been the genesis of the play, has that changed your relationship with the director you're working with?

I don't think there's one single answer to your question. Plays and their productions have come about in so many ways over the years. I think in general it's true to say that early on in one's career one has to have, I suppose, a calling card. You're not going to go to a theatre and say, 'I'm a writer, now commission me!' So the way one gets seen as a writer is to write a spec script. I think the same is true for film, TV and radio. This might not be the play that is ultimately produced, but it's essentially the script that shows you can write, you have the commitment, the enthusiasm, the intelligence, even if you have not yet fully mastered the skill. However, it's rare that this method will be enough to see your work produced in the larger theatres. You have to get your work out there, not only to get it seen, but to begin to understand the process of production and for the larger theatres to believe in your commitment.

At the start of my career I was at Edinburgh University and I used to put on plays – my own and others' – in the university theatre. Ian Brown, who was then the Artistic Director of the Traverse, saw one and he brought me in for workshops with the dance company DV8. That brush with serious professionals emboldened me in my final year to take a play on tour to Ireland, which then got picked up and taken to London and I got an agent. But I think there's a misconception about writers' agents in theatre. They're very different to publishing agents. Because the production of work, new or old, is a collaborative process, it is much more about writers' working relationships with directors, literary managers and artistic directors than 'agent power', which again is different to TV and film. So initially you need to get your work out there, whether with a director, directed by yourself, or sending round a script. There are also lots of courses nowadays – run by the Soho, the Royal Court, the Arvon Foundation and many more – and these help writers develop not only their writing but their understanding of the theatrical process and collaborative relationships.

As for my own work, I've found latterly that I tend to work to commission. However, to deal with another misconception, this is not a case of 'We want you to write a play, here's some money,' and I go off and write it. I meet with a director or literary manager or producer I've developed a working relationship with, or with one who's expressed an interest in my work. We'll discuss what we are working on and areas of common interest and out of that will hopefully come an idea that fires us both – if it doesn't fire us both, there is a problem since it's a long haul from first idea to production. It needn't be the first idea.

Quite often you'll inadvertently mention something and out of that will come an idea. The writer will probably be asked to put down their idea on a page. This is one of those awful, unnatural, but unavoidable documents. I think what directors and artistic directors are looking for is not an exhaustive blow-by-blow account of the play the writer will write, but a brief outline which gives an idea of the subject and the conceit or hook (i.e. the unique approach the writer proposes to take). It's not enough to say 'I want to do the collapse of the economy.' The director needs to know, as does the writer, why is this take different and important? However, I do think writers and directors come at the same idea from different angles. Writers look at the hook or the conceit as the way in to the 'story'. Younger directors especially are in danger of looking at the hook, looking at a proposition, and jumping to their great directorial moments. I think if I was commissioning work like that, I'd really want to know, in very basic terms, 'What's your way in to the story?' (i.e. the hook or conceit). 'What is the journey of the hero?' And, in very loose terms, 'What's the three-act movement of it?' – what are the two major reversals or, in film terms, the 'plot points'.

I'd say 80 per cent of the new plays I see in London have only two acts. And I don't mean there's an interval, an act one and an act two. I mean it in Aristotelian terms; there's only a two-part movement to the story. It doesn't deliver in the third act. Quite often the hardest act to deliver is where the real dénouement and crisis occurs. Ian Brown – who I've gone on to work with again at the West Yorkshire Playhouse – once said to me, 'The only plays you should commission are plays that have already been written.' I think there are two ways of interpreting that. One is that he really does mean he'll only commission plays that are 90 per cent there so he knows exactly what he's getting. But a more generous way of looking at it is that the would-be commissioner knows the writer knows the world of their play, who their main characters are, and generally how the situation they propose will develop. Increasingly I work like that – perhaps that is just my submitting to industry norms, but in a world where money in the arts is diminishing, I suppose people want to know what they're getting for their money.

But sometimes there can be too much interference in the commissioning process. One difficult project I was recently engaged on eventually came to nothing because there was too much intervention from the producing house wanting the (as yet) unrealised product to capture a particular audience we had captured before. While the commissioning process needs to be financially shrewd, I think, at least with original work – as opposed to adaptations and musicals – the market shouldn't lead the writing. Personally, as a writer I also like to completely change each time. It's very easy to fall into a category and at times I've been perceived to fall into a category – being variously perceived as an 'Irish' writer, a translator of classics, an adaptor, art-house collaborator – and recently, because I've written plays about Afghanistan and Iraq, certainly television producers are saying, 'Oh you write about political situations.' I think people like to put other people in boxes; it's safer that way. This seems especially pronounced in the UK. However, as a writer, after twenty years, the only way to keep it interesting is to keep changing. So, yes, I think there are those two stages in your career and when you're starting out you've got to do it for free, you've got to do it for the love and to show your commitment.

Let's say you've been commissioned by West Yorkshire Playhouse to write How Many Miles to Basra?. *When you deliver the first draft, what kind of meeting would you expect and, as a playwright, what kind of feedback is useful for a first draft? What kind of parameters would that meeting have?*

Well, on one level *How Many Miles to Basra?* is actually not a good example because it was a radio play first, so in one sense it was a process of unpicking it and reimagining it as a stage play. That's why every process is different. When I work with Hideki Noda or Kathryn Hunter we start with an idea and a few theatrical images and Hideki brings odd texts in, extracts from newspapers and from classical literature, and we mess around with them. However, perhaps these processes are 'typical' because they are 'untypical'.

But if we talk about the normal 'British' way of developing work, the most typical examples of which I suppose are the National Theatre and the Royal Court, once the writer and the director have their first meeting, a sharing of ideas and homing in on the idea that fires them both; then a second meeting, once the writer's had a chance to research it a bit and think about it theatrically, probably interrogates the identified proposition in more detail. If it stands up and both parties are still as enthusiastic, then the writer might be commissioned to write a first draft.

After this, I think there are three stages in the draft of a play. (You might do ten drafts to get through those stages, but there are three milestones along the way, so to speak.) Writing the first draft of something is often an emetic process – it is the writer spewing out everything that they know or occurs to them about the story and the world of the story. Like directors later in the production process, at this stage writers like to keep options open so there are many plots and subplots and blind alleys, with the result that the first draft is often overlong, unfocused, yet somewhere within it, if writer and director are lucky, it contains the play they both want to produce. This is what might be identified at the first-draft meeting. The director (or literary manager as it often is in Britain) is crucial in helping the writer, who is often snowblind with the possibilities at this stage, in identifying 'what this play is about' and hence 'the story'.

The ideal feedback from a director at this stage therefore is general, non-prescriptive notes. The director might want to argue about the particular, but what is the point when the particular might change as a result of the general 'big' notes? I find radio producers are the best at this; they're brilliant at homing in on what is essential. Perhaps because the medium itself is so tightly focused and because in general each radio producer develops and records up to fifteen new plays each year, they seem to understand that writers don't want any specific notes about scenes, even particulars about characters – unless those characters are superfluous or can be kept 'off' – because it's about focusing on 'the story'.

It's very dangerous for the director at that stage to be either specific or even too concerned with specific theatrical or design moments. It's very dangerous for a director in first-draft stage to start jumping to theatrical solutions and ideas. The theatrical language has to emerge from the text and the text emerges from the story – it can't be imposed on it. The best directors I've worked with keep their options open quite late into the rehearsal process.

So, then the writer goes away and works on a second draft, which might take two or three drafts to get to, and very often you'll find the second draft is about half the length of the first draft; and interestingly it is often overly short because it's been compressed down into that really tightly focused journey.

The director and playwright have agreed what the main story is, so you're cutting away to let that emerge more?

Exactly, so at stage two (which is actually stage four – I said there's the general talk, the one-page talk, the first-draft talk, now the second-draft talk) the director really needs to start offering notes. Again, not necessarily specifically about lines and scenes, but about character developments and layers. And then the next draft is about reinflating the play around this tight structure. Once you've got down to its essentials it's about giving it life and layers, drawing out the imagery – and I don't mean that in a literal sense, but the theatrical imagery, and looking at plot structure and how specific moments and scenes might work within that structure.

Then the writer does the third draft, and let's call that the rehearsal script, and that will, in length, be somewhere between the first and second drafts. The relationship continues on into the rehearsals through to the 'polishing' period, which is when all the tiny notes and details can be introduced and teased out.

As for rehearsals, I tend to be around in the first and last weeks and leave the awkward middle to the director. I think it's good to re-engage with the play after a break. I know there are some writers who police rehearsals and won't let a word of their rehearsal draft be changed. There are writers, like Brian Friel, who emerged from a theatre where there were no directors, or untrained directors, so they have to be directed from the page. My inclination is to hand over my work with as few stage directions as possible so director and cast have to tease out the action from the dialogue.

So the stage directions are in the writing?

I think that makes directors and actors alike interrogate the text more rigorously. It's the reason directors like working with Shakespeare and the Greeks: there are no stage directions telling you how to do it, but actually the theatricality is built into the language. I'm writing a stage play at the moment, and I've got one stage direction at the beginning which describes the continuous action the actors will perform, but I'll leave it to the director to find the exact when and how of it in the spoken text. It's not that I'm completely averse to stage directions, especially impossible ones. In *Monkey!* (an adaptation of *Journey to the West*, not to be confused with *Kafka's Monkey*) I had a stage direction, 'A mountain falls on Monkey!' and 'Then 500 years pass.' I think there should be an excitement of discovery in rehearsals. It shouldn't be the writer telling everyone how to do it – and even directors should have to work, sometimes.

I am aware when writing the rehearsal draft of saying to myself, 'I'm going to write this level of theatricalisation but I'm going to leave another level to the director and the actors to discover or invent.' One very positive recent theatrical experience I've had was with Walter Meierjohann, who directed my adaptation, *Kafka's Monkey*. We had the Kafka short story 'A Report to the Academy', and we had the actor, Kathryn Hunter, who was developing a physical language long before I wrote the script, and many other adaptations we looked at had been content with the original story as the basis of a full production. But adapting from one medium to another also adapts the relationship of the text to the audience/reader/auditor. Walter and I sat down and asked, 'What is the relationship of the stage to the auditorium, what is the theatricalisation of Kafka's idea?'

And for me the story is very much about the split self: the monkey who has become man is ultimately neither one thing nor another. I kept saying to Walter, 'We need two monkeys, two Kathryns.' I didn't tell him how to do it, I just said there are two monkeys and the man/monkey is in conversation with the monkey/monkey, her former self, throughout the monologue. I pointed to the problem and made this explicit in the text, but I did not try to solve it for Walter. In the end, he found a very simple theatricalisation of that idea with the designer, Steffi Wurst. He projected a four-metre-high image of one of the original Hagenbeck monkeys, which was there for the first act, disappeared for the second, and returned for the third. The way Kathryn's character related to the projected monkey in the first act was very different to how you viewed it at the end, so the whole dramatic structure of the play was underpinned by the scenic structure. An audience might not even be aware that they are watching something quite so structured, but that's an example of how we developed a theatrical language from the text, I as author in words, the director in theatrical realisation, but one that was true to the text.

In situations where you've written a play which has been commissioned, rather than the more collaborative process on Kafka's Monkey *you have just described, have you, as part of the three-draft process, had workshops and how have you found them useful, and at what stage are they useful?*

They're useful after you've handed in the first draft, in identifying the story and exploring the theatrical language. After stage two, a workshop is just going to become a reading. It's important to show producers and it's helpful in tweaking moments, and you're always going to learn from actors doing their stuff, but, actually, a 'workshop' workshop as opposed to a rehearsed reading is between stage one and two, when there is an idea and a play world and characters, but pretty much everything else is up for grabs.

And do you and the director have a specific agenda for that workshop, or set of questions that you want to answer?

You've got to have a specific set of questions. For instance, it's a major decision whether you're going to show the work or not, because this slants the whole workshop.

In some ways would you agree that it's more productive if there isn't an aim to show the workshop, in terms of asking diagnostic questions?

I did a workshop on *The Walls* at the National Studio; the idea for the piece was very open and during the workshop we explored it as a theatrical proposition. We had a week on it. As the week progressed we discovered it worked. If we'd decided on the Monday that we were going to show it I think we'd have had a very different atmosphere, but deciding on the Thursday morning, because we knew we had something at that stage, was completely different. So we showed it on the Friday and it was commissioned and scheduled on the spot. There are great benefits to showing the work, but you've got to decide at the outset of a workshop, 'Who is this for? Is it for the producer, or is it for the director, or for the writer?' It's crucial to identify that before one plans a workshop. However, it could turn out, like the workshop we did on *The Walls*, to be for all three.

So by working through the proposition with actors you could test it in a way you couldn't by discussing it with the director?

In television, where the drama language is invariably one of naturalism, there is neither the funding, time or (I would argue) the need for workshops. And I wonder with a naturalistic play in the theatre whether one needs workshops since the theatrical language is a given. A good literary manager or director should be able to iron out the problems with the writer. However, when for instance, I work with Hideki Noda and Kathryn Hunter on projects such as *The Bee* and *The Diver*, we start the workshops with nothing and develop a theatrical language through the workshops.

What do I mean by theatrical language? Most people see this as performance and production style, but something I keep coming back to, and I think is very under-explored, since in naturalistic theatre it's just something that's taken for granted, is the relationship between the stage and auditorium. And actually it's a crucial dynamic. *The Walls* very much explored that, as did *The Bee* and *Kafka's Monkey*. The rhythm of the action is a whole complex layer that needs exploring, but also it comes down to what the audience are experiencing. On the page we experience one thing, but on the stage that live dynamic, which is theatre's uniqueness, is really crucial.

What do you see as your function in the rehearsal room and how do you relate to the actors?

Lots of writers have had lots of bad experiences when their work is in development, and these bad experiences will come to a head in the rehearsal room because rehearsal is the process whereby the writer hands over authority for the play to the director who in turn hands it on to the actors. The path to production is fraught with dangers for the writer–director relationship. For instance, when younger or more insecure directors try to impose their aesthetics on a new play, or show off their talents, it is very difficult. I had one experience like that and it proved very painful. The directing must come from the work.

As Peter Hall says, every new play deserves at least one outing as itself. And to reference another leading British director, I saw Howard Davies say in the papers recently that directors should work with writers of their own age. What I understand by this is that there should be a parity of esteem and of experience. When I worked with Peter (Hall) I was thirty and he was seventy, and I was in a creative team that was Peter Hall (director), Harrison Birtwistle (composer), Alison Chitty (designer) and me: they were an established team, they had two knighthoods and an OBE between them, and about a hundred years on me, and that was very daunting. I'm proud of the work we achieved but it was very much me working to their aesthetics and their precepts.

Some of the best experiences I've had in recent years have been working with Walter Meierjohann, Dominic Hill and Indhu Rubasingham, directors all from very different backgrounds and companies, but all of an age with me and therefore with a range of historical experiences, references and aesthetics in common.

And I'd say with all of the directors mentioned above they found it helpful to have me in rehearsal. But one must respect the dynamic and the authority in the rehearsal room. Unless invited by the director to address the actors directly, I'd always feed comments through the director. It's important for a director to convey to the cast that there is a unity of approach from the creative team. But, for all that, if the writer says something the director might not agree with, he or she should be able to defend his or her position. There is also the potential for the director to use the writer as a third eye. The writer will in general not be worrying about set, costume changes, props, lights, budgets – so can perhaps focus more clearly on the text and action. Just as the director can help the writer out of the snowblindness of the first draft stage, so can the writer help the director at this stage. Obviously if a writer's saying, 'This is the way it has to be,' there's a problem. You'll find that more with naturalistic work.

And indeed, sometimes having the writer present and part of the production discussions can solve problems and save money. In Ibsen's original of *Peer Gynt* there is a hugely complicated shipwreck scene which I had retained through to the rehearsal draft of my recent adaptation, though I was not happy with how I had realised it. The director, Dominic Hill, had intended to perform this sequence on these huge overhead gantries which would drop as the ship sank. I was in rehearsals when the production manager came in and informed Dominic how much it was going to cost: £30,000 I think it was. Dominic blurted out exasperatedly that he didn't even like the scene. I agreed with him. 'So why don't we do it on an aeroplane? If we're updating everything else, Peer should be flying home by budget airline that starts to go down. It's just a line of chairs?' After a moment's thought, Dominic said, 'And you know, there's been this gag I've always wanted to do with oxygen masks.' That scene was one of many show-stopping moments in his production.

At the end of the day the audience only see the show. The vast majority are not interested in how it was made, or whose ego is bruised, or how much anything cost – notice this question only arises publicly when something is not good. Writer, director and everyone else involved have to be prepared to adapt and collaborate towards this end. Quite often the best decisions derive from necessity, from the collective imagination of the group, and when you exclude members of the group there can be difficulties and blame. On one play of mine I was not party to the discussion about the set design. All those meetings and decisions had taken place elsewhere. I'm not necessarily sure I could have found a solution to the design question posed by the play, but perhaps discussions between myself and the designer might have yielded some solutions for him. The writer can be wrong, but if the writer's got a problem with something I think it's good for the director to tease it out, if only at least to confirm the insanity of the writer.

When you come back to rehearsals in the final week do you have a different role? Or do you have a different set of comments?

Generally, by the end of the rehearsal process the director is dealing with so many aspects of the production. I like to see the last few runs in the rehearsal room before the tech. I just ignore the tech because I realise the director's concerned with something else completely. So I think the purest version you're going to see of a play is in its last run in the rehearsal room. The notes I would take would be very much about the language, pace and emphasis. I could feel strongly the blocking was wrong, but again, this should always feed back to the director. Indeed, I don't really comment on the blocking until I see it on stage – since much can change in the tech and look very different in the extended space of the theatre.

Then when I come back to see previews I very much look to see if the same issues I might have had in the rehearsal room runs are still evident and how they play with the audience. For me, the previews are that polishing process for both production and script. Most things are in the right place and you can really start to fine-tune things, but, I know, again, the director's dealing with so much. Sometimes I have been asked to talk to the cast about text while they get on with technical details. It's all about a level of trust. The director needs to feel that the writer's not going to start giving really crazy notes, telling actors how to act. I think it's more difficult in the rehearsal processes when the actors start coming to the writer and start wanting notes from them.

A rehearsal process is a political cauldron as it is, and a writer's relationship to it is very fraught. One obviously has one's own vision of the production, but one must empower the director to realise theirs. When the trust is there and repaid, both director and writer can work better than the sum of their parts. When it's not there one can end up with a divided, difficult and dispirited team trying to realise different visions of the same piece.

Interview with Simon Pittman

Simon Pittman is a freelance theatre director and practitioner. He was Resident Director at the Library Theatre, Manchester, from 2006 to 2007, trained on the MFA in Theatre Directing at Birkbeck, University of London, and attended the National Theatre Studio Directors' Course. He co-directs Rough Fiction, a multidisciplinary company that creates original productions and runs a permanent Ensemble Laboratory that produces unique, pop-up productions of existing plays.

Recent direction includes The Love of the Nightingale *for Rough Fiction,* The Last of the Lake *for Rough Fiction and The Point, Eastleigh,* Not a Game for Boys *by Simon Block at the Library Theatre, Manchester, and* The Interview *at the Arcola. For the National Theatre of Scotland he has provided movement direction for 99 . . . 100 and Mixter Maxter, and was assistant for 365 at the Edinburgh International Festival and the Lyric, Hammersmith. He has also assistant directed for Paines Plough, the Library Theatre and Guildhall School of Music and Drama. He has worked as Creative Learning Associate for Frantic Assembly and as a visiting lecturer at Royal Holloway, University of London.*

There are many companies called devising companies, but is it more of a way of making work rather than how you advertise yourself in Time Out *or in a brochure? Is it a tool rather than a genre?*

I think that when the word 'devising', or the idea of devising, first appeared, it was on the fringes of theatre practice, as a response to a writer-led theatre, and it was about certain companies doing something experimental, avant-garde or 'other' to the mainstream, which were essentially new ways of experimenting with form, finding new ways of relating to audiences and new ways to collaborate in the creative process: people wanted to free up their options to be able to work and say things differently.

When we are talking about contemporary theatre-making, which is a term I prefer to devising, there is no single aesthetic or ideological objective. There are many different genres that have their origins in the roots of devising practice: early examples might be companies as diverse as the Wooster Group, Forced Entertainment, Complicite and DV8. So, whether you work in community work, physically, through live art, or through dance, or with sound or digital media, devised theatre is about finding forms through which to express an idea better, and engage with an audience, and media can extend as far as psychology, sociology or anthropology. For me, the interdisciplinary nature, and the pliability and the porous quality of forms and disciplines, are the keys.

I don't really know which companies would be called 'devising companies' today because playing with form is so much more present and understood throughout the theatre industry: Lecoq, Gaulier, clown work, physical theatre practice, live art, installation, immersive theatre events, site-specific theatre events – all these things now are so much more interconnected through specific choices in a making process, that it makes it a lot harder to define today's different theatre genres. We are really talking about making choices in creative process, style and form, and knowing how that relates to content.

There are some aspects of the work of these diverse companies linked to 'devising' that might be considered as similar and defining. The idea of theatre as an event is important for much of the work: it ceases to be about going to the theatre in a conventional environment to watch actors reanimate an existing text; and it becomes about what is performative, about how one experiences the event. The audience–performer or spectator–artist relationship is so much more at the centre, and so much more considered and rigorously thought out in the process of making devised work. It's not taken for granted, it's an artistic option that is up for question and needs to be investigated.

Several voices in American critical theory have defined devised or contemporary theatre-making as 'collective creation': artists have less traditionally defined roles. For example, an actor is not just seen as an actor but as a rounded creative artist, which then enables the actor to be empowered not only in the shaping of the content, the form and the ideas of a play, but also to have a dialogue within the process of theatre-making about their process and approach. The 'self' of the artist or the performer becomes so much more apparent, important and key to the work: it becomes integrated into the fabric, the content of performance.

Also, within the making of this kind of work, process is foregrounded. Devising then become a process of experimentation, and originating 'a set of creative strategies', as is noted in *Making a Performance*. So part of devising is reconceptualising creative practice in direct connection to the content which you are researching and developing. The relationship between process, form and content becomes much more apparent in the room, so the work is more closely connected to the moment and context of production than is often the case in what we are calling, for the purposes of this discussion, a writer-led theatre.

Devised theatre has enabled us to ask, 'If we are starting from nothing, what are we making, what is it about, where has it come from, and what are our resources?' The starting point might come from an aesthetic, political, social, psychological, anthropological or personal perspective. The creative process may begin with seeking out your creative process or it may begin with an idea and then working out which creative processes will best suit that idea: it completely opens the landscape up, which is why devising is so difficult to talk about and to define.

There are two very useful books that cover the history, forms and processes of devising. The first is Alison Oddey's *Devising Theatre*, which is a very good account of the earlier forms of devising, and the second is the book I mentioned earlier: *Making a Performance* by Emma Govan, Helen Nicholson and Katie Normington, which is a more current account.

What are some of the first questions you may wish to ask to establish your parameters and processes?

The problem with that question is that certain things may already be established from the nature of how you come to the work. For example, people may have existing styles of work as a company, or you may begin with a shared understanding of why you are there and what you are there for, or one person may come with a proposition to explore. Any one of those factors will inevitably lead to given attitudes towards style, content, audience relation and the creative process. So with these key questions one will have a certain number that are variable and a certain number that are fixed: it may be that the proposition is fixed, or the genre is fixed, or the style of the company or the artist involved are fixed. So the first thing to do is to identify what are the variables and what are the givens.

If we assume that everything is a variable, first we may ask what our skills are: as we have certain physical skills, the story is going to be told physically as well as through text. Or we've got somebody who is a sound designer, so incorporating sound from the very beginning is an important element. Second, what do we want to make work about: have we come together to explore a specific issue or theme? Third, how do we want to make it: what making processes do we want to employ? And, perhaps finally, what aesthetics are we interested in and what do we want to use to communicate?

A further key question is about how a group operates in collaboration; to what extent are we democratic or hierarchic in our interaction: who leads, who has responsibility, who has ownership?

I believe all these things have to be clearly questioned and established. For me, where a lot of devised work falls down is that it is very easy to lack rigour in any one of these areas, and if they are unclear it is very difficult to make truly great work through a collaborative group-devising process – to create work as a group in a room without an individual to offer focus, drive and leadership. Who is responsible for dramaturgy, writing, or guiding a coherent structure can be very hard to manage.

Then one has to think about what the art form is. For example, are you talking about a piece that is primarily based around structured narrative and storytelling? Immersive and interactive theatre may focus more on the experiential and have different values, or people can value narrative in a different way, so other elements may be placed higher on the agenda, or be a larger part of what one is offering the audience. That's not to say narrative and story are not important, but it depends on what the aim is, and that can change your relationship to narrative.

For example, in some of Punchdrunk's pieces, or in *You Me Bum Bum Train* each member of the audience experiences the piece, and the narratives, in an individual way, so that they are partly, or significantly, creating their own narratives. One company programmed at the Barbican for BITE this year was Non Zero One, with a show called *Would Like to Meet*, in which you are given a pair of headphones, an iPod and instructions, and you walk about the Barbican and have a personal experience with an audio journey and engage with other participants. There are no performers, it's just the Barbican building and an interesting set of ideas and concepts.

What does need to be established is a collective way of thinking, or what I would call a score, for your process. As an example I'll describe the process for a project we are doing at the moment with Rough Fiction. I am a director and work in movement and as a dramaturg; my colleague is a playwright and will also work as an associate director; and we are working in collaboration with some people who are trained as actors. Although we start our process with just two of us we engage people to go on a creative journey with us, so it is important to 'enshrine expectations' for those involved and be clear about what is fixed and what is open, and which stages of the process will be entirely collaborative and which will require a hierarchy of decision-making.

Can you describe a 'template' version of the making processes, or score, you may use on a project, taking this current project as an example?

In this instance it begins with an idea, or proposition, that we wish to investigate, then asking, 'Why do we want to do it?' and, 'Why us?' Once we're clear on why we want to embark on the project and what the broad idea or focus of investigation for the project is, we then research and develop this idea to a point where we can say, 'We feel we have enough of a proposition here to engage with a larger company.' The next stage is to find that company and to go through a process of researching and gathering more material, then exploring and developing it with the company. We say, 'Here is the theme, here is the wide idea, this is what is important to us, now let's explore it.' But we also set out what the artists can expect in terms of offering ideas, building ideas and taking ownership.

The piece we are working on at the moment is based on the semantic theme of water, so someone might bring in an artist's portrait of his wife in a bath and then explore the ideas behind it and ask the actors to respond to it; or we may ask people to go away and research deep water, or ideas around water's relationship to the mind, and then we explore responses to that research through practical exercises. So there is a sense of everyone having a shared ownership and shared knowledge of this information; they gather a sense of what this thing is, and they are immersed as artists in the creative process just as a writer or director might be.

But then the writer might suggest that we develop this work in a particular direction, so the second stage is developing and building on what comes out of that initial research and material. At this stage the company might also be improvising, for example, around a particular character that has emerged. We might be setting new tasks to refocus the exploration, so during this development stage we are beginning to guide the direction of the final material. At the beginning everything is up for grabs, but then we define what becomes set and what is still up for grabs. We might close rehearsal scores down a bit further and define more specifically what is still open to explore: so there is artistic freedom within given parameters, but those parameters are suggested by the research and exploration.

There has to be a point when one shifts from developing and exploring to ordering and structuring in order to make the material into a piece of theatre – a point where we say, 'We are writing and structuring a play that has come from you, is related to you, is guided by us, and is written for you and made for you to perform.' In this example at least, our process may then shift to become a more traditional playwright–director–actor relationship to the piece, but with a shared history of related experience and exploration supporting it.

Being clear about the different stages of the process and people's roles within it is really important. It can be argued that if you don't enshrine expectations, if you don't get your roles and your hierarchy correct, and the ways you interrelate set and happy, that's where it can all go wrong, and that's what makes devised theatre, if we are going to use that term, so difficult because people don't always know what is expected of them.

So at this stage, for example, we ask the actors questions about different characters. If the actors are unsure about the facts or characteristics surrounding a character it might help the writer hone down where more work needs to be done to form that character clearly; so here there is a different practical process of testing, clarifying and fixing. What's important to us is the absolute mesh between movement, physicality, musicality and text, and this process allows you to work across all of those different media at the same time and for them to be part of that structuring process rather than forced together too late in the day.

We work a lot with building atmosphere and sensory experience, so that involves music and light, but not necessarily huge or complex set designs. The dramaturgy and writing are happening among the other performance languages you are testing and exploring, so content and form are pliable and porous within the creative process.

Finally we are in a position where we are able to hone down, spiral down into a score for performance that ends up closed, set and formed out of that process. However, since all involved have now gained ownership of how the process works, of the form and of the content, I think it is important to remember that you have to work into your process some space and time to be self-reflective as an artist and as a company, and to enable something which had apparently been closed and set to be revisited.

It seems to be inevitable that in many instances there is a need for someone who, at least for a project or a period within a project, is given a leadership role, so they can take it forward and enable everyone to work effectively.

Once we've gone through a proposition, gathering ideas, developing and exploring it and starting to hone it down, clarify and structure it, then a big part of the devising process is about how you analyse what you end up with – just as you would look at a play and ask what is working and what is not. So, as Simon McBurney describes it, we make an 'attempt' – we might present a one-off public performance, or do it for an invited audience of people with whom we have a dialogue and who might be able to help us work. In another model the attempt may become a separate and defined stage of the making process, and you could call it a first development. So you make the attempt and then you analyse the problems or whatever you need to readjust or restructure. In this model, only after the 'attempt' and the subsequent reworking do we 'present' – put it in front of a paying audience.

So the whole process moves from open to closed, from closed to open, in certain directions. I believe, in this example at least, one tries to let the resulting performance text speak, and to serve it and not get in its way. You are ensuring that everything is focused towards a coherent whole, and at the same time you are trying to come to it with a certain freedom, enabling everyone's ownership and input into the work – while hopefully avoiding the bad sort of arguments, and blocking good things from happening!

Practical exercises

Exercise one

One way of choosing a translation is by a game of blind tasting. Having selected three or four translations of a play, select three or four scenes that you consider pivotal, and have a degree of contrast between them, and make copies of the same scenes from each translation. Mark all the scenes from the first translation as A, from the second translation B, and so on. Then find however many actor friends you need for the scenes, and ask them to read the different versions of each scene, in a random order, without letting you know which version is which. Make notes on the strengths and weaknesses of each version, and perhaps even score them.

You may wish to consider the economy of the language, the use of imagery, the modernity or ease of expression, for example, and mark each version against these, or other criteria. Having read all the versions of all the scenes, and then revealed which version came from which translation, you and the actors may have noted qualities about each translation you may not have noted by reading each whole translation one after another, and you may be surprised by which version you choose.

Exercise two

Choose a play by a classic or historic author, research it and work on it in the ways suggested in the chapter, as if you are preparing to direct it. To focus this work on your production rather than on criticism of the play you may wish to set yourself two framing tasks.

First, imagine that you have chosen to give a ten-minute talk about your production before the read-through and model-showing on the first day of rehearsals to the assembled cast, creative team and theatre staff. For the purposes of this exercise, and for envisaging the production, assume that there has been a discussion process with a designer, although you will have designed it yourself. Ideally you will find several friends to role play your audience, and ask you questions at the end about your production, then give you feedback on the whole presentation. Would they like to be directed by you for four weeks on this production?

You will undoubtedly draw on your research on the author and his or her other works, and the world of the author and the world of the play, and possibly critical commentaries on the author and the play, but the purpose of the exercise is not to give a lecture on the play but to find a tone of voice and speaking about your production rather than the play. It might not be useful, even though you may have expended hours on research, to talk about your research in detail, but only to refer to it if it helps your audience to visualise your production.

Given that the people you are talking to will be creatively involved in the process of making the work happen, talk to them as if they can help – indicate how your approach to the play will creatively involve the actors and others in a process rather than describing a closed vision: you will wish to inspire and excite those people you are about to work with over the next month and give them confidence in your approach and production by enabling them clearly to envisage the production.

You may wish to begin by saying why you have chosen to direct this play at this time, and your individual critical and instinctual response to it, and how that will inform your overall production aims and approach. Leading on from this you may wish to outline any particular themes you wish to emphasise; your design ideas for the production; any specific casting ideas for the play, particularly any against type or through casting decisions that affect the production; any specific approaches to the text, or particular rehearsal methods you may wish to employ; any other production elements that are distinctive to this production – which might be choices of music or sound design, for example; a particular target audience or marketing strategy; the close involvement of other creatives such as musical director, fight director, or voice coach.

You may not wish to imagine that this production is for a specific theatre, but it may help crystallise your thinking.

The point of this exercise is to help translate research and initial ideas into concrete production ideas which you can then effectively communicate, and to develop a way of thinking and talking about a production that is pragmatic and will engage fellow artists.

Exercise three

Either separately or alongside this, you may wish to consider how to turn your research materials into a useful rehearsal tool. As discussed above and in Chapter Six, 'The Director and the Production', it is increasingly common for directors to assemble an 'actor pack' or, as Sarah Esdaile describes it, a library of information, in the rehearsal room. Preparing an actor pack, to be copied and given to each member of the cast and creative team is also often one of the first jobs a director will delegate to an assistant director, and, as first directing opportunities are often assisting opportunities, it is worth considering what may go into an actor pack.

The actor pack should be a collection of items that you (and your designer) have already collected in the process of your research rather than material you have entirely constructed for the purpose, so it also provides a useful distillation or paper trail of your research, as well as being useful information and stimulation for others. Ideally, this pack should provide the actors and others with any material that you think they would find useful in learning about the world of the play or the context of the author and play. It should be aimed at informing and stimulating a cast, so it needs to contain a range of written and visual material that is well presented and well annotated. It might include music or a DVD. Huge copied articles with no annotations or cross references will appear boring or forbidding, so it is important to direct the reader's attention to what is most stimulating and germane, and to present the material well and within a context, perhaps even referring to scenes for which a piece of information is most useful. Again, it is about having a sense of a throughline as to how your initial research will inform the final production and production processes.

Weblist

Bush Theatre	www.bushtheatre.co.uk
Bushgreen	bushgreen.org
Canal Café Theatre	www.canalcafetheatre.com
Equity	www.equity.org.uk
Goldsmiths MA in Writing for Performance	www.gold.ac.uk/pg/ma-writing-performance
Hampstead Theatre	www.hampsteadtheatre.com
Independent Theatre Council (ITC)	www.itc-arts.org
Old Vic New Voices	www.ideastap.com
Paines Plough	www.painesplough.com
Royal Court Theatre	www.royalcourttheatre.com
Soho Theatre	www.sohotheatre.com
theatre503	www.theatre503.com
Theatrical Management Association	www.tmauk.org
Tristan Bates Theatre	www.tristanbatestheatre.co.uk
Writers' Guild of Great Britain	www.writersguild.org.uk

Bibliography

Alfreds, Mike, *Different Every Night*. London: Nick Hern Books, 2007.

Barton, John, *Playing Shakespeare*. London: Methuen, 1984.

Berry, Cicely, *From Word to Play*. London: Oberon Books, 2008.

Edgar, David, *How Plays Work*. London: Nick Hern Books, 2009.

Govan, Emma, Nicholson, Helen, and Normington, Katie, *Making a Performance: Devising Histories and Contemporary Practices*. London, Routledge, 2007.

Hall, Peter, *Shakespeare's Advice to the Players*. London: Oberon Books, 2009.

Oddey, Alison, *Devising Theatre: A Practical and Theoretical Handbook*. London: Routledge, 1994.

Stafford-Clark, Max, *Letters to George*. London: Nick Hern Books, 1989.

4 The director and the designer

This chapter begins with an apology – to lighting designers, sound designers and digital media designers. As is common in the theatre, the term 'designer' is often assumed to mean set and/or costume designer, unless otherwise stated. Much of this chapter discusses the relationship specifically between the director and set designer, although many observations made about that relationship are applicable to the relationships with all designers. The reason there is a need for an apology at all partly comes from what is often seen as an inequitable relationship between different designers: often directors begin their collaboration with the set designer and other designers join the collaboration after many conversations have been had and many decisions made. This is a perennial and problematic issue that is discussed later, and in the interview with the lighting designer Tony Simpson.

Training for designers

In contrast to directors, there are very few working designers who have not undergone some level of formal training. As with director training, there is a growing number of short, foundation, undergraduate and post-graduate training programmes for designers. The websites of the Society of British Theatre Designers and the Association of Courses in Theatre Design list courses that are recognised by practising designers, and the industry – and it is only designers listed on these courses who may apply for the most prestigious award for emerging designers, the Linbury Prize. This is administered by the National Theatre and is awarded biennially to graduates from the previous and current final-year students on recognised design courses. Twelve finalists are selected whose work is exhibited in the National Theatre foyer, often in November, and, from those twelve, four designers are chosen and are guaranteed productions at four different theatres, and from the four there is one overall winner. In 2009 the winner was Aleš Valášek from Motley Design School; the eleven other finalists were from Bristol Old Vic Theatre School, Central St Martin's, Central School of Speech and Drama, the Liverpool Institute of Performing Arts, Royal Welsh College of Music and Drama and Wimbledon College of Art.

It is worth visiting the websites of the courses listed on the SBTD website and reading about their content and focus, as this often tells you something about the approaches and skills of their recent graduates. As with actors from drama schools, it is useful to have an idea of the broad differences between the work of, say, Central St Martin's and Wimbledon designers when considering designers for particular projects.

The website *Sceno:graphy* was originally set up by designers from Nottingham Trent University, and is now the online presence of the Society of Theatre Designers and Scenographers. It acts as a forum for designers and other theatre artists to promote their work and communicate with each other. As well as interesting articles on theatre design it also gives the times and locations of many of the annual exhibitions of graduates from the design courses. Although these exhibitions usually begin with a private viewing, they are open to the public for several days or even weeks. Many are held in June and July. Often the designers are present at these exhibitions, and visiting them is a good way of getting to know emerging designers and their work.

From browsing the websites of the design courses you will see that designers have to acquire a wide range of fundamental practical skills such as technical drawing – including the ability to draw ground plans and elevations to scale – life drawing, costume drawing, scenic painting, model-making, costume-making, textile painting and dyeing. They will also usually gain a knowledge of the history of theatre, and in particular the history of theatre building, theatre design and costume design. They will also gain an appreciation of different staging configurations and will work on a wide range of work from new plays in a small studio, or site-specific work, to an opera at La Scala. Depending on the course, they will also become familiar with working with a wide range of materials, from traditional wood and metal to more modern design resources such as perspex and digital media.

As with directors, emerging designers will bring a great range of skills, imagination, enthusiasm and commitment to a first project, but they may not have had the opportunity to work with a full creative team, including a production manager, or had to design to a strict budget. Just as many emerging directors have to be their own producers in order to get fringe or low- to no-budget productions on, designers often have to be their own production managers in these circumstances, and some are better than others at taking on the financial and logistical challenges at the same time as designing the show.

The director as designer

There are some directors who choose to design or light their own productions, such as Terry Hands, while Philip Prowse and Patrick Connellan are examples of designers who also direct. However, as directors who just direct, we also have to decide how much we need to think from a design point of view and how much technical knowledge we ought to have in order to communicate clearly and collaborate fully with stage, light, sound and video designers. To repeat a refrain from many other chapters in this book, the more knowledge we have as directors, the better informed are the choices and decisions we make. We collaborate with artists who are specialists in what they do and we don't have to know their work intimately to be able to work productively with them, but we do need to have a vocabulary which enables us to be clear and specific about what we mean and envisage: my idea of emerald green might not be the designer's; my expectation of how dusk will appear might be quite different from a lighting designer's.

Concrete references and examples not only help to keep the conversation with the designer specific but also build up a shared language and shorthand, so before there is a need to have a range of references for a particular production there is a huge benefit in taking time to widen your knowledge of visual art, architecture and film, and in acquiring a rudimentary knowledge of stage shapes and techniques, and lighting, sound, projection and video equipment and techniques. The interview with Tony Simpson later in this chapter outlines the level of knowledge that a lighting designer finds it useful for a director to have, and it is clear from that interview that it is not necessary for a director to know what a fresnel light can do, but it is useful to have a broad understanding of what can and cannot be achieved with a lighting rig in order to have a practical productive conversation with a lighting designer.

It is worthwhile going to art galleries, exhibitions and installations to stimulate the visual imagination, but even from internet searches of Getty Images and other sites it is possible to build up a knowledge of current and past artists whose work you admire, to download examples or links, and to build up a bank of images. This knowledge of, and sensibility for, visual images can inform your initial responses to a play and widen those responses beyond the literal and intellectual at an early stage of engagement with the play, and they can also be a useful resource from which you can select examples for future design meetings.

Building up a knowledge of designers, lighting designers and sound designers whose work you admire will provide reference points for initial design conversations. Most designers will not mind if you reference the work of other designers and they will probably have seen work by their peers and colleagues – lighting designers are still a relatively small pool of people and know each other's work well. Of course, these are reference points for initial conversations, not requests to design the production 'just like so-and-so designed *A Winter's Tale*'.

The interview with Alison Chitty highlights the power of the object on the stage and the exercises she has evolved really help directors and designers to consider precisely what each object and each element of the design is saying to an audience about the world of the play, and how objects take on new meanings through combination and juxtaposition with each other, and through the actors' interaction with them during the course of the play. It is an interesting exercise to take a play you know well, preferably one with a number of different public and private locations, to envisage a broad design for it, and then to design it in more detail for a proscenium arch, a thrust stage, an 'open' stage (such as the Olivier or the main auditoria at the Sheffield Crucible or West Yorkshire Playhouse), a theatre in the round, a short traverse and a long traverse. This exercise will not only illustrate how different stage configurations serve different aspects of the play, but also their contrasting demands in terms of the amount of objects (including scenery) they require to convey the world of the play and to create that world fully in the different spaces. The exercise also highlights one element of design that can often be forgotten when conceiving a design in sketch form or in a model box: the relationship of the play and the design with the audience.

The tools of the designer

As the designer Vicki Mortimer mentions in her interview later in this chapter, she prefers to go straight to working with a model from the initial conversation with a director. The prime tools of the designer are the model box, the 'white card model' and the fully finished model of the set. Most designers work in a scale of 1:25, that is, the model is exactly one twenty-fifth the size of the actual set, and to work at this scale the necessary tool is a scale rule which is usually a triangular rule that has a number of scales marked on it: 1:10, 1:25, 1:50, 1:100, etc. Final models are always made exactly to scale and are meticulously completed with exactly the right finishes and colours that will appear on the set, because, as Vicki Mortimer says, the model has to speak for itself: the production manager, carpenter, scene painter and others will have the model in the workshop or production office and refer to it to cost and build the set when the designer is no longer there, so it has to be a definitive blueprint for the final set. Designers spend a huge amount of time and effort on the final model, and busy, high-level, designers often employ model-makers. The cost of the finished model for an opera can be as much as £5,000.

To begin to work on a design, perhaps after a series of sketches, a designer will use a scalpel, white tape and scale rule to fashion a model out of white card so that the designer and director can try different stage shapes quickly and move things around in the model box without committing overmuch time or expense to a design idea, which might inhibit further experimentation and development. Both the white-card model and the final model are usually placed in a model box of the same scale, usually of black card, which represents the permanent shape of the theatre space, and possibly of the auditorium (which may be the same thing in a studio or flexible-space theatre). The white-card model is also the first form in which the design will be shown to a production manager and others involved in the design and making, so that the making staff can get an early sense of the design, and what it may involve in principle in terms of making resources, time and cost. Hence the white-card model gives its name to this 'white-card meeting' in the design process.

Once the final model is made the designer or production manager will also draw scale drawings of the set in the theatre space: a 'plan' drawing, which is the set and stage viewed from above; and an 'elevation' or 'section' – the set and stage viewed from the side. All permanent theatres have 'blank' scale drawings on which the set can be drawn. The plan in particular becomes an important tool on which the lighting designer can add the positions of lights in the lighting rig, and for the stage management to lay out in tape an exact 'mark up' of the set in the rehearsal room.

The other time-consuming task of the designer is to provide drawings of all the costumes that will appear in the production. These are usually completed at the same time as the final model, although they may be preceded by less detailed drawings or collages to discuss costume ideas during the design process. Some designers now prefer to Photoshop costume drawings rather than draw them, but they demand the same level of accuracy in terms of cut, material, finish and colour as the final model, and it is common for the designer to attach 'swatches' (very small samples) of the fabric to be used for the costume. As will be discussed later, particularly if costumes are to be bought or hired, or if there are changes to the costume after conversations with the actor who is wearing them, the costumes may change more than the set, but these costume drawings are likely to be used for budgeting, so they do set parameters.

Staging techniques, equipment and terms

Many directors are anxious about their lack of knowledge of technical stage terms, particularly as many of the terms give no clue as to what they actually mean: 'leg', 'apron', 'cyc', 'genie' and 'dip trap' spring to mind. As with the discussion with the lighting designer, it is not necessary to know all these terms in order to gain an understanding of what is and what is not possible in the particular space you are working in.

There follow some questions that might be worthwhile asking. Some of them might appear obvious, but it is still worth checking most of them, as not asking them might lead to problems or confusion later in the production. People won't think you are stupid, they will just think you are being thorough.

In any space the first question is: where can the actors get on and off from? The stage left entrance might be on the opposite side of the stage to the dressing rooms and be a long walk under the stage or through the offices – which are locked in the evenings! How easy is it for actors to enter from the auditorium? Is your set actually cutting off exits, or making entrances extremely long and within sight of the audience? If you leave a gap between the theatre wall and the back of your set can you avoid the trek through the offices? Where will there need to be quick-change areas if actors cannot get to the dressing rooms during the show?

How flexible is the whole space? Even small theatres such as the Bush and the Gate can be completely unrecognisable from production to production because the seating configuration is part of the design.

What, if any, are the sightline limitations? From a small flexible space to the largest pros-arch theatre most stage spaces have some areas which can only be seen by some of the audience. Many theatre plans have dotted sightline markers on them, but not all do, and many elevations do not show that people in the highest seats at the back can see behind the set into the quick-change area.

Does the stage have flying? Flying scenery can obviously give the design much more flexibility, speed, scale and ambition, but there are two distinct types of flying and one is much more flexible than the other. Older theatres have 'hemp' rope flying, by which a piece of scenery is usually pulled up and down by three ropes, but whoever is doing the pulling has to take the full weight of the piece, so unless there are several fly-people there is a limit to the size and weight of what can be flown, particularly during the action. Counterweight flying is what it suggests: there are a number of weights offstage attached by ropes or lines to a piece of scenery, so that its weight is counterbalanced and even a heavy piece of scenery can be flown in and out by one person.

Are there any trapdoors? Again, traps offer more flexibility and possibilities for entrances and exits, either in full view or hidden, but some traps are just a cut hole in the stage and do not have any inbuilt mechanism for quick, easy or elegant entrances.

Is there any wing space? If there are a number of sets in the design is there enough offstage storage space for the sets which aren't being used? How easy and how long will it take to get the stored sets on to the stage, and how many people will it require?

Meeting and selecting designers

How do you contact and meet designers with a view to working with them? If you have been to the exhibitions of designers graduating from design schools you will probably have picked up a brochure which will have the biographical and contact details of the designers. If not, most of the schools have brief biographies of current and recent designers and will put you in contact with them if you say that you are a theatre director and would like to meet the designer to know more about their work. They will usually pass on an email from you rather than giving you their direct contact details.

The Society of British Stage Designers also has the professional details of many designers. Some will have photos of productions, professional credits and contact details; at the very least the site allows you to send an email to a designer to contact them. The site also has an agents' directory which lists the main agents who represent stage designers. Both the site's own list of designers and the sites of the agents can be used to browse the work of designers whose work is unfamiliar to you, and to contact those whose work you have seen and you would like to meet.

As with actors and other creative artists, there are different ways of contacting designers (including lighting and other designers) at different stages in their careers, and it is advisable to consider seriously if a well-known designer, who is much in demand, will be willing to meet you to discuss an unfunded project with a tiny budget. Recently graduated designers may be willing to meet to discuss their work with you with a view to the future without there being a specific project to discuss, but in general it is better to meet a small number of designers, preferably whose work you have either seen in production or in an exhibition, and ask them to bring a portfolio of work to a meeting. Nearly all designers without a large body of high-profile work will have a ready portfolio of production photos, and possibly DVDs, of previous productions to show.

However, although it might be the prerogative of the director to choose, or not to choose, to invite a designer to a meeting and to work on a project, a truly collaborative working relationship will begin with an exchange of information, ideas and tastes at this meeting, which might be viewed as a way of getting to know each other rather than an 'audition' for the designer. If there is a specific project in mind, email the script or project outline in good time for the designer to absorb it, without placing any expectation on the designer to come to the meeting with specific ideas, but rather a sense of whether the project is something they connect with.

It is also important, either at the meeting or preferably in advance, to give the designer as much information about the dates, type of company, scale of the project, finances, budget and making resources, confirmed or possible collaborators, and your CV. The director and designer can then begin the meeting being clear about the parameters of the meeting and possible future work together, and you can both concentrate on making a connection with each other, for which the designer's portfolio is a starting point of collaboration rather than a calling card. As with auditioning actors, it is then professionally courteous to indicate what the next step will be and how long it might be before you contact the designer again – and do contact them again, even if this particular designer is not, in your opinion, the right one for this project.

Which is the right designer for the right project? Perhaps if you are directing a play with ten different locations that requires fluid changes between them, you don't work with someone who has only designed single sets. Perhaps you admire a designer's minimalist style, and how they suggest periods and locations with very few objects or scenery; or their painstaking attention to naturalistic detail; or their choice of colour and textures in bold and unexpected ways. There might be two decisions to be made in choosing a designer: the one with whom you have a natural connection, share artistic tastes and whose overall body of work you admire; and the one who has particular experience of or an aptitude for the demands of the particular production. Ideally, they will be one and the same person, but sometimes you have to make a choice.

The design meetings

At the end of the last chapter, on 'The Director and the Author', the suggested exercise was to take a historic play and research it, conceive a production and prepare for the first day of rehearsals, as if the director had fully realised the design for the production. This was an exercise in taking initial responses to a play and following them through to their practical application in the rehearsal and making stages.

In reality, most directors reach the stage of an overall response to a play, and possibly an overall conception, but would welcome the first conversations with the designer(s) as soon as possible in the process of conceiving a production. However, often the project is a scheduled reality by the time the designer comes on board, which may mean that the venue or company, the stage shape and audience configuration, the budget and making resources and production dates are already fixed. In an ideal world, in order to have a completely unfettered relationship with a designer, the director and designer would conceive the production before the director has to 'pitch' the production to a company, venue or producer, so that the venue and resources fit the production rather than the production having to fit the resources. If it is possible to work with a designer, or designers, who at this stage are presumably working for no money but a belief in the project, before the director and/or producer have to develop the project to the point where there is enough detail to secure the dates and resources for the project, the design conversations will obviously have much more scope and freedom, even if practical considerations have to impact on the design at a later stage. Many companies of affiliated but unpaid artists work in this way and then seek funding to suit the project.

For the purposes of discussing a generic design process let us at first assume that 'designer' means the set and costume designer (not the lighting, sound or digital designer) and that there is a scheduled production and a venue or company, but no fixed staging configuration. In this chapter the designer Vicki Mortimer outlines the pattern of discussions that she usually has during a design process, inevitably with a number of caveats and exceptions, as each relationship with a director will be different, and even with the same director each production will require a particular process depending on its challenges and needs.

It is worth discussing some principles that underlie this pattern of discussions.

The first meeting

From the designer's point of view it is easier to feel engaged with the director and the production if the director can articulate their motivations for wanting to create this production, at this theatre, for this audience, at this moment in time, and the key ideas and themes that inspire the director to want to direct this piece.

Sometimes, particularly with plays with complex or difficult staging problems, it is tempting to 'end-game' the design process: to want to solve the problem and so lock down the design before you and the designer have fully considered the visual language of the play. It is possible to have quite a narrow view of design, but, as George Bernard Shaw pointed out, design is not decoration, and nor is it just problem-solving. A much broader and dynamic conception of design might be to see it as a dramaturgical tool which expresses and releases the world and themes of a play and gives a three-dimensional, stylistic, poetic and metaphorical expression to the inner life of the play, and which also has a dynamic throughout the play which is given life by the way in which the actors, the lighting, the sound and other production elements interact with it.

Perhaps what follows is a heavy-handed example, but it illustrates that through the actor's connection with one object the meaning and significance of that object can change through the course of the play and visually express the changing dynamics underlying the action.

In *Macbeth*, when Ross brings the news to Macbeth that he is now Thane of Cawdor, there are references to 'borrowed robes' and 'strange garments': Macbeth may be given a distinctive coat by Ross which obviously belonged to the Thane of Cawdor. Macbeth is initially hesitant about wearing it because of the witches' prophecies. But he arrives at Dunsinane to meet Lady Macbeth wearing the coat and looking far grander than the muddied soldier we first saw, and her delight in the coat as an expression of Macbeth's new status is evident in the way they react to his new appearance. Banquo may refer to it in their discussions about the future and the witches. Later, after the murder of Duncan, in moments of despair, Macbeth may discard it as an unwelcome reminder of the duality of the honours and curses brought upon him by the witches. Lady Macbeth may wear it in the sleepwalking scene, telling us that the coat has become a substitute for a husband who never sleeps with her and barely talks to her, although she may talk to it during that scene. So, one item of costume comes to symbolise the changing relationship of Macbeth to the honour he is given, to the witches, to his wife, and the couple's pursuit of happiness by the pursuit of power.

When working with a new designer it might be worthwhile to clarify some of the vocabulary and terms you use. For example, many directors use the word 'aesthetics' about a design without really defining what is meant by it. 'Aesthetics' can be taken to mean an artistic style or genre, such as expressionism or naturalism, but very often it means the design itself, which can lead to vagueness between designer and director. Most designers will be comfortable with the use of the following terms and distinctions, but you will have to agree that you both mean the same thing when using them, as they mean different things to different people.

Any play will have a set of visual references, whether that be to places and items in the stage directions, or to locations, colours and objects referred to by the characters: I take that to be the visual language of the play. The play may also be written in a particular genre or style: Strindberg's *Miss Julie* seems to require a 'naturalistic' kitchen, but the scenes and stage directions for the midsummer revels may be perceived as more 'expressionistic': I take those to be the styles, or aesthetics, of the play. So the play has a visual language and one or more aesthetics.

During the design process the director and designer try to formulate a coherent design for the production, which I take to comprise two elements. First, an overall visual language for the design, rather than the play, which may contain one or more 'aesthetics': one overall design which encompasses the naturalistic and the expressionistic elements in *Miss Julie*, but does not make the production appear to have two competing or contradictory aesthetics. Second, there is the physical language, by which I mean the choice and number of elements and objects used to denote or create different locations and scenes.

For example, a Victorian production of *Macbeth* might have had huge gothic windows and arches to create Lady Macbeth's chamber; and a production in the round might have a furry rug and a distinctive lighting state and ambient sound. It would follow that the other scenes in the Victorian production have sets which have similarly realised level of flats, furniture and other objects to create a consistent physical language for the whole play, and that the theatre-in-the-round version has the same level of a few carefully chosen objects which suggest the scene. So the design has a visual language and a physical language, which, taken together, can simply be called the design, or the design aesthetic. Whatever terminology you use, it is worth agreeing with your designer that you are talking the same language.

It may not be necessary to bring a bank of images or all your research thus far to the meeting, but most designers respond to images that express a connection that you have with the piece and illustrate how the play resonates with you. These are not images of how you see act two, scene three, but images that strengthen the shared understanding of the play and inspire the designer to further research. You are not trying to design the play but to share your view of the world of the play with the designer.

If you have done some of the research and dissecting of the play you may wish to share your notes on the given circumstances, and your plot of who is in which scene, of entrances and exits, notes on the length and location of each scene etc.; or you may decide to divide this analysis between you for the next meeting. You, collectively, may also wish to reread the play for references to its physical world in the stage directions and within the text – noting, for example, the different references to water in

Lorca's *Yerma* and the colour palette in his stage directions and the characters' observations. In another play there might be a surprising number of references to the sky, or to food, which are not obvious from a first reading. This visual detective work may lead to a richer understanding of the world of the play and be the beginning of a design.

Some designers like actually to read through the play with the director out loud, perhaps discussing each scene and noting its practical requirements as you go. Sometimes it might be worthwhile incorporating a field trip, meeting at a place which has some connection with the play, or even going to see a production together and discussing it afterwards to get to know each other's tastes better. If possible, you might be able to visit the space where the production will take place. And of course, you might find time actually to get to know more about each other, your work, and any preferred ways of working on a project.

As Vicki Mortimer points out, there are no set number of meetings a designer and director should have before the white-card meeting and there are no hard and fast rules for how long to leave it between meetings, but, as she also says, you will want to keep the momentum going and not leave it too long before the second meeting, otherwise a lot of ground will have to be retrodden.

Ideally, the first meeting and shared responses to the play will lead to further thinking, reading of the play, and perhaps visual and contextual research, including research into other work by the playwright, the playwright's life and contemporary world, including the visual arts. It may seem a little formal, but for clarity it is probably worthwhile deciding and noting who will do what before the next meeting and outlining what you expect to discuss at the second meeting. As Vicki Mortimer also says, she prefers to think about all elements of the design at the same time, and at this stage it is useful to continue the more general and responsive work on the play in parallel with considering the practical demands of each scene, without yet trying to solve one with the other.

The second and subsequent meetings

Depending on the parameters of the first meeting and the agreed tasks for the second, that second meeting could cover a number of areas, but it is probably desirable that by the end of it the designer has enough shared and agreed information about the world of the play and the context of the production to go away and begin to do some detailed design work.

If you have not decided on a stage and audience configuration it is worth discussing this and at least coming to a provisional decision or agreed options for the designer to experiment with. You may both have decided to come to this meeting with responsive images for each scene, or major themes of the play, and hopefully through sharing these images, together with your visual detective work, you will begin to articulate an overall visual language for the design, which may then lead to decisions about what each scene practically requires within a design language which is sustained for the whole of the play. You may choose to storyboard the play together: that is, to do a rough sketch for every scene, indicating what its overall visual and stylistic feel is and what it practically requires, or you may leave that to the designer to do after the meeting, or do it at the third meeting. There may still be unresolved problems, and competing visual styles, but perhaps you acknowledge this rather than trying to solve everything, and leave the designer to develop the design ideas through a series of sketches or a white-card model which can be used at a third meeting to talk through what is unresolved.

The development of a visual language for the design can be particularly difficult for plays which themselves contain several different worlds or styles or for plays such as Shakespeare's, which invite a range of possible worlds, periods and styles. There is no reason why there has to be only one stylistic language when it is clear that the play and the design world have deliberately moved, but how often have critics and audiences complained that the last act of *A Winter's Tale*, set some sixteen years after act four, has no visual or stylistic connection with the rest of the play and that the designer and director have designed the first four acts and not addressed the fifth? There may be different worlds and styles within the play, but also overall design language that encompasses and links these worlds.

The other problem with designing classic plays is that choosing one specific period in which to locate the play, say the First World War for *Much Ado About Nothing*, can be liberating or reductive, and as discussed in the previous chapter, neither reflect either the internal architecture of the play, nor highlight its most resonant themes. On the other hand, multi-historicism can lead to eclecticism – a world in which all directorial and design bets have been hedged and the signposts given to the audience about the world conflict and cancel each other out (which relates to Alison Chitty's comment about the power and meaning of the object on stage). Another temptation is to stick with a brilliant idea which works wonderfully for one or two scenes, but not really for the rest of the play. And finally, in this list of pitfalls is what can be called 'the desire of the interpreter'. Often in the design process, because there has been so much background research and discussion, you may think that an object or scene carries a meaning which the audience will not get because you have imbued the object with that meaning but there is nothing to support it. It is often helpful, at a later stage in the design, to ask other collaborators what they see when they see a particular object or scene with fresh eyes.

Hopefully, by the third or fourth meeting, you have a working visual language which is working for the whole play, is rooted in its agreed world and ideas and has a physical vocabulary that relates to what is required for each scene.

The white-card meeting and final design meeting

There is no limit to the number of design meetings you may have before you have the white-card meeting, but, if you are being employed by a theatre and you live in Leeds and the designer lives in Birmingham, the theatre may only be willing to pay for three or four meetings before the white-card meeting and one or two meetings between the white-card and final design meeting. If you are both working in the same building then it is much easier to have short meetings as and when you need them, but having a notional number of meetings, say five or six, gives a structure and impetus to the design process. If you are contracted to a theatre it is likely that the production manager will send you the white-card and final design dates near the beginning of your contract. Time scales vary from theatre to theatre, but for a regional repertory theatre the white-card meeting is likely to be two or three months in advance of rehearsals beginning and possibly the final design meeting about a month before.

The production manager and other key members of the production staff will be at the white-card meeting. Depending on the theatre and the availability of people, those at the white-card meeting will include the head of the design department, the resident carpenter or head of workshop (if there is an in-house carpentry and making workshop), the stage manager, the deputy stage manager who will be in rehearsals with you, the lighting, sound and video designers, staff from the costumes and wig departments, and possibly the artistic director and chief executive of the theatre.

As well as having the white-card model, the designer might be expected to have a rough idea of how the set is going to be made, what materials will be needed and the finishes of the set and floor. The main purpose of the meeting is for the theatre to check that the design is viable given the space and the resources, and the most important thing to emerge from this meeting will be whether the design is achievable within, or close to, the budget allocated for it. Because this is quite a formal meeting with a number of people present, if you or the designer have had concerns about the feasibility or cost of the design, it is advisable to have earlier, less formal meetings with the production manager. Ideally there will only be one or two meetings between you and the designer after the white-card meeting, so if the design has to be completely rethought after this point it may cause delays and some consternation to the theatre.

The production manager will be aware of the competing demands on the theatre, its staff and the design. These include: the human and infra-structural resources of the theatre – how many making staff there are, how much freelance staff will cost, what resources, such as steel deck and flats, are in stock and can be adapted or used at no cost; the size of the produc-tions before and after yours and the demands they place on the theatre and the staff; any health and safety implications of the design; how long it might take to order things and get things made; and the budget.

Although the main artistic relationship in a design is seen as being bet-ween the director and the designer, the production manager has a pivotal role in realising the final design, and often a production manager will be able to ask why, for example, a wooden beam is eight metres long, and point out that if it could be two four-metre beams joined together the costs would be one-third and a lot easier to construct. At which point, you and the designer have to consider the implications of an upright support halfway along the eight-metre open space below the beam. It is important for you and the designer to go into this meeting with a strong sense of what is fundamentally important to the design and what might be altered to make the overall design achievable: if you and your designer have a strong relationship you should have the ability to respond flexibly to changes in the design to make it more affordable or practical, but also to know what is the essence of your design and how that can be enhanced and delivered, not compromised, by these changes. At its best, the white-card meeting, and prior meetings with the production manager, will help distil and refine the essential design ideas.

After the white-card meeting there may be the need for further alter-ations to the design and some checking back with the production manager. If, during your design process, the play has not been story-boarded in detail, identifying every prop, piece of furniture, piece of set and costume that will be needed, it is advisable to do it now – first, to check that you and the designer have thought of everything, and second, because at the final design meeting every element of the production will be accurately noted and costed.

At this point it is also useful for the director to consider the traffic of the stage. As Vicki Mortimer mentions, it might be possible to defer some decisions about the design until the director and the actors have had a chance to work with the mark-out of the set, and it really depends on the cycle of the making period in relation to the rehearsal period as to what can be deliberately left open: it is obviously easier to be flexible about the number of chairs needed than to leave a decision about the set for a whole scene. More fundamentally, as was mentioned earlier, the design should have the ability to interact with the actors, and vice versa. Because no one would want to 'block' scenes for actors before they have even begun rehearsing, you may want to reassure yourself, for example, that the number and position of entrances and exits and the amount of stage space in a particular scene give you and the actors enough options to explore the scene physically in the rehearsal process. As the director, make sure you have enough options within the design to allow a relatively free exploration of the play and the design, as the set may well have been built by the time you begin rehearsals.

Lighting design

In the interview with lighting designer Tony Simpson later in this chapter, he outlines patterns of discussions with the lighting designer and suggests a toolkit for effective communication with lighting designers for directors who may not have a profound knowledge of lighting. One issue he raises is the point at which the lighting designer becomes involved in the design process, and this can be a serious issue for lighting designers, whose first contact with the design might be the white-card meeting, by which time many decisions have been made. Of course, earlier involvement by the lighting designer, and other designers, is desirable, but because of the number of jobs a lighting, sound or digital designer has to take on to make a living (because they are paid relatively less than the set designer and director), it is often logistically difficult to involve them until late in the design process. But they would appreciate being informed of any design ideas that might either affect their lighting design, such as a ceiling that blocks out much of the lighting rig, or particular or large expectations of the lighting design which become integral to the set design. As both Vicki Mortimer and Tony Simpson point out, lighting designers have the shortest and most pressurised working period, and the more that they can be kept in the loop by phone and email, if not by meetings, the happier will be the lighting designer and the better and more integrated the lighting design.

Sound design

The same issues of availability apply to sound designers, although if you are working in a producing theatre there is a far higher chance of the sound designer being resident than the set or lighting designer. Increasingly sound is being seen as a more important element of productions and there is a growing number of extremely good sound designers, or sound artists.

Sound designers will want to know the same information about the play and the production as the set and lighting designers, and a similar process of establishing a shared vocabulary and taste is just as important. As with sharing images with the set designer, if you have any sounds or music that are expressive of the type of ambience you are thinking of, it might be useful to share them with the sound designer, but even if you do it is still important to be as clear, detailed and precise about the sound qualities you have in mind. The next stage might be for the sound designer to come to the next meeting with rough samples and to discuss them. Unlike lighting and set design, stage time is of key importance to a sound designer, and to be able to give him or her rough ideas of the length of scenes, and scene changes, which can become more precise as you work through the play in rehearsals, will be important for the designer.

Inevitably, lengths of scenes, scene changes, entrances and exits will change during the technical rehearsal, and the sound designer might come with one sound effect of, say, ten, fifteen and twenty seconds ready, or will be able to alter the length of the effect during the tech, but adequate time will then be needed before the first dress rehearsal to re-edit the single effect and to put the effect in the master edit of all the effects and possibly to reset the sound levels.

In considering the sound design it is useful to think of the sound design as having three elements: the technical equipment necessary to create the design and then to deliver or generate it during the performance; the stage and auditorium space, and where the sound is coming from and what speakers are necessary to deliver it; and the audio content itself – the live or recorded material.

Sound designers/artists have varying supplies of their own equipment to create the recorded sounds, and it is worth checking at a first meeting with a freelance sound designer how much of the design they will be able to create themselves and whether they will need to hire equipment or space to create and deliver the design you both want. They will also have different levels of technical skill and knowledge, and, particularly if you are working in a theatre with a permanent sound rig, the sound designer might need to have meetings with the sound engineer or technician with knowledge of the equipment in the theatre early in the design process.

For a production with only pre-recorded sounds, it is often possible for all the effects and cues to be reduced to one track and for all the effects to be operated by one person (who may also be operating the lights). Productions with live, or live and recorded sound will need a mixing desk and a technician to mix the sound live. Preferably this person will be in the auditorium and not in a separate or soundproofed tech box, and this may have implications for a flexible stage and seating space, or on the number of seats that need to be taken off sale so that the operator is in the best place to assess the sound for the whole auditorium.

The more complex the auditorium or playing area, the more complex will be the system of speakers to deliver the same sound to different parts of the auditorium. In a theatre in the round, for example, because there is a need for several speakers, each of which is a different distance from a given point of the audience, there will be time delays between the sound from each speaker reaching that point in the audience, and so time equipment to equalise the arrival times of the sounds has to be installed. In site-specific work it might be necessary to use a series of independent minidisc players and speakers to avoid lengthy cables going back to one desk.

It might be necessary to instal speakers in the set itself. If there is the effect of a window breaking, it really needs to come from the direction of the window, not from the overhead speakers in the auditorium. Small speakers often have to be hidden under chairs or behind pieces of scenery to ensure that the sound is convincing in its direction and volume. A musical requires much earlier collaboration between the director, set designer and sound designer and musical director, particularly if the musicians are on the set. If the 'band' are going to be in full view there are a number of stylistic decisions to be made about the necessary presence of speakers visible on stage, the number of instruments and how, physically and visually, they fit in with and are a part of the design language of the production. Even if the band are hidden, there are similar decisions to be made about the stylistic implications of hand-held mikes, radio mikes on actors' costumes – or hair, or faces, and mike stands. Without taking these factors into consideration, it is possible to come up with a superb set design in the model box which is then completely changed by instruments and sound equipment that are not represented in the model. Conversely, the director and designer might decide the best place for the musicians in terms of their visual impact, only for the musical director to say that the singers cannot hear or see the band, or that the drummer can't communicate with the bass player, and they will have to move.

Projection, video and digital design

Many of the observations about the process with designers apply equally to a collaboration with a video or digital designer, as do many of the observations about the need for stylistic and physical integration of all the design elements. In addition, it is worth considering the size, colour and surface material of the objects on to which images are being projected, whether the objects are integrated into the design of the whole set when they are not being used as projection surfaces, and whether those surfaces will allow the images to be of the right size for the set, the action, and the audience. There is also the issue of how the images are to be projected, where the equipment is – backstage, on the set, or in the auditorium – and if those positions will give a right-sized image of sufficient intensity, and if actors or audience are likely to cut across the projection beams. There will have to be close conversations between the digital designer and the lighting designer, since the lighting will have to accommodate and support the projected images for them to appear to be of sufficient intensity.

It is clear from the above that the more design elements there are, the greater the need to involve all designers in the design process as early and as frequently as is possible. In the chapter on 'The Director and the Production' there will be further discussion of relationships with your other collaborators, such as the choreographer and movement director – and indeed, the actors – and how those relationships need to be woven into the relationships with the designers in the making and rehearsal period.

As a director, one of the oddest things about the relationship with the designers, particularly the set designer, is that it is they with whom you first share your ideas about the whole project, and with whom you have one of the strongest creative relationships, but, by the time you are in the rehearsal room, surrounded by actors, stage managers and making staff, that first relationship can come to seem remote and a distant memory. So it is important to ensure that there is a fundamental understanding between you before the rehearsal period begins.

Interviews

Interview with Alison Chitty

Alison Chitty OBE is recognised as one of the world's leading theatre, film and opera designers: she was resident designer at the National Theatre for eight years; has designed a number of Mike Leigh's films; and has designed for the world's most prestigious opera houses, including La Scala Milan, Houston Opera House, Glyndebourne and the Royal Opera House, Covent Garden. She is an Olivier Award winner. She is also the inspirational director of the country's leading school for theatre designers: Motley Design School. Motley was founded by another leading designer, Margaret 'Percy' Harris, in 1966, and Alison took over as director in 1995. Graduates from Motley are now among some of the world's leading theatre designers.

Much of the following interview has been taken from a speech Alison Chitty made in accepting an award in memory of the designer Misha Black in 2007, which was then reproduced in a guide to the exhibition of her work at the National Theatre to celebrate her design work from 1970 to 2010.

I have two major passions in my life – the theatre and teaching. I love the theatre. I love how the theatre helps us to understand and interpret our lives. The best theatre helps us make sense of the world we live in. As theatre designers we are in the business of telling stories, helping performers to tell stories – live – in the best possible way. We make spaces to hold the performers, we clothe them and we create a complete world that they inhabit. As we design we make order out of an endless, random, succession of variables. We sort it all out, we try to make sense of it and give it some form. We sort out the text – if there is one – we sort out the performance spaces, their potential and their limitations. We start with the text; my way to start is to draw. I couldn't work without drawing. It is essential to the way I clarify what I know, and investigate what I don't – I design from the inside out. The nature of the world is dictated by what happens in the play. I am a designer, not a decorator.

In 1969 I won a nine-month Arts Council bursary to the Victoria Theatre, Stoke-on-Trent, a theatre in the round run by Peter Cheeseman. I stayed for eight years. In retrospect I can see how my work in Stoke was the foundation of my design and teaching philosophy. Working in the round, I began to understand the power of the performer in the space, the power of the object and also the effect of one on the other.

Here is an exercise to illustrate this. Imagine an empty stage. Imagine an eighteenth-century cup and saucer. What do we know? We are probably in the eighteenth century – in any case, at some time since the cup and saucer were made. Add an eighteenth-century chair. What has happened? In many ways – nothing. But, in fact, we are what I call 'more so'. We are more definitely in the eighteenth century, or, of course, another possibility, in an antique shop. How do we know which? Answer – the condition of the cup and the saucer.

Take away the cup and saucer and replace it with a Campari and soda. We now have an eighteenth-century chair and a Campari and soda. What has happened? The chair has become an antique. We are now in any time since Campari was invented and the glass was made, or any time in the future.

Now, take away the chair and replace it with a yellow towel. What has happened? We are suddenly in a more contemporary world, the temperature has changed, and we are possibly even outside. Or we could, of course, be in the sort of bathroom where people drink Campari and throw their towels on the floor. But the nature of these objects in combination does seem to take us outside. I made the towel yellow. It may make us think of sand. The period is dictated by the date when the glass and the towel were made, or any time since, or in the future.

You can see how, with only four objects, we've leapt across a couple of centuries, gone from inside to outside and the temperature has changed. Every decision has enormous repercussions. Every decision must be fine-tuned.

It is easy to see how often in the theatre much of what is on the stage, most of the scenery (and I hate that word) and most of the props, are saying exactly the same thing. Everything is saying 'this is an eighteenth-century drawing room', or whatever it is. Everything is making it 'more so'.

I am fascinated by exactly how much or little I need to evoke a world precisely. In Stoke-on-Trent I began to see how a little goes a very long way. I began to develop some restraint. I worked to select the essential elements that were needed, and at the same time I came to realise that a distilled version of the world of the play was leaving space for the audience to take part – space for them to use their imaginations and contribute. I believe it heightened their experience, and they had a better time.

The important thing is that it's not just one set of responses; there are as many responses as the number of people in the audience, and that can be one of the problems. So one of the challenges is to fine-tune the selection of objects, not only in terms of what they are, but also how you put them in the space and how you relate them to one another. In that fine-tuning, one steers the imaginations of the many people who come to see the production.

For example, the colour 'golden yellow' has different associations for an American from the cornfields of the Mid West and for a Moroccan working in the dye-vats of Marrakesh. So, 'golden yellow' has subtle nuances of meaning for different people. One should never worry about what that is; all you can do is follow your own instincts; try to hone, distil, and refine things to the purest form of what feels right.

Then we need to pass on our ideas; we use drawings, models, storyboards and lots of other ways of communicating what we intend. As theatre designers we need to say clearly, 'This is what I mean.' We work with many people: all the way from directors via production managers to accountants. A drawing can be a simple way of assessing scale and therefore budget. Money is always an issue in the theatre.

Sometimes, and this might sound crazy, a budget can be your best friend, especially if you have a tendency to over-design. It makes you distil your ideas and can take you back to the immediacy of your first thoughts, the work in the sketchbook, or an approach that you might have developed in a workshop.

I remember working with the director Martin Duncan on a production of *Forza del Destino* for Holland Park Opera, where the budget was limited, despite the production being traditionally regarded as expensive, because there is a large cast, and many locations. We did it austerely and economically, and this approach gave the production great strength.

In Stoke, many of our simple visual statements were born out of limited budgets, and, of course, the very nature of theatre in the round. The focus of the space was the floor and we were working sculpturally. I was learning that with distillation, restraint and often a little bit of wit, I could powerfully express any place in any time. I was becoming what I am now – a designer, not a decorator.

After eight years I returned to London and worked with Peter Gill. He comes from the Royal Court tradition. George Devine and the designer Jocelyn Herbert established a simple and elegant style of production there in the 1960s and 1970s. Peter Gill had been working there for many years and had developed his own way, his own aesthetic – again distilled and restrained, but also refined, exquisite and expressive. He has a way of looking at everyday life, and somehow making the simplest things poetic – a woman brushing her hair, or washing her husband's back when he comes home from the mine.

I then worked with Peter Hall at the National Theatre. Peter had been working with the great designer John Bury for years at the RSC and their productions were always extremely exciting and visually very strong. I could see in their work at the National how they loved the bold statement. Great sculptural shapes took control of the space. Their work was often in a very controlled palette, sometimes monochrome, punctuated with bold flashes of colour. They worked with broad brushstrokes.

Collaborating with Peter Hall taught me about working in large theatres. I loved to work at this scale but I wanted to find a way of protecting the performers, holding the actors, framing them, throwing them into focus, not losing them or drowning them in scenery. We worked on many productions, in particular lots of Shakespeare, in the Olivier. Peter's passion for how Shakespeare is to be spoken and played meant that each scene should follow fast on the heels of another with no breaks in between. As in *Antony and Cleopatra*, the plays were often at one moment intimate, the next epic. Our open stage had to be flexible and change quickly in front of an audience.

I realised simple statements work well.

Interview with Vicki Mortimer

Vicki Mortimer studied at the Slade School of Art. She has worked extensively with the RSC and the National Theatre, and has also designed for Random Dance Company; the Royal Ballet; NDT; the Almeida Theatre; Donmar Warehouse; Crucible Theatre, Sheffield; Gate Theatre; Shochiku Theatre, Japan; and the National Theatre, Ireland. Her opera designs include Così fan tutte, St Matthew Passion, The Miserly Knight, Gianni Schicchi *and* Die Meistersinger von Nürnberg *for Glyndebourne Festival Opera;* Jephtha, Jenrefa *and* Kát'a Kabanová *for Welsh National Opera;* The Turn of the Screw *for Scottish Opera;* Salome *for English National Opera. Recent work includes* Beauty and the Beast, Waves, The Seagull, Attempts on Her Life, The Man of Mode, A Matter of Life and Death, The Cat in the Hat, Burnt by the Sun, *and* Hamlet, *all for the National Theatre;* The Wild Duck *for the Donmar Warehouse; costumes for* Fiddler on the Roof *and* Nine *on Broadway;* Jumpers *at the National Theatre, Piccadilly Theatre and on Broadway;* Easter *and* Natt och Drommar *for the Royal Dramatic Theatre Stockholm;* Boy Gets Girl, Mountain Language/Ashes to Ashes, My Zinc Bed, *and* The Country *for the Royal Court;* The Seagull *for the RSC and on tour;* The Real Thing *at the Donmar Warehouse, West End, and on Broadway; and* The Master Builder *at the Almeida.*

How do you like to begin your relationship with a director on a new project?

It's very variable, depending on who the director is and what the project is – but if I were to suggest a state in which I like to be when I first have a conversation, then I suppose I feel pretty uncomfortable if I'm not well acquainted with the text or the music or the libretto that we're about to start working on. So I feel that my preferred state is to know the raw material well but to have no opinions consciously about what might be done with it. Then, in that first conversation with a director, I think my job is to listen to what the director has to say about their views on the piece and only then start to apply it to what I might have received myself, or picked up from a reading. By the end of that first meeting what I hope to have listened to are enough clues for me to start to work out what the kind of visual vocabulary might be – even if it's very vague and associative at that point – so that between the first and second meetings probably what I'd want to do is to source images, as well as to start to think about the geometry of the space and the audience relationship to the space in the theatre, or theatres, in which we're working.

So you start thinking about the relationship with the audience straight away?

It's a key decision, really, how you place an audience in relation to the space – if you've got a choice. Obviously, if you're going into a proscenium theatre, you haven't really got a choice about how to do that, but even if you're working in a pros you can start to make decisions about how intimate or distant, or objective or subjective, you want the audience to feel about how you place things in the space. That relationship is very much a kind of locating decision for me.

Is there anything you particularly find useful for a director to bring to that meeting? Do you like it if the director brings images or things that have inspired her or his response to the play?

I think that can be useful, particularly with a director that I haven't worked with before. If it's a completely new working relationship, those sorts of visual libraries are very useful, but they don't necessarily have to be images that are actually brought to the meeting. It can involve talking about films or paintings and sculptures that you are reminded of, or other theatre productions that you might have seen, so it's about building up a general shared reference rather than necessarily specific images – although I love it if directors have images that have given them something to think about. Without those shared references, the designer has to take the leap very much more boldly, proposing a whole visual language for the piece. It's the only way you're ever going to understand what the other is talking about, because the conversations between designers and directors can be as productive and enjoyable as you like, but you can still end up with completely different understandings of what you've said until you see a picture or a model, or until you have a shared experience.

You think you're talking about the same thing but you're not.

Yes, and that's as true for me with working with Katie [Mitchell], who I've worked with for twenty-something years now, as it is working with a new director. With Katie, I can still turn up with something onstage and she'll say, 'Oh, I didn't think it was going to look like that.' There's just been a part of the communication that we've taken for granted, whereas actually we needed to say, 'Yes, we really do mean it's exactly that geranium' or whatever it is. I think the director–designer responsibility towards each other is to make sure that both we and the people we're working with absolutely understand what we mean, and however you communicate that has to be arrived at between you.

So at the end of that first meeting you like to have a strong sense of a shared visual language, even if you or the director has brought nothing to that meeting. And hopefully, at the same time, you've also both got a strong idea about a configuration or relationship with the audience?

That's right, so when you meet for the second time the opening statements are like a confirmation of what you thought was said at that first meeting: you're reinforcing the shared reference. That's when I would always assume that there would be images and conversation pieces. It's a process of refinement then – about how you use that information in staging the piece. And that's, in a way, impossible to generalise about.

How long do you like between the first meeting and the second meeting, and the second and third meeting?

I wouldn't have a problem with that second meeting happening quite quickly. The immediacy of it helps, because for me first meetings are so improvisatory that you need to maintain the memory of that improvisation for not too long before you're having another conversation – so not much more than a week later. But after the second meeting is the time when I feel the responsibility to have an idea. That's the time when I always think, 'Well, I'm not a proper designer because a proper designer would have had an idea by now, and I'm never going to have an idea again, and what do I think I'm doing?' So that neurosis is the indication that this is the moment when I start to do my concrete work, and it's to do with declaring my hand: 'As the designer on the project this is what I'm proposing' – so it's nerve-wracking in that sense of approaching a public moment.

So although it is of course a dialogue, between the second and the third meeting there's a change in emphasis so that by the third meeting it's you making the proposal and the director is essentially responding to that?

I would say that that's a fair description. I'm sure there are some designers on some projects who turn up at the first meeting saying, 'I've got a great idea for how this might work' but it's not my way!

In your process are you thinking of every element of design – the architecture, the visual configuration, the visual language of it all – at the same time, or do you prefer to look at it from one angle to open it up?

I might expect a normal process to include all aspects simultaneously. There will be thoughts about light (although there is a lighting designer, obviously) or costume, because, in a way, as a designer you are responsible for every bit of visual information physically on the stage. For example, you may not be responsible for the lighting but you are designing the apertures that let light in, so you are effectively responsible for a part of structuring the light. With some shows, it is crucial those conversations happen earlier than with others: where the positions of lights, or the access to lights, or the narrative role of lights is much more important than in other shows, so I prefer, on the whole, to have at least an initial presence of a lighting designer quite early on in the process.

In this country at least, the design roles of set and costume designer are usually filled by the same person, and that enables a visual responsibility. This means that I don't think I could separate out the design processes for each aspect, because in the end we have got the opportunity to make visual choices which can have a conversation with each other. So, for example, you can use costume to highlight a bit of action so that you don't need to use a piece of scenery to do that – because you can pull focus with a person. With colour, scale, movement, reflection, or all of those elements potentially, there's a sort of bargain that you can strike between one visual aspect and another.

So I'm saying that normally I would expect all elements to run in the same track, but that there are shows where early on you think, 'Well, this is really a costume piece,' so then you might move sideways and seriously work through what the costume contribution to this show is and sideline the scenic elements until later. So it varies from project to project.

Whereas if you're only doing part of the process, it becomes a lot more complicated?

It becomes a bit more complicated because it's about negotiating your way through those narratives in a much more verbalised and, sometimes, time-consuming way, because you've got to have the meeting with the person who is responsible for that aspect where you exchange your ideas.

If there are problematic scenes, or there are staging challenges, do you try to crack those by working on them first, or do you leave some of those problems and try and crack them at a later stage?

There are plays that have a shopping list of things to be solved: notoriously, the play within a play in act one of *The Seagull* is one. And with the *Hamlet* [at the National Theatre in 2010, directed by Nicholas Hytner] that I'm working on at the moment, we were really preoccupied at the start of the design process by the ghost, and that felt like a primary problem that would affect the kind of aesthetic choices for the entire show, because it was about establishing a visual idiom, a physical context in which we would answer questions about what frightens us now. But what we are discovering is that, as we've been going through the process of designing the play, the ghost is solving himself: we are getting on and designing the play and the ghost is finding his place within it. Whereas if we'd gone obsessively into how on earth we were going to do the ghost in the Olivier Theatre, I think we would have become really locked down. I don't think that there is a kind of golden rule about not looking properly at a problem, but the shared job of a director and designer is to be aware of what is to be solved and then finding the right point to solve it. What you can't afford to do as director or designer is to leave the elephant in the room – you have to say, 'We know we've got this to sort out but we're not going to do it now.'

A lot of designers start with sketches and then only later go to a model but you prefer to work straight from a model?

My usual way of getting to that next stage is to start working directly in the model box with really rough versions of events. The speed of experimentation that I like to have available at that point is much better served by cutting up bits of cardboard and offering them up in the model box than through drawing, because it's often about proportion and relative spatial relationships, particularly if it's a theatre I haven't worked in before, and I'm trying to get my bearings in three dimensions about the scale of a figure and architecture in the space. Actually, if I were drawing it, I'd need to be in the theatre, which is often not a possibility.

So you actually construct a 1:25 model box of the space?

Yes, and I think what I'm realising in the course of our conversation is that I rarely have design ideas that are detached from the environment that they're in. So stand-alone ideas, if you like, aren't maybe where I start from by instinct – they are in relation to the containment of space that is the theatre, which is why sketching perhaps doesn't serve me as well as it does some other designers, who can come at it from a different direction.

How many design meetings would you normally have before you have a model that you wanted to show to a production manager?

With *Hamlet* we probably had three or four meetings before we got to an idea that I felt needed a production manager's eye on it, which was to do with the management and feasibility of pieces of moving scenery. So I asked him to come and look at it specifically with that in mind and to say, 'Is this affordable, practicable and desirable in terms of the theatre?' I would quite often do that – try and get a production manager involved quite early, so it's not a formal presentation as such.

In terms of formally presenting a 'white-card model', it's probably six or seven meetings. The white-card meeting is for the benefit of the theatre, so that they've got an opportunity to say what they want to about the idea you're proposing – in terms of how it works for the theatre, its affordability and so on. And then normally what happens (if the white-card model is passed) is that the theatre will do a rough costing. So it's not for the benefit of the director and the designer, except inasmuch as you often get very useful suggestions and feedback from the relevant departments. After that I wouldn't necessarily expect to work or meet with a director very frequently: it might just be two or three meetings before the final design is handed in, because my experience on the whole has been that by the time you've got to the white card you've sort of had the conversations. After that it's about the nitty-gritty of working through the events of the play, and just checking that everything's right.

So you might go through the play scene by scene with the director?

Yes, that can be a very useful thing to do immediately after the white-card has been passed by the theatre. With some productions what you're looking at is providing a containing space for the work that will then emerge from rehearsal, so you're not in a position where that scene-by-scene work is appropriate, because that's the work that's going to happen later: you've just got to make sure than that you've got a space with the right criteria for putting that sort of experimentation in.

And so you and the director would have a sense of what is more or less going to stay for the process and then what flexibility there is within the design – so you just identify what's up for grabs and what's fixed?

Exactly. But, as I say, the final model is a crucial tool. It has to be a stand-alone communicator – the model has to speak for itself when you're not in the room with it, which is why I believe it's the tool that you have to invest most in as a designer. The making of the final model is the most labour-intensive, the most costly and incredibly time-consuming part of the whole process. The better and more accurately communicative it is, the more dependable the result will be – the less potential there is for mis-understanding. If, for the model to succeed, you have to be standing next to it saying, 'Well, it's a bit like that, but not quite like that, because actually what I meant was this,' then the model isn't the tool that you need it to be. Therefore, rewinding from that, in the immediate aftermath to the white-card meeting it is crucial just to say, 'Are we both really sure that this is what we're doing? Right, off we go . . .'

Interview with Tony Simpson

Tony Simpson has been a freelance theatre lighting designer for twenty years, working in the UK and internationally alongside a broad spectrum of directors, designers and sound designers. Notably, his UK work has included productions from the National Theatre; the RSC; Royal Court; Welsh National Opera; West Yorkshire Playhouse; Old Vic; Watford Palace Theatre; Mercury Theatre, Colchester; Royal Theatre, Northampton; Rose Theatre, Kingston; Exeter Northcott; Plymouth Theatre Royal; Chichester Festival Theatre and numerous designs in the West End, on the London fringe and on tour. He has been associate lighting designer on Woman in Black *and* An Inspector Calls *for thirteen years in total for PW Productions, and took several designs into London prisons for Synergy Theatre Project. Tony served as chairman on the Equity Theatre Designers Committee for eight years. He is currently based at English National Opera.*

What do you like a director to say to you about a production and a lighting design at a first meeting?

To answer the question, I will take as an example a production in a regional producing theatre of a text-based play, with a three- or four-week rehearsal period, and a five-day production week. Assuming you have met the director before and you both know the circumstances and resources of the production, such as budget, cast size, other creative team members, you are then free to begin to talk about the work itself, which often begins with the story of the piece from the director's point of view. This is an umbrella conversation, loosely covering all aspects of the director's ideas for the play and it will generally involve the director explaining why he or she wants to take the story of the play in a particular direction. These preliminary discussions are vital to a lighting designer, as they ground you in the world the director is beginning to develop. Until this discussion happens, it is impossible to second-guess where a director might want to take a text, no matter how conventional that text might be. This applies even more so with devised work. You might imagine that directors show designers all types of visual stimuli, but in my experience we would initially meet for two or three hours to discuss all aspects of the play and the director's approaches. These early meetings can be the least pressured in terms of practical results, but they can yield much food for thought. If it is your first time working together there is also a need to understand each other's tastes. Ultimately, in tangible terms, what comes out of these first meetings are what I call hooks: these are the concrete, almost non-negotiable, ideas that the director has hooked the play on, and on which I will hook my lighting design. It is rare that these hooks change considerably, but, even if they do, what they provide is a solid foundation and boundaries within which I can work. If a director doesn't have any particularly strong ideas, or can't provide any hooks at all, a lighting designer can feel a little at sea and this may cause problems in a short rehearsal and technical period. Generalisation, in this case, really can be the death of art.

For a director it's very important to be able to find a lighting designer with whom you have a shared taste and language, and if you look at the current practice of theatre directors they often work with the same designer and lighting designer time and time again, because they have developed a shared language, a number of shortcuts in their way of working, and similar production values, despite the variables and uncertainties of each production. There are now many established trios of director–designer–lighting designer, or director–designer relationships that can accurately be described as a 'creative ensemble' – none more established than Katie Mitchell, Vicki Mortimer and Paule Constable, or Declan Donnellan and Nick Ormerod.

Is it not true that one of the reasons it is often difficult for the director and lighting designer to meet early in the process is that lighting designers have to take on far more projects than directors and designers?

Yes. We have to be very busy to make a living as freelance lighting designers, and frequently we have to work on several productions at any one time. The fact is that lighting designers are, relatively speaking, underpaid, and yet they are now being asked to contribute far more to a project than they were, say, twenty-five years ago – particularly on bigger productions, such as musicals in the West End. This is mainly due to advances in the available technology and the complexity of lighting systems which, in essence, means that there are far more possibilities in terms of what a single light can achieve. So yes, the involvement of the lighting designer might be governed by the balancing and crossover of projects.

Notwithstanding the availability problems, how often and at what stage do you like to come into rehearsals?

Time in rehearsals can be split into three different areas. Of course the first day of rehearsal is the most significant time spent early in the process. This is not only when you listen to the actors read through the play, but it is also probably the first time that the director, designer, sound designer and any other creatives involved in the production come together and you are first acknowledged as a creative team by all involved.

Throughout the following couple of weeks, lighting designers will often find the 'meat' of their design, and this comes from being present in the room, and engaging with the work as it develops. Quite often a director may not be able to articulate in a meeting exactly what she or he wants to achieve with a scene in terms of light, but as I watch the scene and hear how the director is working with the actors, I can often begin to visualise what the director needs the scene to feel like. Directors spend much of their time with the actors, and sometimes simply being an eavesdropper in a rehearsal session can feed much more into my lighting design than detailed conversations over several hours.

Lastly, I would want to see as many run-throughs, or partial run-throughs, as possible. The earlier the play is on its feet, the easier it is to tap into its physical shape and map out the peaks and troughs of its mood, stringing the pieces together into a coherent chronological order. The later you see run-throughs the more pressure there is on a lighting designer. For example, you might have a requirement in your contract to produce a lighting design for the in-house technical staff at a particular point – often, in a four-week rehearsal period, by the beginning of the fourth week – a week before the fit-up, because equipment may have to be hired and colour bought.

So it's useful for the director to be aware that a lighting designer has responsibilities to the production department as well as to the production.

Absolutely, particularly as the lighting has to be one of the first things that gets put up in the theatre, before anything else. Usually the lighting needs to be rigged before any scenery goes up, so the lighting designer can end up having a very narrow window between seeing a run-through and finalising the lighting plan.

Once the lighting design is there, if I'm a director with no great knowledge of lighting language and lighting technology, is there a useful language for talking to a lighting designer that will make practical sense?

Yes, and it splits very equally into four distinct expressions. These are the intensity of the light, the focus of the light, the colour of the light and the beam of the light. First, the intensity is the level: in simple terms, how bright is it? Second, the focus is where the light is coming from: is it from behind the actor (or set), above the actor, from the front or side, or is it from below? So the focus is the direction from which the light is hitting the actor and set on the stage. Third is the colour of the light: this speaks for itself, but when you're speaking about colour in lighting terms, the spectrum of possibilities is endless, especially with the arrival of colour mixing – the ability to create any desired colour within a single light. This means that the colour blue, for example, has many variations. And finally the beam: what is the quality of the light? Does it have a sharp edge or a soft edge? Is it very wide, or quite narrow? So intensity, focus, colour and beam are quite simple shortcuts for a director to be able to see the lighting design, analyse it and then discuss it with the lighting designer.

And those are all things that a lighting designer can do something about?

In a heartbeat. If you say to a lighting designer, 'That's very bright, is it possible to see this lighting state with a reduced intensity?' the lighting designer can take the level of the lighting state, which might be 20 lights at 100-per-cent intensity or brightness, down to 50 per cent. You could use exactly the same method in terms of colour: 'It feels too warm and sunny, perhaps too yellow: could the light onstage be cooler?' Or your cool moonlight and my cool moonlight are two different moonlights. The same applies with beam – are the edges of the lights onstage too sharp, are they making rings on the floor? 'Is there anything we can do about the edge of those beams; they look very sharp?' Similarly with focus – the direction of the light: a designer may have employed too much sidelighting rather than front lighting, or strong top lighting, which is casting excessive downward shadows. So immediately there's a method of dialogue, and it gives the director more confidence when referring to the lighting as a whole.

It is important to remember that most lighting designers have come from a technical background: they'll have rigged lights, they'll understand about how to focus a light, how to work with it. The lights are our paint brushes – the broad strokes, the narrow strokes, the blanket strokes. We have a family of three simple tools – basically three different types of light – even though there are many different manufacturers of the same light.

What are those three different types of lights?

We have fresnels, profiles and fixed beams. Firstly, floodlights, or fresnels as they're commonly known, are our broad strokes. They can light areas in a soft way, to create a wash. Commonly you may find a line of six or seven lights at a particular distance to each other to create a blanket of light that covers an area of the stage.

Secondly, we have profiles, which are our fine brushes and with which we can create shapes. For example, if you wanted somebody highlighted sitting on a chair during a speech, you may wish to reduce the general lighting state (the fresnels), over several minutes, and use a tightly focused profile to begin gently to highlight the actor. You can also put gobos – metal patterns – into profiles to create patterns or shapes onstage. For example, in a forest or woodland scene a lighting designer may use a break-up gobo to create the desired mood quickly and unambiguously.

Finally, we have fixed beams or our blanket strokes. Fixed beams are usually powerful lights, but there are no means of altering or controlling the light which it emits: their beams are fixed, like a car headlight. I would use fixed beams to light a cyclorama, for example.

So although we have many different types of lights it is useful to think of them as being in these three categories. Even moving lights, or moving heads as they are often called, which are the most sophisticated types of lights, are simply programmable to operate between the properties of these three categories: as well as being able to move and change colour remotely, they can go from being a fresnel to being a profile, for example.

A lighting designer does not expect a director to have a knowledge of different lights and how they work – that's our job. But thinking about lighting in those four terms – intensity, focus, colour and beam – may be a useful way of discussing how you see the lighting design, even at the first meeting, as well as when the lighting design is realised. Like the director, we are trying to tell a story clearly – we just need to understand the story we are all telling.

Practical exercises

Exercise one

Go to some art galleries. Search the web for free art and photographic images. Buy cheap art books. Many directors have an underdeveloped visual sense and knowledge, which means that they have to start from scratch when trying to think visually about a design aesthetic for the next production. Just as in Chapter One it was suggested that it is useful to have a sense of geography of the theatrical canon over the past two thousand years, it is worth finding 'art readers' that will give you an overview of the main artistic movements, periods and schools to help you develop a range of references to artists with which designers may be far more familiar than you, but might provide a useful common language. It will also help you to develop your own visual and artistic tastes besides having a knowledge of important historic artists – just by collecting individual images or cheap books with a range of modern images, say of architecture or 1970s clothes, you will begin to build up a bank of images with which you have an instinctual connection that may express your response to a scene or character in a play you are directing in five years' time. Create a long-term image bank as well as shelves of plays.

Exercise two

There are also simple exercises to develop your sense of spatial awareness and stage dynamics. You only need a large room and about twenty chairs, but it is possible with no more than this to set out the configurations of an end-on stage, a theatre-in-the-round, a long traverse stage, a short traverse stage and a thrust stage and to explore practically their different properties and qualities.

For example, if there are three or four of you, simply moving around these different spaces will reveal which are strong and weak positions. Which positions and spatial relationships between you add or subtract status from each person? How does the dynamic change when one person enters or exits the space? Does it feel instinctive for you all to want to rebalance the space once that person has come or gone? You might then take one scene which contains several exits and entrances and changing dynamics between the characters, and try the same scene in each of these configurations. Some might give the same scene a very domestic feel, or epic dimension; some might be better for scenes with many entrances and exits; some might be more limited in offering dynamic variations in an extended scene between two characters.

You may then wish to think about where you place entrances and exits within those shapes and to imagine an audience and what sightline problems those configurations might pose. You may then apply Alison Chitty's exercise of introducing one or two objects to convey a place or period and begin to evaluate the inherent design demands for each configuration – or more simply, how much 'stuff' does each configuration seem to need in order economically to create the world of the play? Although these exercises can be very easily achieved with no more than a room and some chairs, they might not only reveal the advantages and disadvantages of a configuration for a play or scene, they may also help you choose the one that best suits your budget and resources.

Exercise three
Going back to the exercise in Chapter Three, 'The Director and the Author', on gathering research material for a play by a classic or historic author, re-visit that material and imagine that you are meeting the set designer and, separately, the lighting designer, for your first design meetings. Bearing in mind the comments in this chapter on design meetings, which of those materials do you think would stimulate the designer and open up a creative and collaborative process? Which do you think might represent stages in your process of conceiving a whole production that would have gone beyond the point of beginning a collaborative process together? In other words, are there ideas and images which might feed into a design process, and are there ideas and images that *are* the design, and might leave less room for collaboration?

Weblist

Association of Courses in Theatre Design	actduk.wordpress.com
Association of Lighting Designers	www.ald.org.uk
Getty images	www.gettyimages.co.uk
The Linbury Prize	www.nationaltheatre.org.uk/linburyprize
Sceno:graphy	sceno.org
Society of British Theatre Designers	www.theatredesign.org.uk

5 The director and the industry

This chapter explores the financial and organisational contexts in which theatre is made in the UK today. As well as giving an overview of the national organisations and funding mechanisms it will also look at how individual theatres are organised and make planning and financial decisions. It will also explore the similarities and differences between the three main forms of theatre organisation and funding: the subsidised sector; the commercial sector; and the fringe, independent, or unfunded sector.

The second part of the chapter will focus on how, as an emerging theatre director, you might approach putting on an unfunded production, setting up a company and finding sources of funding. The interview with Annette Mees, a co-director of Coney, explores the genesis of one company from mounting individual projects to long-term sustainability and non-traditional ways of running a company; the interview with director Elly Green recounts her experiences of directing and producing her own productions at several fringe theatres in London with no funding; and the interview with director and producer Andrew McKinnon discusses the recent emergence of an important new collaborator for directors: the creative producer.

Since organisational and funding structures vary so widely from country to country, this chapter is the most UK-focused in this book. The interview with Walter Meierjohann in Chapter One offered some insight into the nature of subsidised theatre in Germany, and the interview with

Allison Troup-Jensen in Chapter Seven, gives a very different picture of how theatre is produced in the US.

The national picture

Government economic statistics estimate that the theatre industry contributes £4.6 billion to the economy annually. Although it is estimated that the commercial theatre sector contributed £2.5 billion to the UK economy in 2009, the most important single structure to consider is the structure of subsidised arts funding and organisations.

The Department of Culture, Media and Sport

The funding structure begins at Cabinet level. The Department for Culture, Media and Sport is headed by a Secretary of State who is responsible for the arts; broadcasting; the creative industries, including design, fashion, film and music; libraries; museums and galleries; gambling; the historic environment; tourism; sport; and the 2012 Olympics. With such a wide remit it is unsurprising that the Secretary of State is supported by three ministers who have responsibility for different areas within this remit. One of the three ministers is the Minister for Culture, Communications and Creative Industries, whose responsibilities include the arts and, within that area, theatre and performing arts.

The DCMS does not directly fund any arts organisations or individuals but the overall spending for the arts is decided at government level. In order to promote, develop and manage the arts, and to distribute government funding, the Arts Council was established in 1946. Today there are four arts councils: Arts Council England (ACE); Arts Council of Wales; Arts Council of Northern Ireland; and Creative Scotland. Inevitably, the largest of these organisations is ACE.

Arts Council England

ACE has a national head office in London but much of its work and funding is undertaken by nine regional arts councils: East, East Midlands, London, North East, North West, South East, South West, West Midlands and Yorkshire. ACE declares on its website that its objectives are 'to develop and improve the knowledge, understanding and practice of the arts, and to increase the accessibility of the arts to the public'. To this end, as well as distributing government funding, ACE develops strategies to promote and develop the arts in England. The latest such strategy is entitled 'Achieving Great Art for Everyone', and sets out ACE's plans and priorities for the next ten years from 2010. To quote again from its website, it 'is the biggest transformation of arts funding for a generation' and, 'argues for excellence, founded on diversity and innovation, and a new collaborative spirit to develop the arts over the long term, so they truly belong to everyone'. The strategy document can be downloaded from the ACE website.

In October 2010, Alan Davey, the chief executive of ACE, announced ACE's spending plans until 2014 following the government's Spending Review. These involved a cut in funding to ACE of 29.6 per cent over four years, reducing the grant from government from £450 million a year to £350 million in real terms in 2014.

In March 2011 ACE announced its plans for funding arts organisations from 2012 to 2015. In 2010 ACE had 880 'regularly funded organisations', over 200 of them being theatre companies. From April 2012 ACE will have National Portfolio Organisations, a new term for arts organisations who receive guaranteed funding for a fixed period: in this case three years. Of the 1,330 organisations that applied to become NPOs, 692 were successful. Over 200 previously funded organisations lost all their funding from 2012, including longstanding theatre companies such as Shared Experience, the Riverside Studios and the Northcott Theatre, Exeter. The Almeida Theatre saw a 39 per cent reduction in its grant, and the Institute of Contemporary Arts a 45 per cent reduction, in real terms. The RSC and the National Theatre suffered 15 per cent reductions, and many large regional producing theatres reductions of 11 per cent, in real terms. ACE also cut the audience development organisations it had previously funded.

The total reduction in regular funding was £118 million over four years, although this was mitigated by the addition of lottery funds of £85 million, which have been ring-fenced for supporting touring work and work with young people and children. Regular funding was announced for just over 100 companies who had not previously received it, including HighTide and Coney, and there were large grant increases for some theatres, including the Arcola, Punchdrunk and the Barbican. It was one of the largest shake-ups of regular funding in recent years and sets out a new landscape for producing theatres until 2015. You may view the details of the organisations that ACE funds on their website.

Apart from strategic funding for specific initiatives or areas of activity, for which you cannot apply, the other major source of funding from ACE is Grants for the Arts. Funded by the National Lottery, this is open to applications from individuals and companies to fund individual projects for a limited period. There are no deadlines, and applications can be made online at any time. The guidance notes for making an application are extremely detailed and helpful, but competition is fierce. In 2009–10, ACE made 2,795 awards totalling £64.9 million. Although all Grants for the Arts applications are assessed centrally in Manchester, you may contact a theatre officer in your regional ACE office for advice before making an application. You can find contact details for the theatre officers in your regional ACE office on their website.

The ACE website also contains news of recent events at national and regional levels; there is a theatre-specific set of web pages; a number of recent reports that ACE have commissioned, for example, on trends in new writing over the past three years; and much information about which companies are funded, how much their funding is and how they find funding from other sources. For National Portfolio Organisations only receive a proportion of their total income from ACE; according to their website regularly funded theatres receive 33 per cent of their funding from ACE, 50 per cent from earned income (ticket sales, programmes, workshops, etc.), 9 per cent from local authorities, and 8 per cent from sponsorship, donations and fundraising. After considering some other important national theatre organisations we shall look at how that funding mix affects how theatres are organised and plan their work.

National theatre organisations

There are a number of organisations that it is useful to know about, even if you are unlikely to come into direct contact with them, as they form the key structures within which theatre is made. Their websites, listed at the end of this chapter, contain useful information about current and future policies and issues which will shape theatre-making, and also much helpful advice about such matters as setting up theatre companies and rates of pay and contracts with other artists.

The THEATRICAL MANAGEMENT ASSOCIATION, to quote its website, is 'a leading trade association representing the interests of and providing professional support for the performing arts in the UK. Our members include theatres, multi-purpose venues, arts centres, concert halls, commercial producers, touring theatre, opera and ballet companies, sole traders and suppliers to the performing arts'. It represents all of the building-based subsidised theatre companies, and one of its key roles is to negotiate pay and conditions for actors, stage managers, directors, designers, writers, fight directors, choreographers, stage crew and front-of-house staff working in those theatres: the current rates of pay can be seen on its website. It also offers conferences, seminars, legal and industrial advice to its members, and organises the annual TMA Awards which recognise outstanding work in its member theatres. In 2007 its members had audiences of 7.5 million people, having sold tickets worth £188 million.

The TMA shares its offices with its sister organisation THE SOCIETY OF LONDON THEATRE, which 'exists in order to serve, protect and promote the interests of those engaged in theatre ownership, management and production across London'. So it represents all significant commercial producers who operate in the West End and other parts of central London, and although the majority of its members are from the commercial sector it also includes representatives from the National Theatre, the Royal Court and other subsidised theatres in central London. It also negotiates on pay and conditions for artistic and technical staff on behalf of its members' theatres and offers a range of professional services.

Unlike the TMA its members are not the theatres themselves, but individuals who represent production companies and theatres. In addition it produces the official *London Theatre Guide* and operates 'tkts', the discount theatre ticket booths in Leicester Square and Brent Cross, and the national Theatre Tokens scheme. It also organises the prestigious annual Laurence Olivier Awards, celebrating the outstanding work in its members' theatres. In 2009 its members' theatres sold over £0.5 billion worth of tickets to audiences of 14.3 million people, and although the numbers of tickets sold dropped slightly in 2010 the value of those tickets rose slightly, for the seventh year in succession, so the West End appears to be bucking the recession. Under the aegis of SOLT is a registered charity, STAGE ONE, which offers workshops, apprenticeships, bursaries and investment to new producers. It is an important resource for the training and development of emerging producers, particularly those wishing to work in the commercial sector.

The INDEPENDENT THEATRE COUNCIL represents over 600 members, playing to audiences of over six million in 2009. Some members are individual artists. and many are middle- and small-scale companies, including venues and touring companies working in a wide variety of art forms: theatre, dance, opera, puppetry, mixed media, mime, physical theatre, circus, and in education. It offers management and legal advice, networking and information exchange, and negotiates on pay and conditions on behalf of its members. Because many are individuals or emerging companies, it also offers a wide range of training and personal support programmes, and these are also open to non-members. Its training programmes cover a wide range of areas including arts marketing, finding funding, contracts, finance, co-productions, and starting a performing arts company. Although some of the key issues in forming a company are discussed later in this chapter, if you are serious about starting a legally recognised company you will benefit from the detailed and practical step-by-step training and advice that ITC provides.

The EQUITY website says: 'Equity is the UK Trade Union representing professional performers and other creative workers from across the spectrum of the entertainment, creative and cultural industries.' Commonly known as the actors' union, Equity also represents directors, designers, fight directors, choreographers, dancers and stage managers. It is the union with which SOLT, TMA and ITC negotiate pay and conditions for all of these artists. The 'Equity rulebook' governs rehearsal hours, numbers of performances and, indeed, the whole working week for actors, stage managers and directors. Actors working in the smallest of the subsidised regional repertory theatres (known as sub reps) in 2010 earned £352 a week, due to rise to £400 a week by 2016. In 2008 the minimum rate for directors in small sub rep theatres was £2,240 for a four-week rehearsal/tech/opening period, although in practice the going rate in 2010 was nearer £4,000, including relocation allowance if working away from home.

As well as negotiating pay and conditions Equity is also a high-profile campaigner and advocate for the performing arts. Equity members receive a number of benefits and services, including legal advice, representation in disputes with employers, and advice on tax, welfare benefits and pensions. Equity membership also includes Public Liability Insurance of up to £10 million, which would normally cost as much as Equity membership. This is particularly useful for freelance directors, in case, for example, a participant sprains their ankle in a workshop you are running and seeks compensation.

Many directors are members of Equity and the DIRECTORS GUILD OF GREAT BRITAIN. The DGGB does not negotiate pay and conditions for directors, but it does have template contracts you may use and offers legal and dispute advice. It also runs regular workshops on approaches to directing led by leading theatre directors, and holds networking and other events to promote the art and craft of directing. The DGGB's membership includes a large number of directors working in opera, film, TV, radio and other media, and it is a useful way for a theatre director to find out about making connections and working in other media.

The WRITERS' GUILD OF GREAT BRITAIN is the trade union that represents writers in all media and is the chief negotiating body for the pay and conditions of writers with the TMA and ITC. These agreements can be viewed and downloaded from the Writers' Guild website and they offer good general guidance for the commissioning of writers and their rights in respect of working on a new play. The current commissioning fee for a new play produced by an ITC company is £7,650 and £5,810 for a new play produced by a small subsidised rep. You can also find out the contact details of over 500 playwrights on their website.

BECTU is another trade union, which represents over 25,000 people employed in theatre, film, broadcasting and other media. Although its website says that it represents all workers except actors and musicians, it is widely known in the theatre for its representation of stage crew, theatre-making staff and front-of-house theatre staff. Membership is open to freelance workers as well as those employed by theatres.

The MUSICIANS UNION (MU) represents musicians working in a wide variety of media and art forms, including theatre. It negotiates with the TMA and SOLT on pay and conditions for musicians, and is also a campaigning organisation: recently, for example, it has been negotiating with SOLT about the use of 'virtual orchestras' on West End shows such as *Les Misérables*.

The BRITISH ACADEMY OF DRAMATIC COMBAT (BADC) offers industry-recognised training and qualifications for fight directors. Its predecessor organisation, the Society of British Fight Directors, set up with Equity the 'Equity Register of Fight Directors', and fight directors employed by theatres are on this register, thus ensuring the technical expertise and requisite knowledge of health and safety legislation and considerations by fight directors employed by theatres.

Theatre organisation, funding and planning

Theatre companies can of course vary in size from being one person with a computer in their bedroom to the National Theatre and the RSC or the Ambassador Theatre Group. As a template to describe a 'typical' theatre organisation I shall take a medium-sized regional subsidised repertory theatre as a model. Although the number of personnel and departments and size of budgets may vary from theatre to theatre, this organisational and financial structure applies to many funded theatre companies.

Boards and trusts

Theatres in receipt of regular funding are usually legally constituted as 'companies limited by guarantee'. They are registered at Companies House as trading companies and the board oversees the running of the company and ensures that it is financially solvent. These companies have limited liability, which means that if the company is insolvent it is the company that bears the debt, not individual board members or employees of the company. It also means that all contracts are issued by the company, not by individuals. They are not-for-profit organisations: they do not distribute any profits to shareholders but reinvest any profit back into the activities of the company. These theatres will invariably also be registered as charities, which confers additional responsibilities but also certain tax and legal advantages on the company. Charities, or charitable trusts as they are properly named, are governed by trustees, charged with ensuring that the charity fulfils its charitable aims: broadly, in the case of most theatres, to entertain and educate, and to be of public benefit.

In practice many members of the board and the trust will be the same people, and their meetings are usually held on the same occasion. Most boards and trusts meet four times a year. For the sake of simplicity I shall refer to the board as meaning the board and/or the trust: to conflate the two roles, a theatre's board is often referred to as a 'board of trustees', with a chair elected by the board from its members. The composition of boards can vary greatly, but generally they contain three types of people: those who represent organisations that directly fund the theatre, such as councillors from the local authority; those representing organisations with which the theatre has close relations, such as other local arts organisations; and individuals who bring relevant experience or expertise, such as actors or directors, or legal, financial or marketing professionals, or educational experts such as teachers. Officers of the Arts Council or local authority are usually invited to meetings. If they attend they do so as observers and while they can comment or give advice they are not board members or trustees. However boards would rarely ignore their advice!

The board will discuss the recent artistic, organisational and financial performance and future plans of the theatre, often in great detail. The budget for the coming financial year has to be approved by the board, and, in some theatres the actual artistic programming has to be approved, or if not formally approved at least discussed.

Executive director and artistic director

It is usual for the board formally to appoint only two members of the theatre's staff: the executive director and the artistic director. Both attend board meetings to report on and discuss the performance and plans of the theatre. Technically the two directors are then responsible for appointing and managing all the other employees of the theatre. In practice, some board members may be on interview panels for other senior posts and senior staff may be asked to attend part of board meetings to report on matters in their department, but this is the formal relationship between the board, the directors and the employees of the theatre.

Most theatres have a staff structure diagram which is known to all members. This clearly shows the areas of direct responsibility of the executive and artistic directors and how every member of staff fits into the staff structure, and so how they are 'line-managed' within the organisation. The executive director is usually responsible for the finance, marketing, development (or fundraising), front-of-house and catering departments, and any other 'back office' staff. The artistic director is usually responsible for the freelance creative artists, including actors, designers, choreographers, fight directors, casting director, musicians, the literary department, and often, but not always, for the production department, which will include the theatre's workshop, the costume department, the technical department (which will itself include lighting, sound and stage technicians) and any freelance makers. The education and/or outreach department is usually but not always line-managed by the artistic director.

Confusingly, either the executive director or the artistic director can also be the chief executive – the first among equals of artistic and executive directors – and will therefore have slightly more weight and profile in leading the organisation. Increasingly this traditional pairing of the two roles is changing, and in some cases an outgoing artistic director's role is rethought and a creative producer is appointed to plan the theatre's artistic programme and to bring together creative teams, including directors, for individual projects. English Touring Theatre is a recent case in point.

Often the theatre's day-to-day management will be co-ordinated through regular senior management meetings attended by the two directors and the heads of all the departments in the theatre. The senior managers or heads of departments will then pass on information to people in their department. In addition there will be regular marketing, development and production meetings.

The pattern and focus of the cycle of production meetings is discussed in detail in Chapter Six, 'The Director and the Production', which focuses on preparation of a single production; here we will look at the overall planning for a season of productions to identify the factors that inform it.

Three-year plans

As mentioned in the section about Arts Council England, regularly funded theatres have a fixed funding period, often three years. In order to reach a funding agreement with ACE the theatre will have to write a three-year plan for the next funding bid. This three-year plan will cover all areas of the theatre's activity, setting out concrete plans for the development of that activity. It won't necessarily include individual play choices, particularly in years two and three, but it will identify the number of productions, developments in thinking about the overall mix of plays, intended audiences, and how those audiences may change; and then, how the core produced work will relate to touring productions that are brought in, other events, the outreach and education plans, and the marketing and financial plans that stem from that overall vision. Although there may be variations, it has to be a coherent plan for the future of the theatre and becomes the blueprint for the next three years' activity. Within the three years the theatre provides annual reports to the funder to monitor progress and to agree changes in the light of real events in the early years.

Once a three-year plan has been agreed, ACE will be able to indicate the proposed level of funding the theatre will receive over the next three years. As also mentioned above, on average, ACE funding only constitutes 33 per cent of overall funding, so at the same time the theatre may be in negotiation with local authorities, although actual promises of funding from local authorities may be annual rather than over three years. Add to this the typical figure of 50 per cent from ticket sales and other income, such as catering and programmes, and 8 per cent from fundraising, and the theatre can begin to create a budget for the plan, which will, inevitably, be much more detailed for the first year than for subsequent years.

Budgets

Many companies, including theatres, operate on the traditional financial year beginning on 6 April each year. This means that theatres often finalise their budgets between November and January for the next financial year.

A regional producing theatre may have a large season brochure mailout to previous attendees, and if there are two brochures a year the play decision deadline for the autumn brochure might be May, and for the spring brochure October. This means that programming discussions for the autumn season will begin around the previous Christmas, or in the New Year, and decisions for the spring season will be made in the previous spring and summer. As artistic director of Harrogate Theatre I had planned the whole season from September to May by the end of the previous April, even if not all of the plays were announced to the public, because I had to consider the budget for the whole season in order to make play choices.

Taking these two cycles – the budget cycle and the season planning cycle – together, although I had planned the season by the end of April, the budget for that year had already been set in the previous November or January, so that budget covered a season of notional plays with notional resources. So, to take a simple example, you might have agreed a budget for five plays, three of which have casts of eight actors and production budgets of £15,000, two with casts of five with production budgets of £7,000 and one, Christmas production with a cast of ten and a production budget of £30,000. All these notional plays will also have notional box-office targets.

In your three-year plan you may also have identified that at least one play needs to be targeted at a new audience you are trying to develop and one that will tour nationally, or be a co-production with another, as yet unspecified, theatre. The production budgets will also include notional figures for freelance directors' fees, designer fees, and the number of musical directors or choreographers or fight directors you think might be needed. Programme planning is like a three-dimensional sudoko grid: some of the numbers have already been filled in, and you need to fill in the rest of the grid with numbers that fit that prearranged pattern, financially and logistically, while also fulfilling an artistic vision for the company.

This is not the only way to budget: some theatres budget every production separately so that projected income from box office covers all the resources for that production; other theatres have separate season-long budgets for actors, for designers, for freelance staff etc., and then apportion those budgets to individual productions, but the point is the same: artistic directors are nearly always creating seasons from pre-existing budgets, in whatever way those budgets are arranged.

One of the most important budgets to consider is the yearly budget for 'actor weeks'. Although the production budgets already discussed assumed cast sizes, they did not mention rehearsal periods. For example, one of the productions with a cast of eight actors might have a four-week rehearsal period, one week of technical rehearsals and opening and a three-week run, so altogether eight weeks: and eight actors for eight weeks is sixty-four actor-weeks. At roughly the Equity minimum wage, plus relocation allowance (or subsistence) for actors working away from home, each actor week cost might be just over £500 a week, so a production with a cast of eight would cost just over £32,000 in actors' salaries alone.

One of the unenviable calculations an artistic director might have to make is having a small-cast play with a four-week rehearsal period, or a larger-cast play with only three weeks' rehearsals. One of the unenviable facts of life in a producing theatre is that the rates, electricity and phone bills have to be paid and the number of commissions, freelance staff and actor-weeks are sometimes the most vulnerable budgets; and while it is not the only reason, making these precious resources go further and sharing some of the costs is why more and more theatres are co-producing.

Once the budget for the year is agreed you can move the resources around and change the cast sizes, production budgets and freelance staff of individual plays, but the size of the pot for all productions remains the same.

Although, as an emerging director, you may not have these concerns immediately, this relationship, and often the time relationship, between budget, resources and artistic decision-taking, is true for most theatres and for single productions.

It is also worth being aware of the planning and finances behind a theatre's season before pitching ideas for productions to a theatre, and these patterns and resource levels can often be deduced by reading previous seasons' brochures and visiting the theatre's website; reading the theatre's mission statement, or a digest of the three-year plan; looking at the overall mix of plays in a season and calculating average cast sizes for main house and studio productions; and envisaging the target audience for each play. With this background you will be able to make informed decisions about what projects or plays to suggest for that theatre.

Commercial theatre

Commercial theatre comprises a number of independent companies that range in size from the Really Useful Group or Bill Kenwright Limited, to individuals who set up a company and raise funds to put on productions project by project. By definition, in commercial theatre the aim is to make a profit on the production, or, in the first instance, not to make a loss so that you live to fight another day by your own means.

In practice, there is often close collaboration between the commercial and subsidised sectors and they are, in many ways, mutually dependent. Recently, Kneehigh, West Yorkshire Playhouse and Birmingham Rep, three subsidised companies, co-produced *Brief Encounter*. The production was then taken on by two commercial producers, David Pugh and Dafydd Rogers who brought it in to the West End and then on to New York. The commercial producers benefited from the investment of time and money by the subsidised theatres, and could see that it was a good production before taking it on, while the subsidised theatres saw their production taken to a commercial environment where they might not have been able to operate, and from this took kudos, and probably some financial reward for its extended life.

Sometimes a commercial producer and a subsidised theatre will collaborate from the inception of the production. For example, Bill Kenwright Limited and Birmingham Rep co-produced a production of *Cabaret* that went into the West End and on national tour. The commercial producer, who does not usually own workshops, costume departments and equipment stores, benefits from the infrastructure the building-based theatre can provide. But since individual production budgets at subsidised theatres can be very tight, the commercial producer provided extra funding for the production which the theatre could not afford, and so gets a larger and better resourced production. When the production goes into the West End or on tour, both parties will benefit financially, the exact split depending on the relative resources both parties initially invested in the production. These are but two examples of the many subsidised–commercial collaborations that happen every year.

Julius Green, senior producer at Bill Kenwright Limited, at a recent seminar with directors Tamara Harvey and Rufus Norris about working in the commercial and subsidised sectors, said, 'I always explain the difference between the subsidised and commercial sectors as being, as it currently stands, that the subsidised sector budgets for deficit in order to attract the funding that it needs, and the commercial sector budgets for profit in order to attract the funding that it needs. The fact is that overall both sectors end up losing money, and it is often possible to create two projects that are essentially the same and to present it in two different ways: one that demonstrates that it requires subsidy – funding; and another that demonstrates that it could be a huge commercial success in order to attract commercial investment. It is sometimes an unfortunate assumption that there is a huge difference between them, but in reality, the people who work in both sectors chop and change between them all the time. It's true to say that the people who create the work, the commercial producers or the subsidised houses, are passionate about theatre and nobody is in this game with a primary agenda to make a profit. People who work in the commercial sector try to make a profit simply so that they can continue to generate work that they are passionate about. You will find that the actual experience of creating work is qualitatively different – whether the quality of the work is different is a different question.'

Although, as noted above, the West End has been increasing its audience every year, it is also true that seven out of ten West End productions fail to recoup their investment, and that even a successful West End musical can take over two years to show a profit.

From a director's point of view there are some key differences between working for a commercial producer and working in a subsidised theatre, although, inevitably, these are generalisations that do not invariably hold.

The relationship of the freelance director to the artistic director in a subsidised theatre is discussed in the next chapter, but, as noted there, while the artistic director may make suggestions about casting and choosing members of the creative team, they are usually only suggestions. In commercial theatre the director is seen much more as part of the whole creative team that the producer appoints, and therefore the producer also has a much greater say in the make-up of the whole team, and may also take an active role in the auditioning and casting process, whereas the artistic director tends to let the freelance director get on with it.

Particularly for commercial tours, where the producer has to sell the whole production to the touring venues who may or may not choose to take it, there is often pressure on the producer to cast 'names' who will attract publicity and local press interviews. That pressure on the producer naturally becomes a pressure on the director in the casting process. In a subsidised theatre, if the play has been programmed it will go ahead regardless of 'name' casting; in a commercial production the viability of the whole project may rest upon this.

The producer might be more involved in the design process as well because the financial and logistical consequences of a design might be more complex and far-reaching for a touring production, or for a West End run with high weekly running costs for stage crew, than a production in a single subsidised building.

In a subsidised theatre a large number of those involved in the production process may be permanent staff on long-term contracts whose salaries do not necessarily affect the production budget. In commercial theatre producers tend to have only an office and a very small administrative staff, so that every element of mounting the production, and all the staff, are direct costs on the production budget, and have to be financed up front, as the only income is from the box office, once the show opens. This may mean that every stage of the process is a little tighter and quicker than in subsidised theatre: there might be one or two fewer audition days; there may be a three- rather than a four-week rehearsal period; there may be two tech days instead of four. Similar results may well be possible in the shorter time, but it usually requires everyone's working processes and decision-making to be a little bit quicker than in the subsidised sector, and that is one reason why many directors of commercial productions are already experienced directors who can achieve the same results under greater pressures and constraints than might be entirely comfortable.

As discussed in the next chapter, it is always important for a freelance director to ask questions and to establish the budget and time and physical resources for a production before agreeing to direct it, but in a commercial environment where everything has to be acquired and costed from scratch, and there are few built-in resources to rely or fall back on, it is even more important to establish those facts, and then to work within the budget and resources. Even if your production is a critical success, if you have overseen a reckless production budget or racked up a lot of actor overtime bills, you are unlikely to succeed in commercial theatre.

Fringe, unfunded, or independent theatre

Because so many emerging directors begin their careers directing, and possibly producing, in fringe venues, in London, Edinburgh, or other cities, I have included two detailed interviews with directors with recent first-hand experience. Elly Green has directed and produced several times in

London, and Clare Shucksmith, whose interview appears in Chapter One, has directed and produced many times in Edinburgh. Both these interviews offer practical advice about how to direct and produce your own work in these environments.

As Elly Green remarks, the costs and demands of producing on the established London fringe have risen steeply in the past few years, and if you are paying actors and the creative team a 'fringe' fee level, a three-week rehearsal period and four-week playing period can end up costing you over £10,000 – more if the tickets don't sell. What used to be a really simple and cheap way of getting your work on has become complicated and expensive, so now many directors are producing their first work in 'off-fringe' venues or in found spaces. So it is worthwhile asking yourself some questions about the type and scale of production you wish to direct and/or produce and what your aims are in terms of getting your work staged before embarking on a fringe production.

The theatre or venue

Studio Two at the Arcola, like many similarly sized fringe venues in London, costs £1,350 a week to hire, so just over £4,000 for a three-week run. As mentioned by Elly Green, some theatres will not consider hiring you their venue unless you can prove you have £10,000 in the bank. Others will base their fee on a share of box-office income, which makes the upfront hire costs cheaper, but if you do not sell enough tickets it can be more expensive than a straight hire. Established fringe theatres have the advantage that they are well known and have reputations that you can be associated with. They will sell tickets for you and help market your show, and critics and industry professionals are used to seeing work there.

The alternatives are to start from scratch and find a space which may not be a theatre, such as a disused shop, or another property which is empty, and to create your own venue for the production. Of course, the immediate problem with this is that you may have to find everything you need to create the venue, not just the production: create front-of-house areas and find ways of selling tickets and refreshments; even find the seats, unless it is a promenade or Punchdrunk-type production that doesn't need seating; and you will have to deal with entertainment licensing laws, public liability insurance and health and safety requirements to be legal and properly insured, which might be its own nightmare. Alternatively, you may be able to find a pub or café which is covered for all these requirements (and has some seats) with no track record of theatre, but which is willing to let you have the space for the beer or coffee sales but no rent. You may have to compensate for its being off the theatrical beaten track by putting more into marketing, but it may still be financially and artistically more rewarding than just renting space in an existing theatre.

Fee paying

If you already have relationships with the key creative people and all share a passion to put on a particular piece, it is possible to do it without anyone getting paid, or to work for a profit-share at the end of the production. You may even be able to persuade actors you don't know to be in the piece because it will give them a great role, more experience and hopefully exposure to directors and casting directors who might employ them in the future. For the record, it should be noted that legally, no one can be employed for less than the National Minimum Wage except volunteers working for charities and students on work experience. Although it hasn't happened yet, it is possible for someone working on a profit-share production – particularly when there is no profit – to take 'the employer' to court under this legislation.

In 2005 Equity launched an agreement for fringe companies to sign up to, which can be found on its website. This ensures that all actors and stage managers get paid the same, and that the level of pay is in line with the minimum wage, currently being paid at £250 a week on the fringe. It also sets out guidelines for working hours and other terms and conditions of employment. Some other fringe companies have become registered charities and have drawn up volunteer contracts with those working for them: they may not get paid, or just get expenses, but they have contracts that recognise the rights and obligations of the company and the individual and form the basis of a professional relationship.

But as Elly Green says in her interview, there are two issues which are, and are not, just about the money. The first is that, however passionate people are about a project, if there are no fees not only are people not getting paid, it is actually costing them to give up the time to be involved in the production, and this can severely limit the range and calibre of those involved in the project. The second factor is that even if the payment is below the normal Equity minimum, a payment of a fee recognises that person's contribution and importance to the piece, and engenders a commitment to it well beyond the monetary value of the fee.

Budget and resources

If you are going to produce your own production as well as direct it, you will have to do all the planning and budgeting. You may have experience of budgeting production costs, but if you do not it is really worthwhile getting the advice of your designer, a stage manager, or even production manager to think through every aspect of the process and cost it closely. The importance of a creative producer to such a project is discussed by Elly Green and Andrew McKinnon, but it is also worth considering the importance of a production manager – someone who takes responsibility for overseeing all the production resources, logistics and budgets; who can liaise between the designer, lighting designer, sound designer, other designers and stage manager; and who can liaise with the theatre or venue about the technical resources of the venue and ensure that what you are planning to bring into the venue will be compatible with those resources.

Matching your production with what the theatre provides is discussed in detail with Clare Shucksmith about her experiences at Edinburgh, but the same questions and principles apply to any production going into a venue. It may be that the stage manager is willing to take on those responsibilities, but will the stage manager be able to do that and be in rehearsals with you? It may be that the designer is willing to take it on, but it is important to be aware that there are a set of tasks and questions that may not be covered by a designer and stage manager simply fulfilling their own roles. It is also true that some of the highest costs of a production can get overlooked: rehearsal rooms, particularly in London, can cost £300 or £400 a week unless you can beg a favour or do a deal well in advance; workshops and making spaces can be even more difficult to find, and if you have a set that needs a lot of construction and finishing, finding such a space can be difficult and expensive. Does your designer know somewhere? And the other thing that often gets forgotten is the get-out. The venue may need you to be out within an hour or two of the last performance, and finding willing helpers, a van, and, dare one say, somewhere to store your set, at 11 p.m. on a Saturday night is not always easy.

Marketing and ticket selling

If you are at an established fringe venue your contract will set out exactly how much marketing support you will get, but the venue should put details of your production on their website and include it in regular emails to their existing audience database. They will also display your flyers front of house. But you will probably have to commission the print and image design and get your flyers printed, and, if you choose, pay to have them distributed to other theatres and arts venues in the city.

There are numerous individuals and small companies with experience of creating print designs and images for fringe productions. The easiest way to find them is to pick up print for other fringe shows, see whose work you like, and look for a number or website for the designer on the print. Many printers actually offer free, or nearly free, print designs in the printing package. The going rate for setting up a website for your production is about £250, and about the same for creating an image and print design. Straightforward envelope-size flyers cost about £165 for 5,000. Having got the print design, you can of course set up your own Facebook page and put the information and design in an email to send to contacts.

If you are not at an established venue, getting a ticket-office facility and a reliable contact to take reservations and payments can be difficult to set up and maintain. The theatre information site *theatreweb* offers this service for a 12.5 per cent commission on tickets sold, gives you a professional point of contact for ticket sales and relieves you of worry and responsibility. There are other websites that offer this service, and may do so for a smaller commission, so it is worth shopping around. Of course, you will still need to have someone to take and sell tickets on the door.

Who will come to see it?

As Elly Green points out in her interview, unless you are running a production for three weeks it is very difficult to get national press critics in to review the production; and if you are at an unrecognised venue or your opening coincides with that of many other shows, you may still not get reviewed even during a three-week run. It is worth contacting reviewers you are keen to get to see the show a couple of months beforehand, to give them some information about the company, the production and those involved, to arouse their interest in it before you actually send out press invitations.

If, as well as your passion for the project, your main aim is to get peers and industry professionals to see your work, you don't necessarily have to commit to a three-week run: with enough notice you may be able to get the directors, producers and others you really want to see your work to see it with only a week-long run. There is much good advice about how to approach fellow theatre-makers and to invite them to your work in the interviews with Gareth Machin, Studio Associate of the National Theatre Studio, and Sue Emmas, Associate Artistic Director of the Young Vic, in Chapter Seven, 'The Director and Directing'.

Setting up a company

One emerging theatre director I know recently put on a successful fringe production, directed by him, and produced by him from his laptop at home, but under the name of his 'company'. The company existed only as a name on the print for the production: it had no formal status and no bank account – it was a branding exercise that made the production look more professional and better resourced than just under his own name, and the company name may never be seen again. Many shows at Edinburgh are produced by similarly unconstituted companies, and as long as there is no intention to defraud the tax person or anyone else there is nothing to stop you following suit.

However, if you are planning to apply for a Grants for the Arts award, or to seek funding from trusts or foundations, companies with charitable funds, or from local authorities, setting up a properly constituted company, and perhaps registering it as a charity, may significantly increase your chances of getting funding. Simply, becoming a registered company makes your finances and activities open to public scrutiny and therefore more transparent and accountable: it increases confidence that the monies given will be properly managed and spent for their intended use.

It is often at the point, when several people have come together to produce one piece of work and then decided that they wish to continue that collaboration into a longer-term future, beyond just the next project, that directors and producers consider creating a formal structure for their collaboration; and this also often coincides with the point at which the company looks for external funding to increase its resources.

There are forms of association that lie between just an individual or group of individuals and being a company limited by guarantee. It is possible to set up a 'partnership' with one other person, and it is possible to set up an 'unincorporated association' with several other people. But although both forms of association may give the company a set of rules, or constitution, individuals will still be held responsible for losses and the consequences of not fulfilling contracts. It is only a company limited by guarantee that has the legal status to issue contracts and employ people as a separate legal entity from the individuals involved. The individual members (or directors) of the company only have liabilities of £1 if the company becomes insolvent: the debts are the debts of the company, not the individuals. With a company limited by guarantee you can open a bank account in the company's name and have grants and income paid directly into a company rather than an individual account, which is much preferred by funders.

General information about the status of partnerships, unincorporated associations and companies limited by guarantee can be found on the government's Business Link website and information about setting up a charity can be found on the Charity Commission's website, both listed at the end of this chapter, but for specialist help and guidance on setting up a performance company or charity the best organisation and website is ITC. They run courses on 'Starting a Performing Arts Company' and will guide you through setting up as a company and charity through their 'Incorporation and Charitable Status Registration Service'. If you are considering setting up a company, this is the best advice and training available. Setting up a company is relatively straightforward, but gaining charitable status can be complex and you will probably need legal advice.

Finding funding

Grants for the Arts

As mentioned earlier, in recent years the first stop for individuals and companies seeking funding has been Grants for the Arts, which, through ACE, in 2009–10 made 2,795 awards totalling £64.9 million. Individuals may apply for grants of up to £30,000, but the average grant in 2006–7 was £5,825. Organisations may apply for up to £100,000, but in the same year the average grant was for £24,697. Grants may be applied for online and there is no closing date or regular deadlines. If you apply for less than £10,000 you should receive a decision within six working weeks.

The ACE website contains a great deal of information and guidance about making an application – too much to usefully precis here, but there are some observations about Grants for the Arts that apply to any funding application. Like any arts organisation and any trust or foundation, ACE has a set of priorities for the work it wishes to see developed and therefore is more likely to fund. For the period from 2008–11 ACE's four priorities were: digital opportunity; visual arts; children and young people; and London 2012. This does not mean that arts activity outside those areas will not be funded, but that projects which meet these priorities will score more highly. It also has another set of criteria which will increase the chances of your bid being successful: if you have not received funding before from Grants for the Arts; if your project will increase arts activity where there are currently few arts opportunities; if it will engage people who have had little or no arts involvement; and/or, if it will develop the art form. There is more detailed information on the website, but it is clear from the above that your application and your project will have to address a number of priorities and criteria to be successful: just putting in an application to put on an interesting piece of work will not be enough, unless you carefully consider how your project meets ACE's aims.

Other Lottery sources of funding

AWARDS FOR ALL is another Lottery-funded scheme, aimed primarily at community and voluntary organisations that 'improve communities and the lives of the people within them'. The criteria for awards are slightly different in England, Scotland, Wales and Northern Ireland. In England there is a move away from giving grants to arts activities, but it is worth checking the current priorities and criteria in all countries, as they do change. THE BIG LOTTERY FUND funds a range of regional and national schemes and initiatives in the areas of the environment, education and health, and your project will have to meet the specific criteria within these areas or within existing schemes to gain funding. It is only open to organisations that are at least unincorporated associations.

Local authorities and local education authorities

Until the 2010 Spending Review local authorities were significant funders of arts activity, particularly by locally based groups. As the arts are not part of a local authority's statutory spending, it is difficult to say how much of these funds will remain available, but it is worth searching the website of your local authority to see what current funding opportunities exist and perhaps contact the arts officer to discover future plans and to establish a relationship. Your local education authority will also have a website and a drama adviser (or similarly named post) and possibly a youth arts officer, and if you are interested in working in education or with young people it is worth making contact with these people even if there are no immediate funding opportunities.

Arts trusts and foundations

There are many trusts and foundations that specifically support artists and the performing arts. Some of the larger trusts and foundations are listed with their websites at the end of the chapter, and the better-known ones include: Calouste Gulbenkian Foundation; Foyle Foundation; The Paul Hamlyn Foundation; The Clore Duffield Foundation; the Ideas Fund; and the Esmée Fairbairn Foundation. Each of these foundations has different aims and objectives and therefore also different funding criteria and priorities. Some will fund individuals, some will only fund organisations or other charities; again, it is important to read these criteria closely to determine whether you or your project will fall within them. Most charities have very clear guidelines indicating in detail which activities they will, and will not, fund but the commonest reason for funding applications being rejected is that the activity does not meet the criteria, so many applicants are simply not reading the guidelines!

Finding charities, trusts and foundations

There are a number of charitable organisations with websites that contain databases of charities and foundations with searchable information and criteria, and from which you may research trusts and foundations that most closely fit your work. The largest of these is the Directory of Social Change, which has a searchable database and published directory, while its website also contains useful information on fundraising. But you do have to pay a subscription to use it fully, and it covers all areas of activity, not just the arts. From its website you may also find links to similar sites such as trustfunding.org.uk, companygiving.org.uk, governmentfunding.org.uk, and grantsforindividuals.org.uk, and while they also contain useful general information about fundraising, they also charge a yearly subscription, of between £200 and £300, to search their databases. Another website, funderfinder.org.uk, offers similar advice and a database of 4,000 trusts, foundations and companies for individuals and groups, for which you can pay a daily subscription of between £5.50 and £10.

The organisation Arts and Business also offers advice and information on its website and runs courses on arts fundraising, but again, the information and courses offered by ITC are the most relevant to theatre and the performing arts. The Grants for the Arts pages on the ACE website also contain a downloadable document called 'Other Sources of Funding' that is a useful guide to alternatives to Grants for the Arts.

Fundraising guidance

If you are embarking on a serious fundraising drive for your work it is worth reading the general guidance about how to go about it on the websites just mentioned, but it is also worth considering taking one of the courses offered by ITC. As noted in the discussion on applying to Grants for the Arts, it is important to check carefully the eligibility criteria, the priorities of the organisation, and the funding assessment criteria before writing your application. You may find that your project might fit the criteria, but you will have to rethink and reword your written material about the project to hit the target: you may emphasise one aspect of the project, and spend less time describing the elements that don't fit the criteria – or you may decide that you actually want to change the nature and focus of the project to meet certain funding criteria.

There are dangers in this: you may get the funding and then revert to doing more of what you wanted to do in the first instance, and not fulfil the terms of the grant, and so jeopardise your relationship with that funder, or even the actual funding; or you may embark on a project that meets the criteria and sets out to achieve the aims of the funding, but find that your heart is no longer really in it. To a certain extent we all have to tailor funding applications for projects we wish to do in order to fit funding criteria, but there are dangers in just following the funding, and you have to decide where the tipping point is. If you do change the project to fit the funding, grant assessors are skilled at spotting this and you may be wasting your time writing such an application. It is probably better to do more research to find a funding source that matches what you really want to do than to change the project radically to fit the funding in front of you.

Sponsorship

Sponsorship is different from funding in that funding is given to enable your company to deliver work for the benefit of others, whereas sponsorship is a contract about the exchange of goods and services between you and the sponsor. Sponsorship can usually only be sought once the project is definitely happening, not in order to make it happen, and it is usual for the sponsor's name and/or logo to appear prominently on printed and other materials associated with the element of the production being sponsored – perhaps the education pack, the post-show discussion, or the production itself. Local sponsorship for small amounts can be sought by personal contact and can be helpful in identifying your work with the local community. National sponsorship is far harder to come by, and often requires a national profile to secure it. Sponsorship often only lasts for one project or event, but may lead to a longer-term relationship with the sponsor that then becomes a combination of sponsorship and funding, such as the Travelex season at the National Theatre.

In any sponsorship relationship, which is a contract, you have to be honest and clear about the exact 'billing' and exposure the sponsor will get for their sponsorship: some sponsors do not wish to be mentioned at all, others will have detailed descriptions of the type size and positioning of their name or logo. Even in a buoyant economic climate, significant sponsorship is hard to secure, particularly from national companies, whose sponsorship policies and budgets are centrally determined. Some larger companies have guidance about their sponsorship aims for the coming year on their websites. With many national companies it might be best to find out what good causes they are currently supporting and to apply to their charitable section rather than trying for straight commercial sponsorship.

Donations

Donations usually occur through a personal connection with the donor, and although you may receive a donation out of the blue, most donations are the result of relationships developed over a long period of time. Some funding relationships, and particularly those that result in donations, are built from keeping those people who are stimulated by your work involved in your development: if someone has seen your work and responded well to it, you may wish to keep them informed of your plans and future productions – then it may be some time before this relationship naturally develops into funding or a donation. It is possible for donors to offset their gifts against their tax, and if you are a charity it is possible to add to the value of donations through gift aid. The Charity Commission website and other funding websites mentioned above will give more information about the mechanisms for claiming these tax reliefs. They also contain information about legacies and bequests, but going down this route assumes a certain longevity for your company – as well as the donor!

Support in kind

The Grants for the Arts application has a separate section for acknowledging the value of support in kind towards your project, and it can be a vital element in any production budget. As was mentioned in the discussion on fringe theatre, finding affordable rehearsal and making space can be very difficult, and a rehearsal space can easily add over £1,000 to the budget. It might be possible to find benevolent arts organisations that will give you a very reduced rate if their spaces are not being used, or perhaps you can find a community hall that will let you have the space for nothing if you organise an open run of the play for other hall users; or you might offer the type of presence on the publicity material you would offer to a sponsor, for support in kind. Good stage managers are highly skilled in the art of 'propping' – acquiring or borrowing props for no money or perhaps a credit in the programme. It is worth acquiring their attitudes in approaching any project, not just thinking about sources of conventional funding.

Other sources of information

This chapter is not an exhaustive overview of the many ways in which theatre-making is organised and funded in the UK today, or an exhaustive guide to setting up a company and putting on work, but it does offer a route map, setting out the main organisations that form the infrastructure of the UK theatre industry and the main considerations you may face in putting on a piece of professional work. One recent book – *So You Want to be a Theatre Producer* by James Seabright – was written for producers, but also gives information and practical advice about producing that can be useful for directors who wish (or have to) produce as well as direct.

There are many websites listed at the end of this chapter that will offer more detailed information in all the areas outlined here. It is worth bearing in mind that if you have a relationship with an experienced director or chief executive, or producer, they are often willing to look over budgets and funding applications to offer advice and feedback: you are not asking them to do it for you, just to comment on what you have already done.

Interviews

Interview with Annette Mees

Annette Mees makes immersive theatre, interactive experiences and adventures. She is a co-director of Coney, an award-winning agency of adventure and play (http://youhavefoundconey.net). Coney tells stories in which the audience can become the heroes, and which are always live and responsive and an adventure. Coney's work mixes live performance and play with digital and online storytelling. Coney is a community of artists, makers and players, operating as a secret society which is, of course, run by a Rabbit. Within Coney, Annette focuses on developing new interactive narratives and experiential models, developing new work with writers and actors, and the integration of digital technology and theatrical live events. She has been awarded the Writers' Guild of Great Britain Theatre Encouragement Award for her collaborative work with writers, was named 'an artist to watch' by Courvoisier's Future 500, and holds a Masters in Theatre Directing from Birkbeck. I asked her to describe the artistic policy and work of Coney.

We call ourselves an agency of adventure and play: what that means is that when we make theatre we create stories in which the audience is the hero and the stories take place wherever the audience is. The projects take many different forms: we've done projects that are primarily in theatres but that have an online component; we have made things that are purely live, and work in public spaces, galleries and schools.

Can you give some examples?

Yes. *Rabbit:NTT* was a commission from the National Theatre in 2006 as an experiment in audience development, to create an adventure that would bring people into the National building who normally wouldn't cross the threshold. *Rabbit:NTT* played out over the summer. It was a story of an usher who went missing, a friend of Rabbit's, who had wandered into a shadow of the National – a story that had been built from the real history and present activities of the building. One starting point was a deliberate misprint in the National Theatre brochure which led to a postcard online from Rabbit. If you contacted Rabbit, you would be emailed an invitation to go to the National. There was a sign by a broken paving stone and if you stood there and called the number you'd been given in the email you were led on a journey that was the most exciting way to enter the building, from its basement to its rafters, before ending up in the bookshop. There, if you bought a pamphlet on the history of the National Theatre and asked for it to be gift-wrapped while winking at the bookshop staff, you were given a bag which contained a gigantic map that led you into the story.

More events and happenings then proliferated over six weeks, both in the building and online. It culminated with everyone who had followed these trails gathering on the north bank of the Thames at 7.23 p.m. on a Saturday night, opposite the National Theatre. People had been told to bring a radio and that they would get a message but they didn't know how. At 7.30 p.m. the gigantic advertising sign on the front of the building suddenly turned on to read 'Hello, this is Rabbit. Please tune your radio to . . . ' Then there was a live radio play broadcast and the audience, having crossed the bridge to the building, now found the means to cast themselves into the story to save the day. So, in that project, although Coney worked with actors, as a participant you constructed your own narrative within the broader event.

A Small Town Anywhere was a show we co-produced with BAC, which was the story of a small town under pressure – a small town anywhere – and the originating principle was to tell a story without actors in a room. In this show the audience are the citizens of the town, although not characters so much as their real selves as citizens. So you enter this small town and become a member of its community: you get a badge which says Le Baker or La Mayor so you are, say, Rob Le Baker, and you also get a hat, and you've got a space in the town, where you live. The play then takes place over a week in narrative time, two hours in real time. The story is played out through a town crier, who is a disembodied voice-over, live from backstage. The sound effects and lighting are also being done live, so everything is really responsive.

As the pressure on the town mounts from the big country, the people of the small town have to make decisions and play out their fate. There's a Small Town Historian as gatekeeper who provides a framing narrative both live and online, so you can get in touch before the performance with the historian and you can create a backstory for yourself, and invent your own secret, so you'll come in with a richer narrative; but alternatively you can go into the Historian's office when you arrive, before you enter the town.

It was a very important show for us because we had the opportunity for sustained development and it gave us a real opportunity to discover how to make a narrative that truly responded to people – whereas often with interactive work it doesn't really matter what you say, because the narrative has been set out so strongly. *Small Town Anywhere* was very different every night and it really mattered that Rob was Le Baker that night. And then there is what we call a tail, after the show: by email, you get the town newspaper that tells the story of your small town experience and how the Historian compares it to other towns.

How did Coney begin?

It's evolved from 2005 where it was just the agent of Rabbit, and a small group of artists and others who worked together in the shadows helping Rabbit, recognising that the potential for participation was the most exciting quality of the work. More and more people started joining. The name Coney was born during the adventure at the National (just before I started making work with them), when it became necessary to have a front organisation that looked like a company rather than a rabbit. Coney then took on a life of its own in 2007 but continued to evolve towards its current professional structure, with the three of us now left standing as its current co-directors and runners: myself, Tassos Stevens, and Tom Bowtell. But Coney can be anyone making play.

How do the three of you work together?

Coney works more like a creative agency than a traditional theatre company. We call ourselves runners because we both serve and run the company, and we juggle various roles, including creative producers, as well as being co-directors, making decisions on the direction, artistic and otherwise, of the company. So far most projects have had at least one runner among the lead artists making them, but it's rare for projects to have all of us – *Small Town* was one of those.

I think the structure of Coney reflects the work and the work reflects the structure. We make this kind of work because we became interested in how the story, or an experience, really starts when you first hear about it and stops when you stop talking about it, and often those parts are just occupied by marketing at the start and talking with friends at the end. For us it became really exciting to use that space before and after the actual event for as much story and artistic content as possible. Digital technology now makes it easier for us to do that and part of our work is exploring what that means. It also becomes a more personal experience because you experience and unlock the content in a different way from somebody else, perhaps because you have an interest in one particular story strand rather than another. So from the beginning point you are making up your own narrative within the broader narrative.

Our company structure reflects this. We have office space but it's not necessarily where the heart of Coney is: we have digital platforms so that we can keep in touch with each other and so that the company grows. Just as we like to distribute narratives, we can work in a distributed way, and it means we can do more work more quickly than by conventional means: you don't have to meet in order to communicate. It's also very democratic.

The unusual and exciting thing about Coney is that it has an artistic core but that's not all it is. Coney is also a secret society. The secret society is made up of people Coney has worked with - so there are lots of actors, sound designers, writers, and so on, and people who have played brilliantly as audience. So there are people who started out as a player in something, and contributed something special and so have been invited into the society, from where they might end up working on projects or even in HQ.

We wanted to set up something really playful because playfulness is a key quality of our work. For us it's really important to create a community around our work, so there's a space online where people develop ideas and we can talk about what we're doing. People contribute and discuss ideas and sometimes we meet people if their ideas might be suitable for a project. You don't have to talk about your own expertise: so actors talk about sound design and sound designers talk about narrative. You log in under your code name, and other society members don't know your real identity, which creates a really open, safe, space for people to say things. For example, we have a couple of eighteen-year-olds who are very active, and there are also artistic directors of theatres and people from the Arts Council - and they don't know that they're talking to each other, so they don't feel inhibited. It's our way of creating a creative community around the work and it's really fertile. We now have hundreds of codenames, in places including Beijing, Melbourne, New York, Barcelona and throughout the UK.

There are also live events, like Playdays and gatherings where people come together and make things through playing together, and some of those pieces created have had life beyond the Playday. Like the rest of the work it's a combination of live and digital activity. We are really interested in the digital – we think it's great as a tool – but we're not interested in it as an artistic expression. We're interested in the digital as an opportunity to facilitate communities and creativity in an open, egalitarian way.

How are you funded?

There are really two main ways. The first is by initiating a project and then seeking the funding: so, for example, I'm developing a project called Art Heist, which is initiated by us, and we developed that with the New Art Gallery Walsall, and so we applied for, and got, funding from Arts Council West Midlands. The other way is getting a commission to create a piece: so, the Tate Britain Henry Moore project was a commission. *Small Town Anywhere* was supported by both the National Theatre Studio and BAC in its development phases; and then BAC and Coney jointly got the money for the full production from the Arts Council, which was only the second piece of direct public funding that Coney had received.

The core creative team, as directors and producers, has also worked with freelance producers. Why is that?

We've worked with several freelance producers for the expertise that they bring to the company in particular fields. And we work in many different settings and fields, from galleries to theatre, to the streets, from digital broadcast to theatre, to education, and to more free play. It is more fruitful to bring in different producers with the right skills for different fields of operation. We've also been supported at the centre by some producers with extraordinary strategic oversight: Tim Jones (who is now at motiroti) took us forward for several years, and recently Nick Williams has facilitated continued organisational development.

Do you work with actors, writers and designers project by project as you need them?

Yes. With every project we try to go to the society first because we have developed particular ways of working. It's slightly abstract for us to make participatory work, so we have a very participatory way of working. Work is created very democratically. I work a lot in Coney with actors and with writers and with sound designers and I really encourage people to bring ideas to the pool that are outside their own expertise. I'm thrilled if an actor says, 'We could do this with sound.' I absolutely believe in expertise, and I want a sound designer on my project if I'm working with sound, but if an actor really understands the piece they're part of they might have a good idea about sound.

For me often the writing is more about the construction of narrative than it is about saying it beautifully – that almost comes in at the end when we've constructed what the whole narrative is and who says what; but because the actors are often responsive we need to give them ways of speaking about things rather than saying, 'These are your exact words.'

In this kind of work you learn not to be precious: there are certain writers that we work with really well because they understand that they're writing something that is in motion because it's responsive to an audience. And the same with actors: so we are going to run some workshop for actors specifically about interactive and responsive acting. I think some people who are amazing actors on stage might not always be suited to this work: people need to find it exciting rather than scary to work in something that's fluid.

How do you see the company developing?

The thing that we would really like in the future is for there to be chapters of the society of Coney both across the UK and internationally, because we think that meeting in person is as important, or more important, than the digital interaction that helps glue everyone together. We're hoping that we'll be able to help start playful communities from disparate and diverse individuals in lots of different places. The development of this kind of work is, I think, really exciting because it takes different skill-sets and brings them together in new ways, and tells stories in new ways. It's about growing that work and growing audiences for that work – so the more it can spread the better.

Interview with Elly Green

Elly Green trained on the MFA in Theatre Directing at Birkbeck College and took her BA in English Literature and Drama at the University of East Anglia. She is a member of 'Forward Theatre Project' and a Senior Reader for the Royal Court Theatre. Her directing credits include: My Balloon Beats Your Astronaut *by Kerry Hood at the Tristan Bates Theatre,* About Tommy *by Thor Bjorn Krebs at Southwark Playhouse,* Copenhagen *by Michael Frayn at the Tabard Theatre,* Skylight *by David Hare at the Stephen Joseph Theatre, Scarborough,* The Beach *by Peter Asmussen at theatre503, and* The Zoo Story *by Edward Albee at the Etcetera. She was Staff Director at the National Theatre on* Oedipus, Mrs Afleck *and* Her Naked Skin *and has also assisted at the Almeida, the Royal and Derngate Northampton, Nottingham Playhouse and the Stephen Joseph Theatre. Her drama school work includes* Beyond Therapy *at Birmingham School of Acting,* Pillars of the Community *and* Summerfolk *at Northampton University and* Three Sisters *at Arts Ed. I asked her to outline the productions she had directed and produced on the London fringe in relation to their scale and their costs.*

The first show was *The Zoo Story* at the Etcetera Theatre in Camden with a cast of two. There was no designer and no one got paid anything, so the whole budget was about £500. The second show, *The Beach*, was at theatre503 in Battersea, with a cast of four, a designer, lighting designer and sound designer, and again, done on the basis that everyone involved really wanted to do the project and so were willing to work for free or expenses – for that the budget was under £1,000. The third show was *Copenhagen* at the Tabard Theatre in Chiswick, and the cast of three were paid £150 a week, all the creative team were paid a fee, and the cost of that was approximately £12,000 (including the theatre hire which was taken from the box office). The fourth show was *About Tommy* at Southwark Playhouse, for which the cast of three were paid £250 a week and all the creative team were paid fees, also the design budgets were higher than my previous productions, so that ended up costing £16,000.

That's a rising scale, obviously – was that largely due to the level of fees you were paying?

The costs were directly related to what I paid the actors and the fees for the design team, but basically the amount of time you're asking actors to give up – the rehearsal period and the length of run – is going to determine how big the 'fees budget' is. *Copenhagen* and *About Tommy* were both four-week runs. On the fringe, fees determine the budget: a rehearsal space can often be found very cheaply, or for nothing, and you can usually find a way of keeping the set and costume costs very low.

How much were you paying the designer and lighting designer for Copenhagen *and* About Tommy?

For *Copenhagen*, the design fee was £400, and the budget was £400 too. For *About Tommy*, the design fee and budget were £1,000 each, so £2,000 for design in total. For lighting, it was only about £500 for *About Tommy* and half that for *Copenhagen*.

What's really important is that if I hadn't offered those fees for both those productions I would not have got those actors or creative teams. There is no way any of the people in those two casts would have been able to do it. So I would have had different casts and different productions, and I believe they wouldn't have been as good. The same goes for the creative teams: there's no way I could have got Signe Beckmann to design *About Tommy* without a fee and reasonable budget. This is a production that had its genesis a couple of years before we put it on at Southwark, so I'd been working on it with a creative team for some time, who by then had established careers, so I had to give them something. They were still all working for far less than they usually would. Even if you don't have such a long lead-in process, the designer and lighting and sound designers are putting in work, and coming to meetings over a period of months before you actually start paying them, and even then you're paying them a flat fee no matter how much work is involved.

What's interesting about fringe theatre over the last five years is that the production values have just gone right up. So suddenly it's no longer acceptable to have someone with no lighting experience lighting your show at theatre503 or the Arcola – theatres which used to be 'fringe theatres'. The kind of scratch-it, do-it-yourself, 'everyone's doing it for the love of it' thing, presumably still exists in London, in another 'fringe to the fringe', in smaller theatres, but it doesn't exist in what we think of as fringe theatre any more because the production values have just gone through the roof. Perhaps it's because the funding cuts around the country have meant that really experienced professionals are doing jobs for less money, or for the love of it, or for favours: so you're seeing a creative team, for example at the Arcola, that is just amazing – it's a National Theatre-standard creative team.

Paying a fee is also a sign of commitment from you. It's you saying, 'I value your service. I think that we can afford to pay you this much and I'm absolutely guaranteeing you that you're going to walk away with that.' And I'm sure that my designers still went away from the productions using some of their fee to supplement the design – say, to get a slightly better piece of costume. They probably didn't submit a receipt, because from the start you've said, 'I think your services are worth something.'

What's the planning time scale for putting on a fringe production?

The reality is that many slots at fringe theatres come up quite at the last minute, and you have to make a decision whether to go for it or not. And you probably don't have the lead-in time that the scale of the production requires. That's just my experience, of course. So, for example, I was offered a spring slot at Southwark Playhouse in the late autumn – less than six months' preparation time. I could have said, 'This is a really great offer but I need more time to raise the funds and, if you really want the production at your space, you'll wait until we're ready and we've got the money to do it.' We may never have got that funding. Also the play was topical at the time, so I went for it. In retrospect, I could say, 'Oh well, I wish I'd waited another year,' but then that slot may not have come up again, or it may have only been offered to me because there was a gap in the programme.

So how did you fund, or finance, About Tommy and the other productions?

The short answer is I financed *About Tommy* myself, through savings and from paid work before and after the production. For both *Copenhagen* and *About Tommy* I applied for funding to the Arts Council through Grants for the Arts, and didn't get anything. For *About Tommy*, with the help of a co-producer, we applied to eight other funds, but had no success. We'd counted on getting a minimum of £5,000 funding, so before we even started we were £5,000 down.

I also wrote a lot of letters for both productions and we got a certain amount of funding from very generous actors and directors. We also raised some money for *About Tommy* through a fundraising gala at the People Show, for which the People Show lent us the space, and a well-known band played for free. We raised £2,000 from that. So we put on a show to put on a show.

As director and producer you're not paying yourself anything, so financially the price of the production is not just the cost of the production: it's the cost of the two months or more that you've put in without pay, and that is an unacknowledged cost of the production. And after the production is over there can be further loss: if you've promised people fees, you've got to back it up. I spent six months in a non-theatre job after *About Tommy* to ensure I paid people back for the show.

So, in answer to the question, 'How did you finance it?' the real answer is we financed it on a wish. We financed it on the anticipation of money to come from the ticket office: and when that money doesn't come you still have to pay the fees you promised. If you've promised a profit-share at the beginning, as is quite standard in a fringe, then you just don't pay anyone.

What's the financial arrangement with fringe theatres – do you simply hire them, or do you and the theatre share the financial risk?

It varies. But the theatres protect themselves, as of course they have to, against financial risk. Usually there is a hire fee and when the ticket-office income exceeds the hire fee, then you and the theatre split the income. The split can vary but often it is 50 per cent each or 60 per cent to you and 40 per cent to the theatre. At the Etcetera we simply paid the theatre £500 a week and we took the ticket office. At theatre503 it was an Edinburgh-period summer slot, so at that time we got a simple box-office split. At the Tabard we had a hire fee taken out of our box-office, but retained remaining box-office, and at Southwark Playhouse we had to pay a deposit upfront towards a hire fee for each week, the remainder of which came out of box-office, then – in theory – we would have split any further ticket income. So, for example, the deposit at the Southwark was £2,300 and the weekly hire fee was £2,000, and you only have to find the deposit money upfront: the rest of the hire fee should come out of the ticket office. But in the event that you don't make any profit, it means a four-week run will cost you £8,000 plus VAT before you've paid anyone or spent any production or marketing budget.

With both *Copenhagen* and *About Tommy* we created a budget where the ticket revenue was going to cover all our costs – we thought – but we overestimated the audience. And time and time again in fringe theatre that's what enthusiastic directors and producers – and director/producers – do, particularly because they don't take into account the ticket offers that they will have to make.

With Southwark, it was really bad maths on my part, because of the airline system of ticket pricing. There will be, say, three ticket price bands: £8, £12 and £20, and the further you book in advance the more likely you are to get an £8 ticket, but when the allocation for that band is sold, the tickets go up to £12, and so on. But actually, if you don't sell a certain number of tickets, you're never going to reach the next price band.

So, if you only get 10 per cent audience attendance, instead of the 40 per cent that you estimated, not only are you going to not make any money, but you're going to get a bill at the end – because the ticket-office income hasn't covered the weekly hire fee. And that's what happened. That production was only meant to cost £12,000 and it cost £16,000, because of the bill. Even though we made budgets and spreadsheets and we thought we'd got all the percentages right, we hadn't taken into account what happens with the airline system or what happens when you give away free or reduced-price tickets because you're trying to get people in. It's really important to get an accountant or somebody with an experienced business brain to check your budgets.

I would have thought that if you put on a production at a large fringe theatre, like Arcola One, and paid the Equity fringe minimum of £250 and paid the creatives a decent fee, I'd be surprised if anyone could do it for less than £25,000, and five years ago fringe theatre production really wasn't that kind of beast. I've heard some fringe theatres ask you for evidence that you can afford a £10,000 budget before they'll let you hire the theatre.

So, as an emerging director I think it's about seeking out new spots, because although some of these theatres will provide you with a certain amount of marketing, unless they're co-producing the show they're never going to have the investment in the production that means they're going to go the extra mile. So you may as well find a space that is less well known and pump the money that you're not pumping into venue hire into the publicity.

Did you work with a producer on these productions, or did you produce them yourself?

I produced the show at the Etcetera with some friends. For *The Beach* I had a co-producer; I produced *Copenhagen* at the Tabard myself; and had two co-producers on board for *About Tommy* at Southwark.

How do you produce when, as the director, you're actually in the rehearsal room for the weeks leading up to the production?

You just get on the mobile every lunch and tea break you've got, and when you get home you're on your laptop until very late. When you're in rehearsal, the rehearsals get you through because you're part of a process you believe in, and you believe in it so much that you are willing to give up every other part of your life in order to do it. I think that psychologically it's damaging to be a producer and a director at the same time: you're juggling, your mind is on different things, and I think it's impossible not to let that into the room. I can't see how anyone could leave those stresses completely outside. And it means that as a director I will not be able to spend as much time on things that I'd like to outside the room. I was really lucky on the show at Southwark because my co-producer took on so much of that for me and, when I went into the rehearsal room, I was able to go into that bubble.

When you were self-producing, did you do all the marketing, press and publicity yourself? With a co-producer, did he or she take on those roles?

With the Tabard show I did a lot of it myself but the general manager at the time was also an invaluable help, as were many of my friends in helping me with images etc. We flyered extensively around the venue, at the tube station and residentially: much of that was just me on foot.

I think that a criticism of the fringe is that people end up producing theatre that is only seen by people working in theatre and by their friends and family, and that they're not actually reaching the public. When you select your venue, you need to find out what their connections are with their local community and if they have a returning public that is affiliated with the theatre, who may then come to your production.

But I think the real secret is collaboration with other theatres so that you're either flyering outside their theatre or you're getting your credit on the bottom of their flyers or e-flyers. Theatre503, the Gate, the Arcola, the Tricycle, the Finborough and theatres of that scale are all advertising each other's shows: that's where e-marketing really works.

Depending on the scale of the production, the producer is going to take care of all the marketing and publicity, whether they outsource it to somebody else or not. With the Southwark show we had a co-producer on board who was working on a profit-share basis, and who took over contacting the press. This made such a difference for me. I think it's really important that, as a director, you're not contacting the press personally.

The other problem with reaching the theatregoing public is the fight for the audience. Because you can go to the National Theatre for £12 and the Royal Court for £1 it's very hard to get people into fringe theatres. The reduction in prices and the offers that you can get at mainstream theatres in London at the moment mean that selling people a piece of fringe theatre, especially by an unknown writer, or with an unknown director, or, heaven forbid, both, is going to be very hard to sell.

How easy, and how important, is it to get the leading critics in to fringe shows?

Firstly, you're not going to get a review if you do anything shorter than three weeks. It really helps to sell tickets if you can get reviewers in early, to create some hype around the production: for example, I got a five-star review in *Time Out* for *Copenhagen* on the Tuesday of the last week, which really made a difference in audience attendance but, while as a director I was happy, speaking as a producer it came too late. It can be difficult to get the main reviewers in unless you have a name in the cast, or you have built up connections with the reviewers beforehand.

But reviewing is changing now because of blogging and internet reviews, so making connections with people who write blogs and internet reviews can be as important for publicity purposes as getting the broadsheet critics in. It's interesting that we place such importance on reviews, because in my experience it's not that which gets you jobs: in that sense, it's more important to get other directors and artistic directors to see your work.

Was that a prime reason for producing and directing these shows: so that you could invite other practitioners to see your work?

As a director and a producer, the prime reason you put on work on the London fringe is because you're passionate about putting on that play: you have to be. But as an emerging director you're also trying to get your work seen, and I had lots of people who had said, 'Oh well, we'd like to consider you for this but we really need to see your work,' so you have to think, 'Right, I'm just going to put something on,' even if it means I've got to work for a few months to pay it off. And, actually, because of *Copenhagen* I got an interview at the National Theatre and got nine months of paid work as an assistant director there, and that was the job that I really wanted as the next step for me, so the financial and other stresses for that production were absolutely compensated for by the fact that I managed to get the experience at the National.

But I also think, karmically, every time you commit yourself, not just financially, but emotionally, personally and professionally to a project, it will pay off in the long run. At some point I believe that someone who saw *About Tommy* will say, 'Oh yeah, she can actually do it, so we can trust her with this job, because I saw that production of hers.' The experience in itself is worth it and you never know how it might pay off.

Interview with Andrew McKinnon

Andrew McKinnon is an experienced professional theatre-maker, writer and teacher and currently Programme Director for the Birkbeck MA in Creative Producing. He is a former Artistic Director of York Theatre Royal, Northern Stage, Newcastle, and Perth Theatre; and Associate Director of Nottingham Playhouse. He has written several degree courses, including Drama Centre BA Acting and Birkbeck MFA Theatre Directing, and has been a consultant to many arts organisations. He was a co-founder of the Arches New Directors Awards 2000 and mentored award winners for several years. In 2006 and 2007 he was a mentor on Scottish Arts Council's Creative Producer project. He was involved with Edinburgh International Festival's Insights programme for a decade, conducting public interviews with artists and directors including Bogart, Breth, Bieito, Leon, Purcarete and Stein. He has considerable experience of international projects, and mentoring and developing professional theatre-makers and producers in the UK, Holland, Germany, Greece and Egypt. He continues to make theatre (devised and text-based) with his company 'wayward scot'.

Could you define what is commonly meant by a 'creative producer'?

The term itself is quite contentious because there are a lot of producers who think including the word 'creative' is some kind of insult to them, because they say that everybody who is a producer is a creative producer. Many commercial producers, particularly in mainstream theatre, take that binding together of the two functions for granted, because part of their job is to select directors, select designers in conjunction with directors and so on.

But there's a kind of snobbery about the commercial model. The production of all theatre until the war was all broadly speaking commercially based, of course, with the exception of the regional reps and the Old Vic and Sadler's Wells, although even those enterprises were largely driven by what we might now call creative producers – Lilian Baylis, Barry Jackson, Terence Gray and so on. But when we're talking about producers who were working in the 1920s – to take Cochran as an obvious example, he produced commercial revues and large-scale musicals and so on; but he also took a chance on a Sean O'Casey play no one else would touch. He was a commercial producer; but he was a producer who was exercising exactly the same skills and range of creative inputs as any current creative producers are today. It's just that the funding of these roles has tended to build a wall between them.

Tate Wilkinson, who was the eighteenth-century manager of the York Theatre Royal and who managed the whole of that northern touring circuit, was called a 'manager'; but in effect he was a creative producer, in that he put together a group of creative people. He had a wonderful phrase: 'a manager is a carpenter of genius'. He didn't mean a carpenter who is a genius. He meant a carpenter of the geniuses of other people.

Where there is a kind of snobbish differentiation between, say, a rather traditional murder mystery, as opposed to a brilliant or shocking play by a new writer, it's all only about the piece, the play - the topic and the subject matter. It's got absolutely nothing at all to do with the work of producing. That's one of the hardest things to recognise - for people who have been brought up purely in a funded mentality. Of course there are a few people who float easily between the two sectors, but not very many.

If you are a commercial producer and you want to raise £750,000 to do a big tour, that money - except on the very rarest of occasions - doesn't just fall out of the sky. It has to be argued for, to be sought out: you have to go through hoops for it. And that's a description of the funding process - you have to argue for it. It's exactly the same thing. They are different hoops, but the producing processes directly reflect one another.

The term 'creative producer' was mainly coined out of a need by Arts Council England to classify specific people who were not just enablers or managers but who were actively involved in the creation of either new work or festivals or other pieces of work, and who were sitting at the table from the beginning of the creative process. Putting in the word 'creative' was a red rag to a bull in some ways, but it did allow funders and funding bodies to identify that specific role; and so when ACE started to see it as their job to fund these people, they used 'creative producer' as a way of differentiating them from managers.

It was part of the seemingly eternal struggle between funding bodies and the profession to come up with a way of resolving who should be in charge - of a theatre, an organisation, a performance company, or a funding application. Should it be the artist? Should it be the administrator? After artists and artistic directors had been in charge for quite a long time in theatre, they started to become 'seen with suspicion' by funding bodies – we're taking about the late 1980s and 1990s here – so they tended to be replaced by what people called 'hard-headed' businessmen and women, otherwise known as general managers or chief executives.

Creative producers were being developed in the 1990s by the arts funding bodies partly relieving the artist of some of the responsibility, but mainly to bring about a wider view of the work. In a sense the creative producer is the third point of a triangular relationship – producer–work–audience. So there is a feeling that the creative producer has a foot in both camps: in the camp of the creative process and the camp of the receivers, audience and participants. They are mediating between the creative work and the audience; and there have been a number of creative producers who have been able to do that very successfully. But quite a lot of those people are also programmers: programmers of festivals, programmers of extended events, or sometimes of buildings. When, a few years ago, ACE started to fund bursaries specifically for creative producers and pushed towards their big publication called *The Producers: Alchemists of the Imagination*, there was a specifically created funding niche acknowledging the term. And although quite a lot of these people talk about producers rather than creative producers still, they don't necessarily quite equate the two.

The other thing that became very significant was the spread of large-scale outdoor work and site-specific work, which requires a different kind of sensibility in the producer; and where there is more of a necessity for the producer to interact with the creative team, in terms of things like health and safety – and also simple practicality, because you're not working within a closed system like a theatre. If you're putting something in a park, then you almost always have to start from scratch. And there was quite a lot of resistance – there still is – to that kind of setting aside of the creative producer as a separate individual; reaction against it from creative teams, and particularly from directors, who thought that they were muscling in on their patch.

And it has been true that in certain theatres artistic directors have been replaced by producers or creative producers.

Yes. Though that change is almost always decided upon – or so they *say* – in order to give the artists, the directors, more freedom. But if you look at the way David Aukin, say, ran Hampstead Theatre in the 1980s, in a sense he was working like a commercial producer. The crucial moment in the funded sphere was when he went to run the Leicester Haymarket and was able to demonstrate that a very good producer could commercially produce things that were aimed at the West End, but could equally run a season of new work in the studio and develop new writers.

The situation now is complicated by the fact that, having created this category of crucial people in theatre and performance, the Arts Councils have largely shied away from fully acknowledging them within funding structures. So there is currently only rather patchy funding for developing producers. East Midlands Arts ran a scheme recently; Creative Scotland funds training schemes via the Federation of Scottish Theatre; and of course the original push from ACE encouraged people like Bill Gee and David Micklem – but that ACE impetus happened and then it stopped.

It seems to me that the consolidation of training and acknowledging the creative producer is at the point now that twenty years ago the training of directors had reached. The circle that was closed with the establishment of good director training is yet to be closed with creative producers. You know the bottleneck that all the young directors feel – about trying to get through into the next stage – it's exactly the same for young producers.

It's partly to do with the fact that a lot of people don't know what a creative producer does. Significantly, a lot of young directors think of producers as being merely fundraising functionaries, and not being in any way involved with the creative material. Probably two or three times a week I get appeals mostly from young directors who are 'looking for producers'. A very few genuinely are looking for producers; but most of them are looking for fundraisers who will raise money but not necessarily have any point of contact with the work. Some people will always work like that. But the duties of a creative producer require that person to be intimately associated with the creation of the work – not necessarily to be in charge of it, but to have a seat by right at the table, to allow creative exchange with the other members of the team. It's that kind of collaborative give-and-take that brings out the best in the relationship.

Sometimes – perhaps even quite often – creative producers think of the idea themselves. They can't *do* it. But they can *think* of it. This is very common for commercial producers of course – though several of them have been and indeed still are directors.

So, to be really schematic: in an old-style conventional, commercial set-up, one might expect the producer not only to be in charge of the financial resources but actually to lead the project, appoint the director and in some cases appoint the rest of the creative team, like the designer.

That's very common – usually in conjunction with the director, but not always. If you look at the majority of commercial tours that are being done around the larger number-one houses, most of those are done on the impetus of the producer, who then engages the director – if they're starting from scratch. It is different if they're being taken up from publicly subsidised houses like Birmingham or Nottingham – and here the recent tour of *The History Boys* is a very good example. It opened at the West Yorkshire Playhouse and then did a commercial tour. But nobody's saying that the play's director had no hand in its success, and of course it was programmed by the artistic director of the theatre.

So at the commercial level the producer is the head of the triangle. At the other end of the spectrum, there is a danger of directors thinking of producers, as you say, as just being functionaries, who will raise funds and sort out the marketing. But in fact, a creative producer is somebody in the middle, who is an equal and a collaborator.

It's not that uncommon for experienced directors to engage purely administrative producers who simply do all the jobs. It's relatively unusual for young or recently trained directors to be able to do that.

The situation's made slightly more complex by the expected reductions in Grants for the Arts and funding generally. So the whole funding situation for any given project is a lot more complex than it used to be. It's not just a question now of a director originating a project and filling in a Grants for the Arts application and expecting the cheque to arrive. Is that another impetus or reason for there being a greater involvement with creative producers?

It has become progressively more difficult to get anything other than the barest research and development grant without a really substantial amount of input from somebody who understands how to raise funds. But it's not so much to do with being a 'fundraiser'. It's more to do with understanding the mind-set of the funder and being able to translate the work into a form that will convince them.

And, very often, understanding the mind-set of the funder can be a very demanding thing for a young director – or for any director. Because to get funding these directors have to justify something to other people that they have already fully justified to themselves. Why they need the assistance of a producer, generally speaking, is so that the producer can take on the role of justifying it to other people, and the director can get on with the work. There are some very good directors who can write very good applications. And quite a lot of them who can't. Their main constraint is time.

It is necessary to learn how to ask for the funding in a way that doesn't expect it as a *right*. And one of the difficulties is that young directors very often think, 'I'm very good and therefore my project should be supported.' But many don't know how to construct the appeal or the application to the funding body.

I think it's asking a great deal of a creative person or team both to make creative work, with all the complications that generates today, and at the same time be completely aware of the wider context. The biggest job that producers have to do is to see where that context, that ecology, is weak or strong and where there's a gap to be filled.

But if directors have strongly evolved and strongly created their project without any input from a producer, they open themselves more to potential producers turning them down, saying, 'Well, this sounds great but I can't have any input into it, because it's all already there.' And then the only course for that director is to employ fundraisers, and good fundraisers are very expensive.

So, just as you wouldn't fully conceive a production without involving a designer – you wouldn't design it yourself and then get a designer – the same is true of a creative producer.

That's a very good way of putting it.

Are there forums and networks through which directors might contact creative producers and propose projects?

My experience in recent years is that the easiest and most productive way of meeting producers is to look for them within the audience and within the structures of the kind of work that you want to do. So if, for example, you're interested in the mime and physical theatre area and you don't go to see any of the performances in London at the international mime and physical theatre festival, you're passing up a huge opportunity to encounter people.

Very often one chance experience leads to another. People will encounter one another, and there will be knock-on effects and people will say, 'Well, I can't do it, but you might think about X,' and so on. Directors should always bear in mind that producers are looking in the same direction as they are. Producers want directors. Directors want producers. So it's like two sets of lonely hearts trying to get together.

Often producers are more aggressive hunters than directors. Directors often need to make themselves more visible. Devoted and Disgruntled is a very good example of an assembly of artistic and creative people which is set up with one set of aims – to discuss the present state of the theatre – yet it has another effect, which is to pull together lots of young people who listen to each other and think, 'Well, that sounds interesting . . .' The informality of these events can often bring members of a team together.

Ironically, the more specialised the form, the easier it is to find people who are interested in it. 'Street arts' is an obvious example. All right, you're not going to meet every single person at a National Association of Street Artists meeting, but if you have an interest in making work in the street, sooner or later you'll become involved with some of their meetings and introductions to producers will follow.

I see the Arts Council's work with creative producers as being a job half done – as unfinished business. It seems to me that they've gone a long way to creating this role, or developing this role and making it necessary, or essential, but they haven't found a way of funding its development – funding its professional maturation.

For example, a key aspect of the work of the creative producer is being able to go and see a lot of work. Now of course, if you're living in London, and working in conventional theatre, that's really not terribly difficult. It might be quite expensive, but it's not difficult. But if you're interested in large-scale outdoor work, you have to go to France, Germany or Holland, for example. Until there is funding or support in place to allow these kinds of professional development, I think the role of the creative producer will always have a sort of unfinished air about it – in terms not of the job they do, but in terms of how it could be developed. It needs an overview to pull it together, an informed awareness of what is actually happening.

There are some theatres that particularly support producers. BAC has an almost evangelising role, partly because the artistic directors David Jubb and David Micklem are themselves experienced and very good producers; and partly because they are training up a core of young producers, specialising sometimes in particular kinds of performance, but none the less with skills that can be applied more generally. The Young Vic does fantastic work; and the Old Vic has done some very good work with new producers. But the number of those looking for opportunities is of course far greater than any of these institutions can ever service.

Practical exercises

Exercise one

Using the interview with Elly Green as a starting point, take the figures that she mentions for the payment of fees to actors and designers and the weekly theatre hire to work out a budget for a fringe production. Perhaps envisage a production with four actors with a three-week rehearsal period and a three-week playing period. Elly Green mentions several scales of payments for fees and theatre hires, and you may firstly wish to create a budget for a profit-share model with modest creative fees and production budgets at a smaller fringe venue; and then create a budget paying the Equity fringe minimum of £250, the higher creative fees and budgets and a larger theatre-hire fee. Then consider other items of expenditure and create budget headings for them: for example, £300 a week for rehearsal rooms; £250 for a website; £250 for flyer design and £165 for printing. You may also wish to consider workshop or making space, transport of the set and get-out costs, as well as budgets for the set, costumes, lighting, sound and other equipment hires and writer royalty payments.

Then go to the websites of some of the smaller and larger fringe venues mentioned and find out their usual full and discount ticket prices and seating capacities. Choose a figure between the full and discount ticket price to arrive at a guestimate for the ticket yield – the average amount all the tickets will sell for. If you have a three-week run and six performances a week, you will have eighteen performances: then multiply the ticket yield by the number of seats, then by the number of performances, to work out how much you would take in ticket sales at 100 per cent, then at 80 per cent, 60 per cent and 40 per cent. For the purpose of this exercise do not factor in ticket handling fees, VAT, or other deductions the venue may make to the total box-office income in addition to the weekly hire costs, in order to get a rough overall figure for total box-office income at these different attendance levels. At what percentage of attendance will you match your costs for the production?

This is not a full budgeting exercise, and, as mentioned in the chapter, you are advised to get expert help with a budget before committing to a project, but very quickly this exercise can tell you if you cannot recoup your costs at even 100 per cent, or only at an unfeasibly high attendance level, in which case you may wish to reduce your costs; seek another, cheaper venue (but possibly with fewer seats and lower ticket prices); or look for additional funding to bridge the gap. This is not a full budgeting exercise but it is a useful and quick feasibility study.

Exercise two

Envisage a fictional theatre company and first project. Follow the weblink to ACE's Grants for the Arts pages and fill out a Grants for the Arts application for your company. (This does not mean you have to submit it!) As mentioned in the chapter there is a lot of very useful information on the Grants for the Arts web pages and the form itself asks a number of very useful questions about your notional company's size, status, previous activities, artistic aims, and about the individual project for which you are applying for funding. It also asks you to fill out a basic and clear budget for the activity, so the form itself offers useful guidance for planning any project, whether you are seeking funding or not. In addition to this, as was also mentioned earlier, in order to have a reasonable chance of securing funding your project will have to address one or more of the Grants for the Arts' six criteria for funding, and it may be an activity within its four areas of priority. Reading the guidance notes and thinking of your project in terms of the six criteria and four priorities is a useful exercise in matching your project to a funder's priorities. Other funders will have different priorities, but the Grants for the Arts application offers a useful template for writing funding applications. It is worth practising making such applications before you have actually to submit one, as they are an art form in their own right.

On a technical note, in order to gain access to a Grants for the Arts application form you do have to register and log in to fill in the form online, but firstly you can save your draft application at any point and come back to it (although it will eventually time out), or if you select the option to print the application it will then allow you to download a PDF of the application form (before and without having to actually print it), so you can study the form on your computer without having to have live access to the ACE site.

Weblist

Arts and business	artsandbusiness.org.uk
Arts Council England	www.artscouncil.org.uk
Arts Council of Northern Ireland	www.artscouncil-ni.org
Arts Council of Wales	www.artswales.org.uk
Awards for All	www.awardsforall.org.uk
BAC (Battersea Arts Centre)	www.bac.org.uk
BECTU	www.bectu.org.uk/home
The Big Lottery Fund	www.biglotteryfund.org.uk
British Academy of Dramatic Combat	www.badc.co.uk/home
Business Link	www.businesslink.gov.uk/bdotg/action/home
Calouste Gulbenkian Foundation UK	www.gulbenkian.org.uk
Charity Commission	www.charity-commission.gov.uk
Clore Duffield Foundation	www.cloreduffield.org.uk
Companygiving.org.uk	www.companygiving.org.uk
Creative Scotland	www.creativescotland.com
Department of Culture, Media and Sport	www.culture.gov.uk
Directors Guild of Great Britain	www.dggb.org
Directory of Social Change	www.dsc.org.uk/Home
Equity	www.equity.org.uk
Esmée Fairbairn Foundation	www.esmeefairbairn.org.uk
Etcetera Theatre	www.etceteratheatre.com
Federation of Scottish Theatre	www.scottishtheatres.com
Foyle Foundation	www.foylefoundation.org.uk
Funderfinder	www.funderfinder.org.uk

Governmentfunding.org.uk	www.governmentfunding.org.uk
Grantsforindividuals.org.uk	www.grantsforindividuals.org.uk
Grants for the Arts	www.artscouncil.org.uk/funding/grants-arts
Ideas Fund	www.ideastap.com/ideasfund
Independent Theatre Council	www.itc-arts.org
Musicians Union	www.musiciansunion.org.uk
National Association of Street Artists	www.nasauk.org
The Official London Theatre Guide	www.officiallondontheatre.co.uk
Paul Hamlyn Foundation	www.phf.org.uk
The Society of London Theatre (SOLT)	www.solt.co.uk
Southwark Playhouse	southwarkplayhouse.co.uk
Stage One	www.solt.co.uk/stageone.html
Tabard Theatre	www.tabardweb.co.uk
theatre503	www.theatre503.com
Theatrical Management Association	www.tmauk.org
Trustfunding.org.uk	www.trustfunding.org.uk
Writers' Guild of Great Britain	www.writersguild.org.uk

Bibliography

Seabright, James, *So You Want to be a Theatre Producer?* London: Nick Hern Books, 2010.

Tyndall, Kate, *The Producers: Alchemists of the Impossible.* London: Arts Council England and the Jerwood Charitable Foundation, 2007.

6 The director and the production

So far we have explored the director's relationship with the actor, from the point of view of acting methodologies; the director's various kinds of relationships with authors and the text; the development of a relationship with designers; and the organisational and financial contexts of making a production. In this chapter we will be drawing these elements together and discussing the director's role in the whole production process from the beginning of planning, through pre-rehearsal planning – including casting, design and production meetings, marketing and education meetings, and patterns and strategies for shaping a rehearsal period – to the technical rehearsals, previews and press night, and finally maintaining the production during the run. In addition to relationships with the actors, author and designers, those with other creatives will be explored: for example, musical directors, choreographers, fight directors, dialect coaches, and the production staff and marketing and education departments.

As the theatre director Peter Cheeseman often said, the most valuable resource in theatre is time. The production process will be explored along a timeline from the first decision to produce the play to the end of the run. For the purposes of discussion it will be assumed that you, the director, have been asked to direct a production at a producing theatre, whether that be at a funded producing theatre where there is an organisational infrastructure with staff to support the production, or at a fringe theatre where you and the producer have assembled the funding and production resources to support the core creative team and the production. This is so that we can discuss how the director relates to key collaborators and resources without straying into those areas which might also be the role of a producer.

Eighteen months to a year before press night

In general, the larger the theatre, the longer the planning cycle. Opera companies often contract a director and designer two years before the production and can expect the design a full year beforehand. A regional producing theatre may have a large season brochure to send to its mailing list, and if there are two brochures a year the play decision deadline for the autumn brochure might be May, and for the spring brochure October; this means that programming decisions for the autumn season will begin around the previous Christmas, or in the New Year, and decisions for the spring season will be made in the previous spring and summer.

Fringe theatres may have shorter planning periods but they are still likely to be programmed six to nine months in advance. So if you wish to pitch an idea to a producing theatre it might be wise to consider a fifteen-month cycle from the first meeting to the production. Of course, not all such cycles go to plan and it might be that a production that was planned does not take place, in which case a theatre might be looking for the perfect replacement at much shorter notice, but this is highly unlikely to be less than six months. Eighteen months is a fairly luxurious time scale in many cases, but this allows the different stages to be clearly marked out.

Rights and writers' agents

As mentioned in Chapter Three, if the writer of the play you are directing is living, or has died within the past seventy years, the work will be in copyright and you, or the theatre, will have to identify the writer's agent and approach the agent for the performing rights. If you search for the writer on the web you will probably find out who their agent is through one of a number of playwright databases, such as doolee.com, or through the agent's website. Some of the larger agencies, such as United Agents, have details of all their clients with biographical details about the writer, which member of their team handles that writer, and how to contact them. If the agent cannot be found through a web search it is possible to email or phone the play publishers and bookshop, Samuel French (aka French's), who, as well as publishing plays, handle the amateur rights for most published plays. However, if you ask for their professional rights department, they will be able to tell you the writer's agent.

Phone or email the agent with the name of the company, the venue, or venues, and dates, and they will quickly tell you if (and possibly why) the rights are not available. It might be that another company has the rights to produce the play in the near future, or that a theatre has an option on a play for a given amount of time, which means that no other theatre will be given the rights while that option lasts, which might be more than a year. If the rights are technically available and your company is not known to the agent, the agent might ask for more details about the production and who is involved in it. It might be that the agent has to contact the writer to get their approval. There are fairly standard rights contracts which will include conditions about how the writer's name and the play's title appear on the publicity, and clauses about not making alterations to, or omissions from, the approved version of the play.

There are variations in what agents will charge for the royalties, but a standard rate is between 8 and 10 per cent of the gross ticket-office receipts – so the agent will need to see properly produced reports on ticket sales over the whole run. If the theatre company is new, or unknown to the agent, the agent may ask for an advance payment against royalties, based on the projected audience size, to secure the rights. If the venue is small and the ticket-office income is likely to be low, the agent might ask for a minimum payment for each performance against percentage royalties. For example, the agent might want a minimum payment of £60 per performance or 10 per cent of the ticket-office receipts, whichever is the greater. If you are being employed by a theatre, the theatre will usually deal with the agent and getting the rights.

The process of commissioning a new play obviously makes the planning cycle much longer. A standard contract for a new commission might give the writer between six and nine months to produce the first draft, then another month to respond to the theatre's notes from the first draft. On receipt of the final play the theatre then has approximately ninety days in which to decide whether to produce the play. If this option to produce is not taken up the theatre may pay more to extend the option, or the rights will revert to the author and the play can be offered elsewhere. So it can take two years from commission to production of a new play. For a large regional theatre or a new writing venue the size of, say, Hampstead Theatre, the writer will receive approximately £6,500.

Rates of pay

The payment rates for all those involved in a production will vary according to the size, or agreed scale, of the theatre. The union Equity negotiates payment rates for theatres belonging to the Independent Theatre Council, which represents over 600 small- and medium-scale companies, often not building-based, and for theatres belonging to the Theatrical Management Association, which represents mainly building-based theatres. Equity also negotiates pay rates with commercial producers. There is no formal negotiation between Equity and fringe theatres or companies which do not belong to these organisations, but there is an informal fringe scale which is widely observed, and which currently offers actors £250 a week. The current ITC actors' minimum is £400 a week.

Although some of these pay rates are only accessible to members, there are current rates of pay for actors, directors, writers, designers, fight directors and choreographers on the Equity website. The Directors Guild of Great Britain also offers advice to its members about rates and standard contracts for directors. If you, as a director, are offered a contract by a company which is not a member of one of the recognised theatre bodies, it is worth getting your contract vetted by someone knowledgeable before you sign it. Membership of Equity or the DGGB will provide you with this advice.

Resident and freelance directors

If you are resident at a theatre, as assistant or associate director, you may well have been involved in the whole programming of the season of work, including the co-productions, touring productions and one-night events, as well as those the theatre will produce in-house. You may also attend regular senior management meetings and marketing meetings, in which case you will be involved in the budgeting and marketing of the production you are directing from the moment it is confirmed. You may also begin to talk to the education, outreach and/or continuous learning departments about information and events which will be connected to the production. The staff in this department will wish to discuss particular groups and age ranges for which additional activities are most appropriate and to begin putting information for teachers and target groups on the website. The range of activities will also be discussed: workshops in schools, workshops in the theatre before or after the performances, education packs with curriculum-related activities for teachers to lead. Whether or not you are asked to devise, structure or lead such activities, you will be expected to know enough about your production to offer indications of how it might connect with different groups and what it might look like or contain which are not apparent from reading the play. The marketing department might also be looking for the same type of information about how your production will be distinctive from a simple reading of the play, and may wish to discuss the target audience, distinctive marketing strategies, and early ideas for an image for the production. You may be asked to write a 'blurb' for the brochure and website, or at least to comment on all the above.

At this stage it is not necessary for a director to know everything about the play prior to production, but it is necessary to know enough about what your production might be like in order to convey your ideas to others. There can be an alarmingly short period of time between the play being chosen and announced to other members of staff and your colleagues wanting to have meetings about it. The other person whom you might want to meet quickly is the production manager, with whom it is worth having an early meeting to discuss the ideas for the production in principle and to get a rough idea of the resources available, both in the budget and in the theatre's stock and equipment. Although you don't want to close down the possibilities that will arise from your relationship with the designers, there is no point in spending hours designing a play on a revolve if that would swallow the entire production budget.

If your production is going to require a musical director, a fight director, choreographer or movement or dialect expert, it may have been factored into the production's budget at the point at which the play was confirmed by the artistic director, and it may also have a production budget assigned to it.

As a resident director you may also have a close working knowledge of stage designers, lighting designers and other collaborators whose work you have seen and who know how the theatre works and what is and is not possible in the space you are working in. If there is a resident lighting designer or sound designer, for example, you may be able to work with them at a much earlier stage, and much more frequently, than you could with a freelance designer. There is a set of choices to be made between working with collaborators who know the theatre well – designers who have good, established working relationships with the theatre's staff and know how to make the most of its resources – and working with new designers who can bring fresh approaches and ideas and may produce a kind of work as yet untried in that theatre.

As a freelance director your relationship with the theatre might be much more distant, and a number of decisions about the marketing, production-related activities, and the setting of a budget will probably be taken by the full-time members of staff. Simply because you might be working on another project and distant from the theatre, any consultation or involvement might be limited to emails and phone calls in the first three or four months after the play has been programmed. There is also a similar, but different set of choices about collaborators to be made. You may have a designer in mind with whom you would really like to work, but the theatre might also have a designer they are keen to work with again.

The chief electrician may also light half the shows in a season and be suggested to you as your lighting designer. If the theatre really wants you to work with a particular collaborator, the artistic director will usually bring this up at the point at which you both decide you are the director of the play, but it is worth discussing at a very early stage those members of the creative team the theatre imagines will be theatre staff, those which are the theatre's strong preferences, and those which will be chosen by you alone. If you don't know them, it might be that you agree to meet with the theatre's suggested designer or choreographer to see how you get on before a final decision is made. Another option is that you and the artistic director pool suggestions and you, or both of you, meet several possible people. If the theatre has already budgeted for the expected creative team and there is a fight director who lives in the same town, but you really want one you have worked with before who lives 200 miles away, it may have an impact on other areas of the production budget, or on how many fight calls can be afforded.

This is the point at which artistic and financial decisions really begin to impact on each other and the production, and although the factors that influence your decisions might be slightly different for a production at a large producing theatre or a small fringe theatre, the nature of the choices and decisions, and their implications for the rest of the production, will be very similar.

Six months before press night

By now the main images and publicity material will have been produced and tickets may already be on sale. Other activities and workshops around the production will have been planned, and information circulated about them. You may have the set designer, lighting designer, sound and other designers on board and begun meetings. As was mentioned in Chapter Four, there is no set number of meetings that a designer and director may have before a white-card meeting, which is usually two or three months before the rehearsal period begins, but, if the director and the designer live far apart there may be a finite number of meetings for which the theatre is willing to pay expenses. The theatre will usually have a number in mind and this might be three or four meetings, in which case it is worth planning for each meeting to be a whole morning or afternoon to make it worthwhile. If it is possible for director and designer to meet without incurring costs there is no problem with more meetings, but both will probably have other projects and commitments, and planning four or five meetings might focus the process and keep the momentum going. As also mentioned, lighting designers tend to have several projects at the same time, and get paid less, so it is common for the lighting designer to come to only one of these meetings, or not to see the design until the white-card meeting: the interview with lighting designer Tony Simpson referred to this less-than-perfect situation.

The period between six and four months before press night is also the time to find the other members of the creative team who, depending on the demands of the play, may include: other designers, such as sound and film and projection; a casting director; a musical director (often called the MD) and/or composer; a fight director; a choreographer; a dialect expert; a movement expert; an aerialist; any other skills specialist. At the point of approaching these people to work on the production they will need to know not only what the project is, and to read the play, but also to have an idea of how much of their time will be required. This is a triangular calculation based on: what has been budgeted for their time and what their fee levels are, or what can be afforded, if there is flexibility in the budget; how long the overall rehearsal period is; and how much time the specialist estimates it will take to teach the skills.

Varying lengths of rehearsal period are discussed below, but if, as is common, there are only two weeks' rehearsals for a panto but there are ten songs to choreograph, there may not be time to choreograph all the songs to the same level of complexity, so you may have to nominate five that have detailed choreography and five which have quicker-to-teach choreography, and try to get them all learnt on one day, then tightened and polished on a second day, and then set on stage in one session in the tech. Fight time can be calculated with the fight director, but as there is a higher level of risk involved, there are finer judgements to be made about the complexity of a fight and how long there is to teach it to the point where it is absolutely safe: a very rough calculation of how long it takes to teach a moderately detailed fight might be one hour's rehearsal time for every minute of action, with additional time at the tech.

Each specialist will need a brief about how many actors are involved, what the set will look like and the story of the song or fight. To take another example from *Macbeth*, how much information would a fight director need to prepare for the killing of Banquo? How many conspir-ators are there? Is there a relationship of competence and incompetence between the conspirators? What weapons will be used – short daggers, broadswords or others? Although the dialogue suggests a certain number of events and cuts, the fight could last between ten seconds and more than a minute, so – for how long? And how much resistance does Banquo put up? Is there any other information about the production which might affect the story of the fight? Although a number of these questions can be discussed at the first fight call, the more information the fight director has, the better he or she can prepare, and not waste time over it at the first fight call – and the weapons may have to be decided on and hired in order to be there for that call. A final note on fight directors is that, as there are so many health and safety issues concerning fights, it is highly advisable only to work with fight directors who are on the Equity Register, who have been trained to consider the health and safety issues raised by fights in a theatre.

At a later stage, approximately one month before rehearsals, the actual dates and times for the calls with these specialists will have to be set. How to integrate these specialist sessions into a rehearsal pattern is discussed later in this chapter. If you are working in a producing theatre, having agreed in principle with the specialists that they will work on the production, and the approximate number of sessions or days required, the theatre will negotiate the fee and issue a contract. If you are working on the fringe with a producer, you and/or the producer will have to do the negotiating and contracting. The Equity rates are a guide, but depending on the experience of the specialist you are working with, you will have to agree a figure for the contract.

Three months before press night

If the director's involvement in the production has been sporadic thus far, it now begins to intensify and time appears to speed up. Design meetings increase, and one aspect of the production becomes paramount. This section is deliberately detailed as, without actually being involved in professional auditions, there is little information readily available for directors about one of the most important tasks of the director: casting.

Casting and auditioning

Some theatres begin casting earlier than two months before the beginning of rehearsals, particularly if the casting involves looking for very experienced actors or 'names'. Some directors are still casting the week before rehearsals, which is not ideal, but two months before rehearsals is a reasonable mean. If the casting process begins much earlier than this, actors, and their agents, may not be prepared to commit, putting the whole process on hold. Many producing theatres begin casting two months before rehearsals, but they have well-oiled machinery and are well practised; and as the sequencing of auditions and offers is critical to the process, if you are working on your own or casting professionally for the first few times, you may wish to begin three months rather than two months before rehearsals.

Casting directors

Depending on the theatre, or the budget, there may be a casting director involved. They can do anything from just suggesting a list of names for each character to overseeing the actor searches, sending out the production and casting information (called breakdowns), to booking the audition room and the actors, liaising with agents and making offers. Casting is an intricate, delicate, often protracted process, so it is well worth having a casting director if you have not auditioned or cast professional actors before. There is the Casting Directors' Guild, which has a website and contact details of its members, whom you can contact directly to ask about levels of service and fees. For a full support service for a cast of six or eight, a fee in the region of £2,700 might be expected; for a list of twenty names for each part, with some phone and email support, it might be in the region of £1,000.

Spotlight

Even if you cannot afford a casting director, there is one service that you cannot do without for professional casting: *Spotlight*. Access to the online services of *Spotlight* costs £200 plus VAT for a year or £80 plus VAT for three months. Almost every working actor and every agent subscribes to *Spotlight*, which is a searchable database of actors with each entry including a photo, or photos, and possibly a voice or showreel; a selected list of stage, TV, film and other credits, which may include the theatres worked at and directors worked with; personal information including age bracket, hair and eye colour, etc.; information about skills, such as accents, horse riding, vocal range, instruments played, fighting and dancing abilities etc.; and, of course, the agent's contact details.

It is possible to search an actor by name, but you can also search for a native Liverpudlian between forty-five and fifty who can sing and play the guitar, and who has worked with, say, Cheek by Jowl or Rufus Norris. You will then be shown all the actors who meet those criteria (probably none in this case, as the more search criteria you put in the fewer actors it will provide) and you can create your own online shortlist of actors to contact. There is one flaw: the actor or agent has to input the information for it to be searchable, so if the actor has not said that they are from Liverpool or can play the guitar, they won't appear.

The other important half of the service is that it allows you to send out a breakdown of the production and the parts you are casting, and even the pages of the play you wish actors to read at an audition (called 'sides' as in sides of pages). This breakdown can then be sent via the website to every agent who subscribes, or to a list of agents and others you compile, and the replies will come back to your *Spotlight* account pages, and from the submissions you can compile further shortlists. The breakdown pages guide you through the information required, but you will need to know the production company, venue and production dates; who is directing and producing; the casting dates; and the type of contract or payment.

You will also be able to write a brief breakdown of the play and of each role you are casting. Agents are busy people, so keep descriptions brief and pithy. If you are casting *Macbeth*, you might assume the agents know the play but they will want also to know anything distinctive about your production. And if you are casting the role of Macbeth itself, you will want to indicate an age range, perhaps some physical description or character traits you are focusing on, and any skills required, such as: 'Macbeth:

late twenties. He is a physically imposing warlord who fully investigates the moral consequences of his actions, and although he later acts as a tyrant, we never lose sight of his own suffering caused by his actions. Ideally the actor should have previous experience of playing Shakespeare and an ability to use a broadsword.' This may not be the perfect breakdown, but if you give too little information clients won't pop into an agent's mind; give too much and you might be cutting down possible suggestions. Ideally the suggestions will give you a fair range of actors to see. Timing is all with casting: you may wish to allow two or three days for agents to respond and then give yourself a week to go through the (many, many) submissions and schedule the first auditions to begin about ten days after the deadline. If you do not get what you are looking for you can send new, refined, breakdowns. I regularly received as many as 100 submissions per role for productions at Harrogate Theatre, and that takes a long time to sift through.

There are other casting services such as Casting Call Pro and CastNet through which you can receive submissions.

Drawing up audition shortlists

Auditioning costs money: the hire of the room, the travel, and the time of other collaborators in the auditioning. In TV casting it is normal to see perhaps four actors for each role. If you are being employed by a theatre and the theatre is paying for the room, the travel and the time of those involved you might be allocated a certain number of audition days. To begin with, a rule of thumb might be to select six actors to see for each role. However good a *Spotlight* search and submissions process might be, you only have the information about the actor that has been supplied to you. Ideally every director will have their own database of actors whose work they have seen and whom they would like to work with. There is no substitute for seeing actors' work: an actor might be much worse at auditioning than they are on stage, or they might not display the qualities in an audition that you have seen them display in a part.

For the same reason, although you may subscribe to *Spotlight*, the input of a casting director can be invaluable, as they will have seen many productions and auditioned hundreds of actors in the past year or so. If you only have six 'slots' for each role, the more information you have about those you select, the higher the chances are that they will be worth seeing. Take suggestions from directors, actors and designers you know: if they have worked with someone they will know them as a person as well as an actor!

Although the 'industry norm' might be six actors for every part, as an emerging director, if it does not cost too much, you may prefer to see more than six in order to meet and get to know more actors.

Sometimes directors and casting directors leave only a week between the closing date for suggestions and the auditions, but by the time you have selected the actors, phoned or emailed the agent, the agent has contacted the actor, and the actor has dropped out or is not available for the time and date you have chosen, and you have gone to another actor, and the actor has received the pages to read for the audition in good time, seven or ten working days have whizzed by.

The first auditions might be the first time you have heard the play read, and although you have made certain decisions about the characters, and how the characters will relate to each other, in choosing the six actors to see for each part you might wish to choose six who, so far as you can tell from their submissions or from seeing them before, will bring different qualities to the role. For example, a part like the Porter in *Macbeth* could be cast in a multitude of different ways: you may have asked for an aptitude for verbal and physical comedy, but the submissions you receive might expand the possibilities of the casting in your thinking, and provoke you into thinking about the part in new and interesting ways, so choose four to six actors who might bring very different interpretations.

It is often the case that a director's understanding or conception of a character is significantly changed by meeting actors and hearing the part read for the first time, so do not limit your own thinking and possibilities in choosing the actors. It might be that meeting the first actors makes you realise that you have been looking at the part in the wrong way and that you need to see another three actors who bring different qualities to it in a second round of auditions.

The first audition or meeting

Auditions for musicals and 'meetings' with highly experienced actors will be discussed separately, and these auditions will differ from the most commonly used audition processes discussed here. Not every director employs the same audition techniques or processes, but this is a template used by a large number of directors. An initial decision, before the first audition, is whether you will audition in two stages: first auditions and recalls. If you decide to do recalls, the first meeting might be quite short – twenty or thirty minutes is quite common, sometimes seeing as many as twenty actors in a day.

If you have used *Spotlight* you may have sent the pages to be read, or sides, with the breakdown, and the agent will have passed them on to the actor to read before the audition date. Many directors prefer to send the whole play, particularly if it is a new play, or one that it is difficult to get hold of. This is particularly important when casting large parts as it enables the actor to have a sense of the whole project, to see where their character fits in to the whole play, and to have a much better idea if they are interested in the part or the project. This is not only fair to the actor, but will save you time at a later stage if the actor decides sooner rather than later that they are not that interested in the part. If you are going to ask every actor you audition to read the play you may need to allow more time between the closing date for breakdowns and the auditions.

Most actors are happy to read at an audition. In the past actors recently out of drama school were asked for their audition pieces, often a classic piece and a modern piece. This practice is now unusual, but a surprising number of actors are dyslexic and some might rather 'do a piece' or an extract from something they have recently been in than read from a script, particularly if they have only read the scene outside the audition room.

This is a highly prescriptive format for a twenty-minute audition, but follows usual practice. Actors have often taken time off from paid work and travelled to meet you, so be welcoming, and introduce the actor to everybody in the room: it is offputting not to know whom you are about to audition in front of, not to say discourteous on your part. Perhaps begin with a brief chat about their journey, something on their CV with which you have a connection, or a production you have seen – just something so that you can make a connection with each other that is not directly to do with the play to break the ice. Check that they have received the pages, or play, to read and perhaps ask if they have any questions about it. Some actors might feel rather put on the spot if you say, 'What did you think of the play?' so asking if they have any questions allows them to lead the conversation.

You may then wish to say something about the production or give a brief bit of backstory to the scene if the actor has not read the whole play, but keep it brief or the actor may have information overload and not be able to focus on the key considerations for the reading. Ideally you have chosen a passage which is not more than a couple of minutes long in which the actor's character is speaking for the majority of that time. Ideally one of your colleagues rather than you will 'read in' the other parts, so that you can focus on the actor.

At the end of the reading you may wish to make one or two observations about alternative ways to read it – in other words, give a note or two – but again don't be too complicated. Actors are used to being asked to read a passage a second time, and may feel cheated, or that you have dismissed them, if you do not ask them to read again. Also, giving some succinct notes after a first reading and asking the actor to take on board those notes before doing a second reading may tell you how an actor will respond to notes later: they may not technically be able to respond to the note, or they may be resistant to it, or they may not understand what you are trying to convey (which may be your fault or theirs), but it may indicate a failure of communication between you. The purpose of giving a note might not be to elicit a perfect reading of the part, but just to see how the actor responds. Alternatively, choose a second passage to read, but if you have not sent it to them in advance, you will have to give the actor a few moments to look it over.

At the end of the readings, thank them, perhaps say if and when you might be holding recall auditions, when you might get back in touch with their agent, and ask if they have any other questions about the project: not all agents are assiduous at passing on all such information. Some directors like to talk some more at the end to get a sense of whether this is a person they will be able to have a creative and productive relationship with in rehearsals. If you have a specific way of working you may wish to talk about this, both to gauge the actor's openness and to let the actor know that this is the approach before they accept a recall audition.

At the end of each audition make sure you have made enough notes to recall the audition in enough detail. This says more about directors than actors, but after a day of seeing twenty actors it is easy to confuse one actor and another, particularly if you have seen several actors for one part. If you don't cast or recall the actor the agent may ask for feedback several days later: you don't have to give it, but it helps your relationship with the agent and the actor if you can offer constructive feedback from your notes. Also, auditions are research exercises, and it is important to make detailed notes about actors you meet so that you can remember them several months or years later, as well as during the casting process.

It is unforgivably common for auditions to overrun: build in the odd blank audition time to catch up, apologise to the actor if you do overrun and try to keep to the times. Running late will make the actor more nervous, worried about getting away on time – and give the impression that you or the project might be disorganised.

At the end of the day you and your colleagues might go through everyone you have seen and provisionally decide whom to recall or offer a part to, draw up a list of reserve offers or recalls, and a list of whom not to pursue: if an agent asks if you are still interested in an actor and you definitely do not wish to recall them or offer them a part you can let them know straight away.

As was mentioned in relation to the Porter, you may see three or four actors and decide to rethink the parameters of what you are looking for. If you have begun the casting process early enough you may be able to do a first round of first auditions, seeing half of the six actors you have selected for one part, and to schedule a second round of first auditions a few days or a week later, so that you have time to amend your parameters, rather than seeing all six actors in one day, leaving no options for this.

Recall auditions

If the first round of auditions are quick 'getting to know you' meetings, the recalls might be slightly longer and in more depth. There are many ways to conduct recalls: perhaps another reading with a single actor of another passage which explores another facet of the character, so that you can get a view of the actor's range for the part – an actor might be very good at the comedy, but is there the level of vulnerability you are looking for? If you are casting a husband and wife or two characters who have to work closely together, it is possible to call them together, asking them to read with each other, or set up a form of 'rolling' auditions where one Lady Macbeth reads with two successive Macbeths, and each Macbeth reads with two Lady Macbeths. If Macbeth has already been cast it is possible to pay the actor for the day to read in. Asking actors to read with each other relaxes them, makes the work feel more real, and gives you the opportunity to see how different combinations of actors might work together. If there are particular skills required, such as choreography, it is possible to set up a workshop audition in which there are individual meetings and readings, and group work on the specialist skills.

As long as you let the actor know through the agent that he or she is likely to be in the audition for forty-five minutes or an hour, most actors are willing to participate in longer recall auditions in which they are allowed actually to work rather than just read. Of course, it is courteous to thank the actor for giving up so much of their time, but it is also worth checking that the actor knows the dates, the pay, when you might be able to let them know by, and to ask if they have any offers or commitments that might clash with the dates, and finally, if they have any other questions. This series of questions might save a lot of time if you do make an offer, and might speed up the actor's response. It may also reveal that the actor has three filming days in the first two weeks of rehearsal, which the agent may not have told you about.

Auditioning for musicals

If you are auditioning for a musical you may need several other people in the room. Firstly the musical director (MD), possibly the choreographer, and possibly a piano player, so that the MD does not have to play for the songs. If you are casting actor-musicians, you may also need a piano and a drum kit; actors should bring their own portable instruments. Which skills do you audition for first? Very often musical actors are used to ten- or fifteen-minute auditions in which they are asked to sing a song they have brought, or one you may have asked them to prepare, and to play their instruments, each for one or two minutes to judge their level of ability. There is very little time to talk. As these skills are fundamental to the role, it is often not a good use of time to ask each actor to read for the part first, only to find out that they cannot sing or play the instrument at a later stage. At the recall, actors might be asked to prepare another song, read the part, and possibly go through some steps with the choreographer. Again, it is possible to organise a recall with a combination of group movement exercises, and single meetings to play, sing and read.

Auditions or meetings?

Many directors, actors and agents prefer the word 'meeting' to 'audition': it suggests a more civilised coming together of equals who have something to offer each other rather than the power relationship inherent in the word 'audition'. It is also more commonly referred to when the actor concerned has a long and illustrious career, and it is assumed that you will know their work. The questions are not so much concerned with getting to know the actor's work but rather whether the actor is right for the part, is interested in the part and the project, and whether the two of you feel that you wish to work together. Such a meeting may not include a reading but a discussion of the play and the part, how you both view them, and how you plan to work on the production. Having said that, even some highly experienced actors are willing to read, or may offer to, but whether an actor of stature might be willing to read should be established with the agent before the meeting. In some cases it might be more politic to meet the actor in a café, or invite them to lunch, one-to-one, to talk, rather than meeting in an audition room.

In some cases, the agent will suggest that if you are interested in the actor, make an offer, or have a meeting to get to know each other on the assumption that you will make an offer, and the actor will then make a decision about whether to accept the offer after the meeting. These status-laden niceties are best sorted out with the agent, clearly, before any meeting, so that you and the actor can have a productive conversation about the work rather than the politics of the offer. It is definitely worth leaving the discussion of payment to the agent and the theatre if you are employed by a theatre, or between the agent and you or your producer if you are in an independent company or working alone.

Making offers

Hopefully, by the end of your auditions, meetings, and recalls, you will have a first choice and a second choice for each role. It might be as simple as making offers to all your first choices and crossing your fingers, but, if in your recalls you have decided that you need Beatrice to accept before you know which Benedick to cast, it could be a long time before you make an offer to your second-choice Benedick when your first-choice Benedick has turned you down. It is often important to work out a clear sequence of offers, particularly with actor-musician shows in which you are completing a musical line-up as well as a cast. If the actor or agent is keeping you waiting, you may say that you have to know by the end of the week or will withdraw the offer, or you possibly face losing actors who are waiting for you but auditioning for other productions. Sometimes when the options just do not work out, you find you have no actors for the part, and you have to conduct more auditions – which is why it is worth getting to the offers stage a month before rehearsals begin.

Design and production meetings

At the same time as the casting, there will be an increasing number of design meetings, the most important of which are the white-card meeting and the final design and budget meetings. As was discussed in Chapter Four, 'The Director and the Designer', the white-card meeting is the one where the director and the designer show a white-card model of the set to the production manager and other members of the production staff, and possibly the artistic director and chief executive of the theatre, chiefly to assess the demands and viability of the design, and a rough estimate of costs. It might be that the production manager and other staff suggest changes to the construction or even conception of the design, in order to make it achievable with the resources and budget available, and therefore to make it necessary for you and the designer to get together soon after the white-card meeting, to work through the suggested changes.

Even if there are no changes, you will wish to go through the design again, both with your designer and on your own, to check that you have thought of every element of the set and that the design gives you and the actors enough options to work with in terms of the traffic of the stage. How long is that entrance? Can the actors get behind the cyc? How steep is that rake? If you have not done so by now, you and the designer may wish to storyboard the whole play to check such elements. The next time you see the model it will be a fully finished, realised version of the design, so speak now if you have any questions or concerns.

It might also be the first opportunity you have to discuss the production and the design with the set designer, lighting designer, sound designer and digital designer all together. You may also be able to show some of your casting options to the designer, which will feed into their design, and into costume designs. The white-card meeting might be the first time that all the design collaborators are in the same building together, so it will feel as if all the different strands of the production are finally coming together.

Two months before press night

Design and budgeting

The final design meeting will often be a month before rehearsals begin, so that the making process can begin shortly afterwards. The same staff will be at the design meeting, and in addition, there might be members of the finance staff, since the main purpose of the meeting will be to go through all elements of the design in order for the production staff to go away and cost it. So the design meeting might be followed by a budget meeting a few days or a week later.

Different theatres and production managers budget shows in different ways. Here is an example of a simple production budget. One way of budgeting is for the production manager and finance staff to assign each element of the budget a projected sum: so, for example, £5,000 for the set, £2,000 for lighting, £1,000 for sound, £1,500 for costumes, £500 for design-made props, £300 for stage management props, £200 for transport, and £500 for contingencies, giving a total production budget of £11,000. Each design element will have to come within its own budget; if the set looks like costing £5,500, then that extra £500 will have to be found from another source within the overall budget: this will be negotiated at the budget meeting, and hopefully all the production staff will leave the meeting with approved budgets and be able to get on with doing the work.

Another, perhaps more organic way to budget, is for there to be a global budget but no individual budgets, then to see at the budget meeting what each department needs to make its element of the design. Each budget is analysed, to see if there might be savings by combining resources, or doing things slightly differently, then the finance manager calculates all the agreed budgets to see if the total comes to less than £11,000. If it does not, further savings are sought; if it does, everyone leaves happy. There are variations between these two forms of budgeting which will allow the production manager to assess the likely outcome of a budget meeting well ahead, and to negotiate with you and the making staff and to find compromises and ways forward before the formal budget meeting.

Marketing

Members of the marketing department may also come to the design meeting to see the set and to get a clearer idea of the production, as they will now be beginning to focus on your production and conceive marketing and press strategies. As the director, you may be asked if there are any elements of the production which might provide good press stories, such as newsworthy casting decisions, or unusual (photogenic) skills which the actors might be being taught, and possible field trips for the cast. You may also be asked to write an article for the programme, or the theatre website, and to contribute a regular blog from the beginning of rehearsals through to opening night, or parts of a press release about the production. You may also be asked to be interviewed by print, radio and TV journalists about the production.

This is the point at which your initial responses to the play, having been tentatively articulated to the designer, and then more fully to the production staff at the design meeting, become more public, and have to be more focused, encapsulating the main ideas of the production in a way that is going to be concise and interesting to the public, without being facile or giving the wrong impression of the production. Some directors are much better at this than others, but it is worth giving some thought to how you are going to articulate the production to those who know nothing about it in very few words.

Education and outreach activity

If you are a freelance director you are unlikely to be directly involved in workshops related to the production but you may be asked for further information about the production so that the education and outreach staff can plan more information to schools or groups, and other activities. You may be asked to consider holding some open rehearsals or inviting certain groups to run-throughs or tech or dress rehearsals. If you are a resident director you may be involved in devising and running workshops prior to rehearsals and during the run, and leading pre- and post-show discussions with the cast.

Pre-rehearsal planning

It may be expensive, or not financially possible for you, but the fewer commitments you have in the month before rehearsals, the better and more enjoyable will be your final preparations, and the more you will feel confident going into rehearsals. This is the time to begin to outline your overall rehearsal pattern, finally considering how you are going to work through the play week by week and day by day, working out exactly when the fight director, the MD, choreographer and dialect person and aerialist are going to best interweave with each other in the process, and booking those times. There will be further discussion of this under the section on the rehearsal period itself. It is also time to fill in any gaps in your research and to consider distilling your research. You may wish to compile a pack of research materials that you either have available in the rehearsal room for the actors to dip into, or compile into an 'actor's pack' to give to each member of the company, and stage management, in the first few days of rehearsals. Many actors will do their own research on the play, the world of the play, and their character prior to rehearsals, others may simply not have had the time. Without imposing it on the actors, or making it feel like homework, an 'actor's pack' of selected written information and visual information about the writer, the origins of the play and contemporary events and art, the world of the play, and some of the images that inspired the design, can help actors become quickly and imaginatively immersed in the production. Finally, find time to have one or two slow close readings of the play, now reading it in the light of the design which has been finalised and the cast that you now have in place, considering how those real factors may alter your response to the play, and how you can tailor your rehearsal methods to those real actors and circumstances.

As is mentioned in the interview with Sarah Esdaile, you may ask the actors to do some work on the play before rehearsals begin, such as going through the four lists: What do I say about myself? What do other characters say about me? What do I say about other characters? What does the author say about me? – or to do other background work on the play, or even to learn their lines. If you are going to ask actors to do this you will probably have forewarned them at the auditions but you obviously want to give them as much notice of the pre-rehearsal work as possible. It is very frustrating if only half the cast have done the work by the first day of rehearsals.

From one month before press night to the first day of rehearsals

Rehearsal periods

One month before press night will only be the first day of rehearsals if you have a three-week rehearsal period and a week of tech and dress rehearsals followed by two or three previews in the same week – then a press night at the beginning of the following week. This is a common rehearsal pattern in many producing theatres, but many larger, or better funded, theatres are able to have four or five weeks in the rehearsal room, before the technical work begins, and the National Theatre and the RSC often have six-week rehearsal periods, but with some limited availability of actors who are in productions already in the repertoire. Of course, in principle, five weeks is better than four, and four is better than three, and although I am no advocate of shorter rehearsal periods (which are often out of the control of the director anyway), it is surprising how quickly actors and directors adapt to working within the time available: you just have to choose a pattern that is going to result in at least two runs of the play in the rehearsal room towards the end of the last week, whether that be the third, fourth or fifth. For the purposes of this discussion, it will be assumed that there are four weeks in the rehearsal room.

Apart from the director and the actors, there will be one or two key people who are always present in the rehearsal room.

The assistant director

The role of the assistant director is one of the hardest in the theatre: first, because his or her duties mean very different things in different situations; and second, because the assistant is organisationally (and often actually, physically) somewhere between director, actors and stage management.

Whether you are the director or the assistant it is really important to establish the exact role the assistant will have before rehearsals begin. An assistant director's duties can be expected to include any of the following:

➢ be involved in the casting;
➢ attending the major design meetings;
➢ undertaking research before and during rehearsals and preparing information materials, including actor packs;
➢ liaising between the director, stage management and specialists, such as fight directors and choreographers, and with other members of the creative team;
➢ liaising between the director and stage management on rehearsal calls;
➢ taking rehearsals, including running parallel rehearsals with actors not in rehearsals with the director, or with members of a community cast or with children;
➢ going through lines with actors;
➢ taking notes and contributing ideas to the production;
➢ taking understudy rehearsals;
➢ looking after and noting the production once it has opened;
➢ taking the production on tour and putting it into new venues.

Or it could mean just sitting quietly at the farthest corner of the rehearsal room and doing nothing apart from making the coffee.

Some directors are better than others at fully involving their assistant in the production, but working out a job definition and lines of communication between the assistant and all those in the rehearsal room will prevent the assistant from either feeling excluded or making contributions which the director does not really want. For example, one director might welcome the assistant 'chipping in' during work on a scene, but another might prefer the assistant only to contribute when invited to, or to make notes and observations which are given to the director after that day's rehearsals. It is also true that in the eyes of the acting company the assistant director only has the status that the director gives. If the assistant has been a completely non-contributing presence in the room, it is difficult for the assistant to assume the director's role when looking after the production after it has opened, or is on tour.

The other danger for the assistant is getting caught in diplomatic cross-fire. Sometimes an actor will ask the assistant for an opinion about a scene, or what the actor is doing, and it is easy for the helpful assistant to offer advice which the grateful actor then tries out, only to find that it is not consistent with the director's thinking, to the chagrin of both actor and director. It is also essential for the assistant to understand the director's conception of the whole production and their working methods and strategies in order to represent the director effectively: as an assistant you are enabling someone else's production and vision.

The deputy stage manager

The stage management team is divided into three, sometimes four, roles: the stage manager (SM), the deputy stage manager (DSM), and the assistant stage manager (ASM). Larger teams may be led by a company stage manager (CSM). The stage manager leads the team and is responsible for, or delegating, all the work of the team: organising rehearsals, including making a mark-out of the set in tape on the floor of the rehearsal room and providing substitute props and furniture for rehearsals; the budget for the stage management props, and acquiring those props; organising rehearsal calls and other calls for the acting company; liaising with guests and other specialists who come into rehearsals; liaising between the rehearsal room and other production departments; organising the back-stage areas; often, running the tech; running the show.

The stage manager and the ASM are not usually in the rehearsal room: they are out propping – buying and borrowing the props and furniture for the show, making props, and liaising with other departments to ensure the smooth running of the rehearsal and production processes. The centre of communication between the rehearsal room and all these other activities and departments is the DSM. He or she is 'on the book', the book being the prompt copy in which the DSM records all the cuts and changes made to the script, all the moves and actions the actors make, and, during the tech process, all the lighting, sound and other technical cues. In the rehearsal room the DSM will also make detailed notes of any significant events or changes and communicate them to the rest of the stage management team, other production departments, and occasionally, the rest of the theatre.

For example, the DSM must know and note if a prop is cut, or additional props are needed, or an actor asks for a pocket in a costume, or the latest estimate of the length and timing of a sound cue, and rough timings of scenes and acts when they are run. The communication also works the other way, and the DSM will ask the director for the call for the actors for the next day, which should be available to the actors as soon as possible after that day's rehearsals. The DSM will also let the director know if actors are needed for costume fittings, photo and press calls, and other calls which will have to be factored in to the rehearsal call by the director. The DSM also prompts the actors in rehearsals – and the show, if necessary! Once the production leaves the rehearsal room the DSM runs the show, giving all the technical cues and calls for actors, and often the calls to the audience, from the prompt desk, a console with cue lights, cans (headsets), a mike to backstage and front-of-house areas, and usually a monitor relaying the live action on the stage.

The DSM is often the director's closest colleague in the rehearsal room and an efficient and diplomatic DSM is of enormous benefit to the director and the production alike.

The first day of rehearsals

I have always found the first day of rehearsals far more nerve-wracking than the press night. It is the first time that everyone involved in the production is in the same room, and, if it is a production in a theatre building, there might be a good number of the theatre staff from finance, administration, marketing and front of house, as well as the production team, to 'meet and greet' the new company and to find out about the production. For the director the first day of rehearsals is in itself a performance.

Everyone in the room will want to learn more about the production and whom they are working with, so you might ask everyone to introduce themselves, saying what their role is, and follow this by giving a brief talk about the production. It is wise to keep it brief, and concentrate on why you are all doing the production and what it will look and feel like rather than going into the details of your research: look forwards, not backwards. If it is a new play and the playwright is there, they may be willing to say a few words, and you might then ask the designer to show the model and costume drawings and to discuss the design. This may provide enough information for those not directly involved in making the production, and some people may wish to leave at this point. You want everyone there to feel involved and excited about the work to come: it is about creating a positive beginning rather than disseminating too much information.

Then comes the question of a read-through of the play. Some directors and many actors detest read-throughs, particularly in front of a large number of people they have just met for the first time. Actors can feel pressured into giving a 'performance' and that they are being judged at first sight, which is not good for the sense of positive camaraderie you have just tried to engender. However, the read-through can be a valuable way of sharing the play with the group of people who are collectively going to make the show, but will all disappear off to their offices and workshops over the next four weeks. Sometimes, indeed, the theatre staff request a read-through, or feel excluded from the production if there isn't one. Some directors find a compromise by asking the actors to swap parts with each other, or by asking one person to take the first piece of speech and the person sitting to their left to take the next speech, and so on, in clockwise rotation, so that the whole play is shared out randomly. The play is shared, but no one feels they are being asked to perform or being judged on their performance. Some directors and actors just accept that it is a form of medieval torture that has to be gone through and try to enjoy it as much as they can.

After the read-through might be the first time you, the actors, the assistant director and DSM are alone in the room. You may ask the designer to stay to go through the set and costumes with the actors in more detail than was possible earlier – there is a limit to the amount of information about the design actors will take in on the first day, but all of them will want to have an idea of what they are wearing. This might be the time to say how much flexibility there is in the set and costume designs – what is fixed and what is up for grabs. The costume department will also wish to measure the actors.

After this it might be a good time to outline the working pattern for the next four weeks, both in terms of how you are going to work through the play and when the actors are likely to be called – what the weekly pattern will be, and if you will be working evenings but not Saturdays, or vice versa – and whether you are calling the whole company most of the time, or just the actors who are in the scene you are working on.

You may wish to distribute the actor pack, going through some of the material, or show a film, invite in a guest expert to talk about an aspect of the play, or go on a field trip. If you are directing a musical, you might go straight into learning a song which includes all members of the company.

The first day of rehearsals is a nerve-wracking day for everyone, and particularly if everyone is working away from their home, it will be a long day, even if the rehearsal call is shorter than a normal working day. Hopefully the first day is informative, positive and relatively short, leaving everyone looking forward to the real work beginning on day two, and going off to find their digs.

Rehearsal patterns

How you arrive at your rehearsal pattern is discussed in detail in Chapter Two, and will be determined by the play, the time available and the way you think it best to work with the actors. Whatever pattern you choose will be scheduled within the Equity-approved working week and the DSM will advise you about the actors' hours available to you and the lengths of rehearsal sessions and breaks. Particularly if you are working with actors who are in an evening performance, and when you get to the production week, the calls for actors become quite complicated, and unless you wish to learn the Equity rule book by heart, you need the advice of a good DSM.

The other factor that will affect your rehearsal pattern is working with MDs, choreographers, fight directors, etc. In your pre-rehearsal discussion about their hours and sessions, you will also need to discuss with them the sequencing of those sessions. For example, the MD will need to have taught the singers, and possibly musicians, a song before the choreographer can work on it; you may wish to have worked through the scene that includes a fight so that the actors know their situation and intentions in the scene, so that the actors, fight director and you are all telling the same story in the fight as well as the scene. And choreography, fights, other physical skills and dialects are about actors building up muscle memory, so the earlier that they can learn the skills, the more chance they have of making them second nature and integrating them into their performances.

As the director Stephen Joseph once commented, the most important job of the director is to schedule the coffee breaks. Outlining an overall rehearsal plan on day one and sticking to it inspires confidence, and even if there are good and bad days over the next four weeks, there is a plan to have the play rehearsed by the time you leave the rehearsal room: it won't be perfect, but it will be a firm foundation for the actors to work from.

Whatever your working methods are in the rehearsal period, it is worth planning backwards. It is usual (and comforting) to end the rehearsal period having had at least two full run-throughs of the play, and possibly runs of each act as you work through them before that. In the last week of rehearsals you will want to work on individual moments or scenes, but never leave other parts of the play alone for too long, otherwise coming back to them will be a step backwards, not forwards. So if you consider that half of the last week's time might be spent in runs rather than working on scenes, it tells you how much time you have in the preceding three weeks to work through the play in detail. How you do that is determined by your own toolbox and a consideration of the three factors mentioned above: the play, the time available, and the cast.

The tech

The tech is usually the first time that all elements of the production come together on the stage: actors, stage management, technicians, set, costumes, lights, sound, video or projection, flying and any other technical elements. The tech is for the stage management and technical staff to bring all these elements together, and the role of the actors and director is to support this process rather than thinking of it as a continuation of rehearsals. Although the DSM is 'calling' the show in terms of giving all the cues to the actors and technicians, the tech is usually run by the stage manager or production manager, who will start and stop the tech. The director usually sits in the auditorium, often with the lighting designer, in the best position to see the stage and hear the sound and music as the audience will.

Usually the tech is preceded by a lighting session at which the lighting designer, director and DSM go through the play without the actors, creating the lighting states and cues; the cues then go in the DSM's book, so that the DSM can call them at the agreed points (these lighting sessions are also called plotting sessions). However, many lighting designers prefer to plot many of the states and cues during the tech, because the lighting is as much, if not more, about interacting with the actors, as the set; this is particularly true in theatre in the round, where it is virtually impossible to judge how an actor is going to be lit working on an empty stage. Even if all the lighting states have been plotted before the tech, there will be many alterations during the tech, and often the director's main focus is the lighting.

How long is a tech? Usually the production manager or stage manager will draw up a schedule for the whole technical process, from getting the set in to rigging the lights and sound, focusing the lights, the lighting sessions, and the tech sessions with the actors, and then the dress rehearsals up to the first previews or press night. Elements that make a tech more complicated are the number of set changes, the number of quick costume changes, and the number of lighting, sound and video cues. A tech for a play with only two or three actors, with no quick costume changes, with a single set and fewer than fifty lighting cues may only take one session; a tech for a large musical with over 300 lighting cues, many quick changes, and several set changes, including flying and the use of traps, may take two or three long days.

The actors will be getting used to costumes, the set, the backstage organisation of set, costumes and props, and the changed vocal and focus demands of being in an auditorium rather than the rehearsal room. It can be a strange transition from the comforting world of the rehearsal room to the stage and auditorium, so it is often advisable to suggest to the actors that they 'mark through' the scenes in terms of the level of acting and concentrate on orienting themselves to their new circumstances.

The tech is primarily for the technical staff, and it is not a good idea for the director to treat the tech as an extended rehearsal session, because it will eat up precious technical time and disrupt the technical process, and, as just suggested, actors will be marking rather than giving performances. However, sometimes there will be lighting replotting times, or times when a quick change is being organised backstage, and the director can use these 'down times' to talk to the actors about the new demands of the set and the auditorium and finesse stage positions and business in the light of actually being on the set, which may save time and notes later on. Although the tech is run by the stage or production manager the director does have the prerogative to ask them to stop the tech and go over something – but don't try redirecting the scene!

If the tech is taking much more time than was envisaged, the director and production manager and/or stage manager need to discuss how to speed things up, as the times for the first dress rehearsal and other dresses are important to keep to for the whole process, and for contractual reasons. You may have to ask the lighting, sound and digital designers not to plot as the tech continues but to make notes and plot afterwards: often the priority has to be on the sequence of set and costume changes that happen on stage and backstage so that actors, stage management and crew know the sequences of their jobs.

Dress rehearsals

Ideally there will be two dress rehearsals before the first public performance, whether that is a preview or press night. It is often worth considering a purpose or point of concentration for each dress rehearsal. For example, if the first dress is on Tuesday evening, the second dress on Wednesday afternoon and the first preview on Wednesday evening, the actors are not going to want to give a 'performance-level' performance on Wednesday afternoon, particularly in a physically and vocally demanding production. So, even though the first dress might come hard on the heels of the tech, the first dress is the only time the actors are going to be able to give a full-blooded performance. Also, in this scenario, there is usually very little time between a final dress and the first public performance to give copious or complicated notes or to work on moments, so you will want to note a performance-level run-through after the first dress, either giving notes at the end of the first dress and working on moments on Wednesday morning, or giving notes and working moments on Wednesday morning. If the scheduling is different, or you have more than two dress rehearsals, you can choose different focuses for each dress rehearsal.

Previews

Once the production has been in front of an audience, it is not productive for the director to want to continue to work on the whole play, but rather to give notes on moments in the light of seeing the production with an audience, and only to work on those moments which really need changing or clarifying. Ideally you, the director, have enough confidence in the production and the actors to allow the actors themselves to develop their connection with the play and the audience.

Press night

Of course, the outcome of the press night is press and other reviews. Hopefully, all your reviews will be unreservedly marvellous, but occasionally a review will criticise a particular aspect of the production, or, worse, a particular actor. Some actors never read reviews and would rather they weren't all posted on the company notice board or discussed, and it is worth asking actors if they feel this way during the rehearsal period and, if so, liaising with the marketing department to ensure the reviews aren't posted.

Occasionally you will have to decide if you do want to discuss the critical reviews with individual actors or the whole company. Critical reviews can be very damaging on company and/or individual morale. You may have to decide to mention it at a notes session, address it and show your support for the company or individual. You may decide not to mention the criticism publicly, but that might leave the individual or the company suspecting that you agree with it.

Looking after the production

After each dress rehearsal and performance the DSM will write a show report. This will give the timings of acts and the whole performance, and will note any missed or mistimed cues, any unusual events during the show, and any technical problems that need fixing. It is a factual report and unless there are strong audience reactions, will not comment on the acting or make artistic judgements. The show report is always posted on the company notice board and emailed to all the relevant members of staff. If you leave the production after the press night, the DSM will email the reports to you, and usually phone you if there are any serious problems.

Most directors leave the production alone for some time after the first night, but there is a balance to be struck between leaving the actors to find their own relationship with the play and audience and not letting them feel that you have lost interest. You may wish to see the first performance in the week following opening night, or the first matinee, when the sheen of opening night may have worn off, in order to show support for the actors and the production. If you are a freelance director working at a producing theatre you may be contracted to come back to see the production and note it once or twice during the run. If there is an assistant director the assistant is often required to see the show once a week and to note it, reporting back to the director if there are any major problems.

It is strange that after perhaps a year's work you may only see the production two or three times . . .

Practical exercises

Exercise one

Using the example of the casting breakdown for *Macbeth*, write a brief description of a production you are directing in no more than forty words, if it is a well-known classic or historic play focusing the description on distinctive aspects of the production rather than outlining the plot. Then, using the same example, write breakdowns of no more than fifty words for four of the main characters, including possible age ranges, any important physical qualities, skills or accents required, and a brief description of their actions, storyline and essential characteristics.

Choose two main characters who are dramatically closely linked in a play. To use Shakespeare as an example, it could be a father and child, such as King Lear and Cordelia, Macbeth and Lady Macbeth who are married, or Beatrice and Benedick, who will eventually be married: in each case the casting of one might affect the casting of the other. Using your knowledge of actors, and possibly programmes you have kept, 'cast' four actors for each role. Consider the possible age range, physical type, and character qualities you envisage for each character, in principle, and then 'cast' actors who offer different possible interpretations, as you imagine them.

How does the casting of 'real' actors alter your perceptions of the character; does it widen your thinking and interpretation? You may then wish to envisage what effect different pairings of the actors for the two roles will have on the casting of each actor; the interpretation, and perhaps chemistry, of the relationship; and then the effect these different casting choices might have on the whole production. For example, if you cast Macbeth as being in his forties and Lady Macbeth being in her early twenties, what effect does that have on their relationship and the whole play – and vice versa? What different readings and interpretations result from these four different pairings, and which of the four, individually, and as pairings, would you finally wish to choose and why? Even at a reading rather than casting stage, this exercise may open up possible interpretations of the characters, their relationships, and your overall view of the play that you might not otherwise explore.

Exercise two

Read the section on the casting process and, using a diary or week planner, work out the timeline of each stage of the process. It is helpful to work backwards from the absolute date that you need to have your cast in place – and add a week or two! It is surprising how long it takes.

Exercise three

This whole chapter has been written as an eighteen-month preparation cycle, which, as noted, is somewhat luxurious. Again working backwards, from the press night, using a diary, or week planner, draw up a timeline of deadlines, meetings and tasks that have to be completed by a certain time for all elements of the production process in parallel: do this over eighteen months, twelve months and six months, then discover your own timeline in terms of preparation for these deadlines and how much or how little time you have for other projects or earning money at different points in the process.

Exercise four

Break down a large-cast script into character entrances and exits with page numbers in order to have a table of who is in which scene and for how long. Using this as a table for working out rehearsal calls, draw up a rehearsal call for a three-week and four-week rehearsal period for the same play, judging how much time to allocate to each section of the play and what might have been achieved by that point.

Exercise five

Write a 400-word briefing email to a fight director for a play in which the weapons and the actual narrative within the fight are not prescribed – for example, the killing of Banquo. What weapons are used, how many murderers are there, what is the narrative of how he fights, how much does he protect Fleance, and how long does the fight last?

Weblist

Casting Call Pro	www.uk.castingcallpro.com
Casting Directors' Guild of Great Britain and Ireland (CDG)	
	www.thecdg.co.uk
CastNet	www.castingnetwork.co.uk
Samuel French	www.samuelfrench-london.co.uk
Spotlight	www.spotlight.com
United Agents	unitedagents.co.uk

7

The director and directing

This chapter explores the director's final relationship – the director and directing. It will focus on two aspects of becoming an independent self-aware theatre-maker: the practical and philosophical, the director as a one-person business and the director as an artist.

The practical elements include information on getting plugged into the current theatre ecology as a director: theatres and organisations that offer support, advice, training and networking opportunities specifically for directors, and between directors and other creative artists; awards, bursaries and competitions for directors; and organisations and websites offering networking and information. There is advice on how to become self-employed and submit your own tax return; the point at which you may wish to find an agent; how to approach directors and theatres for work, and how to build those relationships; and how to present your CV and write effective letters to theatres and directors.

The philosophical aspects concern developing a personal aesthetic and a defined sense of the theatre you wish to make that you can readily communicate to others; developing the art of critical evaluation of your work in order to keep learning and evolving; and having a sense of where your work is taking you over the next few years.

At the end of the chapter, in two interviews, Gareth Machin, Studio Associate at the National Theatre Studio and Sue Emmas, Associate Artistic

Director of the Young Vic, offer invaluable practical advice about how to begin and develop relationships with theatres and how to approach meetings with directors and others who might take an interest in your work, as well as offering an overview of the early career stages of current emerging directors. The interview with New York-based director, Allison Troup-Jensen, offers an insight into the world of emerging directors in New York and elsewhere in the US, drawing interesting comparisons between the possible career paths of US and UK directors.

Getting plugged in

As this is the last chapter it is about developing your knowledge, skills and tastes as a theatre director, and is intended primarily for those who may have directed one or two productions at university, or taken shows to Edinburgh, or directed one or two productions without inviting professional peers, and who are now ready to make their work more widely known and to engage with professional peers.

It is interesting to note from the interviews with Gareth Machin and Sue Emmas that many emerging directors they meet do not have current knowledge of actors, or companies that are creating work in new ways. Focused on the work they wish to make, they are not well informed about the wider theatre world. As Gareth Machin suggests, being able to discuss the work of directors, actors, writers and designers whose work you have seen is often the first way in which a peer director will try to get a sense of your tastes, passions and work before deciding whether to see your next piece of work.

It is not necessary to reiterate here all the observations made in Chapter One about seeing work, making lists of the work of practitioners you admire (and why); keeping up with issues and debates about the theatre industry; and developing a better understanding of the different artistic policies of theatres and the 'how and why' of current theatre-making. But it is worth drawing together some of the observations made in other chapters about maintaining a current knowledge of work and practitioners. Perhaps it is worth making diary notes to see final-year productions at some of the drama schools, to visit one or two design exhibitions at design schools and to go to theatres where new writers and companies are first showing their work.

Being a director can feel a very solitary existence, but over the past five years support, advice and information for emerging directors has rapidly increased, and although many of the opportunities are London-based, they are also web-based, and it is possible to feel connected to a wider community of directors and to know about what is current anywhere. There follows a brief description of some of the theatres and organisations that offer support and information specifically for emerging directors. These are the more permanent and better known sources of information, but through them you can learn about many new initiatives and one-off opportunities for directors provided by other companies and individual directors. Their websites – the first and best way to find detailed information about them – are listed at the end of the chapter.

Support and information networks for directors

THE YOUNG VIC GENESIS DIRECTORS NETWORK is the largest for emerging directors, providing a website where directors may communicate with each other, with producers and other practitioners, find useful information and ask other members for advice and information. It is also the portal for discovering the range of bursaries, assisting opportunities, workshops, debates and research and development (R&D) resources offered by the Young Vic. The interview later in this chapter with Sue Emmas, Associate Artistic Director of the Young Vic, provides more detailed information about the Directors' Programme and the Young Vic's engagement with directors.

THE NATIONAL THEATRE STUDIO also provides a range of bursaries, assisting opportunities at the National Theatre, training opportunities, R&D resources, and advice to emerging directors. More information about the work of the National Theatre Studio may also be found later in this chapter, in the interview with Gareth Machin, NT Studio Associate.

OLD VIC NEW VOICES (OVNV) have kindly provided the following statement about their work:

Old Vic New Voices (OVNV) aims to support emerging talent, inspire young people and open up the Old Vic Theatre to new and diverse audiences. For emerging actors, writers, directors and producers, we offer two year-round strands of work: the New Voices Club (London) and the New Voices Network (New York), as well as high-profile projects and showcase opportunities.

To become a member of the Club or Network you will have to be selected to take part in either The 24-Hour Plays: Old Vic New Voices or The T.S. Eliot US/UK Exchange. To hear how to apply you will first need to sign up as an Associate member of OVNV at www.ideastap.com – it is completely FREE to do so. If you have any queries, please email newvoices@oldvictheatre.com.

New Voices Club For those embarking on a professional career in theatre, the New Voices Club offers UK-based actors, directors, producers and writers, aged 18–25, the opportunity to learn from industry professionals, receive support for projects they are passionate about and network with like-minded peers. We now have over 200 members and in the last year alone offered our members over 600 hours of free rehearsal space and 200 hours of professional development sessions.

Recent events have included talks by Hal Prince, Anthony Head, Tom Stoppard, Anna Mackmin and Alan Ayckbourn, together with workshop sessions on personal branding and taking a show to the Edinburgh Festival. Our newest initiative, Time Warner IGNITE, offers members an exceptional opportunity to propel their careers to the next level. Over the two-year programme participants are offered the opportunity to showcase their work to industry audiences, and transform their talent for theatre into a flair for film. Membership is through The 24 Hour Plays: Old Vic New Voices.

New Voices Network The New Voices Network is a unique opportunity for actors, writers, directors and producers, between the ages of 21 and 30 and based in New York, to participate in our award-winning programme.

Similarly to the Club, we offer year-round activities dedicated to supporting our members' professional growth, including unrivalled career support, a dynamic programme of master classes and networking events. Recent events have included talks with John Guare, Eve Best, Mary Stuart Masterson and John Lahr, and workshop sessions on interpreting classic work and producing from scratch. Membership is through The T.S. Eliot US/UK Exchange.

The 24-Hour Plays: Old Vic New Voices A co-production with The 24-Hour Company, this adrenaline-fuelled event is now in its sixth successive year. The project provides 50 young actors, writers, directors and producers, aged between 18 and 25, with the opportunity to prove their theatrical skill on a grand scale. Following intensive auditions and workshops, the team of seven writers, seven directors, seven producers and 31 actors gather on a Saturday night in the Old Vic's large rehearsal room, bringing with them a piece of costume and a prop. Each artist introduces their items, as the writers make notes for inspiration.

The meeting finishes and the writers are whisked away to begin their formidable overnight challenge: create an original ten-minute play for a hand-selected cast of actors by six the following morning. Actors, directors and producers leave for a night of (fitful) sleep. By 8 a.m, the whole company returns and, with the ink still wet on the pages, the scripts are distributed. Fevered rehearsals, with mere minutes of technical stage time, follow. The climax of this nail-biting process is a performance of the freshly minted plays in front of 1,000 friends, family and industry VIPs at the Old Vic that evening.

The creative bonds forged during this high-pressure process always lead to new projects and dynamic artistic collaborations, and each member who participates is awarded full membership of the New Voices Club.

The T.S. Eliot US/UK Exchange   The T.S. Eliot US/UK Exchange is the ultimate transatlantic career opportunity for emerging talent aged 21 to 30, aiming to develop artists' understanding of their industry in a different country and to help them find new opportunities for collaboration and professional development.

Each year, 50 emerging British artists and 50 emerging American artists travel across the Atlantic to experience an intense mix of workshops, specialism-specific meetings, devising sessions, networking events and theatre trips.

In 2010, British artists enjoyed meetings and workshops with representatives from the Wooster Group, the Public, Manhattan Theater Club, New Dramatists, Lincoln Center Theater, Soho Rep, David Stone, Commercial Theater Institute, Theatre Row, 59E59, Abrams Agency, The Flea, Ars Nova and Playwrights Horizons. The pinnacle of the week is a professional showcase of short original works onstage at a high-profile Manhattan venue (in 2010, we were hosted by the legendary Public Theater).

By assisting the development of strong relationships between like-minded artists on both sides of the Atlantic, OVNV hopes to form international partnerships that will bear dividends for years to come. It is thrilling to report that innovative new projects between the 2010 London and New York Exchange participants are already at production stage, with many more in the pipe-line.

THE DIRECTORS GUILD OF GREAT BRITAIN (DGGB) runs regular workshops on approaches to directing led by leading theatre directors and holds networking and other events to promote the art and craft of directing. The DGGB's membership includes a large number of directors working in opera, film, TV, radio, and other media, and is a useful way for a theatre director to find out about working in these areas and to make connections. You have to become a member of the DGGB to participate in some events but many workshops are open to non-members (but may cost more).

THE ROYAL SHAKESPEARE COMPANY (RSC) does from time to time organise public conferences and workshops for directors and other artists but the key way to make contact with the RSC is to write to or email the producers. They regularly interview emerging directors and from that interview will consider a director for assistant directing posts and workshops specifically for emerging artists, including directors, with their own directors and members of their voice and movement departments.

There are other organisations that support emerging artists across a range of art forms, including theatre and performing arts. IDEAS TAP is the largest and longest-running of these and now has 34,000 members (partners include Old Vic New Voices). It offers opportunities to network, promote your work, find creative collaborators, and search for jobs, while its Ideas Fund offers funding to arts projects. A similar organisation is YPIA – young people in the arts – which focuses on music and theatre and offers information and networking opportunities and runs regular talks, seminars and events for and about emerging artists.

The INDEPENDENT THEATRE COUNCIL (ITC) offers a range of extremely useful workshops for directors and producers on matters such as forming a company, becoming a charitable trust, fundraising, budgeting, contracts and employment law. If you become a member of ITC you will also receive specialist advice on legal and other industry issues.

Conferences

Another useful way of meeting other artists and keeping abreast of current debates and issues is to attend conferences such as 'Devoted and Disgruntled', organised by Improbable Theatre. The main D&D annual event is a three-day discussion forum in London, usually in January, but there are also D&D meetings in other cities throughout the year and smaller meetings in London every month. For the past two years the RSA (the Royal Society for the Encouragement of Arts, Manufactures and Commerce) and ACE have organised a 'State of the Arts' conference in London in the spring at which leading figures in the industry, including government minsters, the chair of ACE and leading theatre directors have discussed the future of the arts. 'Shift Happens' is curated by Pilot Theatre Company, based in York, and is about how theatre engages with new technologies – not just onstage, but in terms of networking, reaching audiences and as an art form amid a changing culture and new technologies.

Competitive opportunities

There are a number of bursaries, awards, assistant directorships and production opportunities emerging directors can apply for. Many have age limits and all have their own criteria and guidelines that must be read carefully on their websites before applying. Here are brief descriptions of the major competitive opportunities not already mentioned.

THE REGIONAL THEATRE YOUNG DIRECTOR SCHEME is the most influential and long-running training scheme for directors. It began in 1960 and for much of its history was funded by various independent television companies (hence it is often referred to as the ITV RTYDS scheme). It is now administered by the Young Vic. The scheme offers a secondment to a producing theatre for a year, and supports the director with a £15,000 tax-free bursary for the year. Each year theatres apply to provide the secondment, and many leading regional theatres such as West Yorkshire Playhouse, the Royal Exchange Manchester and Sheffield Theatres, as well as the Royal Court in London, regularly have RTYDS directors. Many current artistic directors and leading freelance directors, including Michael Boyd, Vicky Featherstone and Rupert Goold, trained on this scheme. During the year the director will gain an understanding of all aspects of a producing theatre and assist on productions; the year may be followed by a production at the theatre. The deadline for applications is usually in March. It is intended for directors at an early stage in their careers, but there is no age limit, though applicants need to be over twenty-one,

The most prestigious and sought-after award is undoubtedly THE JMK AWARD, administered by the JMK Trust in memory of emerging theatre director James Menzies-Kitchin. The winner of the JMK Award may find it a dramatic turning point in their early career: winners have included Thea Sharrock, Natalie Abrahami, Bijan Sheibani and Joe Hill-Gibbins. The winner receives a production at the Young Vic and several runners-up receive support towards a production or a workshop, while other finalists are offered advice and workshops. The JMK Trust also offers 'Direct Access' workshops, talks and events around the country for emerging directors; you do not have to apply to the JMK to attend these events, details of which appear on the JMK website. To apply for the JMK Award you have to be under thirty and to have directed no more than two productions with professional casts. To apply you choose one of 100 plays listed on the website and write about a proposed production of that play. The lists of plays are chosen by Michael Boyd, Nicholas Hytner, David Lan, Sam Mendes and Katie Mitchell, and are in themselves an interesting checklist of the classic and contemporary canon.

Each year since 1994 the DONMAR WAREHOUSE has offered a bursary to a director to become its Resident Assistant Director, working on all aspects of the Donmar's productions for one year. This is another highly sought-after position, with previous Donmar RADs including Josie Rourke, Sacha Wares and Rupert Goold. The Donmar now also show-cases productions by previous RADs at the Trafalgar Studios for twelve weeks every year. Applicants are expected to be at the beginning of their careers. The closing date for applications is usually in the autumn preceding the year of the residency.

THE OXFORD SAMUEL BECKETT THEATRE TRUST AWARD is open to directors, other practitioners and theatre companies with two or three fringe productions behind them, but not open to those in full-time education or in receipt of regular funding. It is primarily for those looking to mount their first fully resourced production, and offers up to £50,000 in resources. For 2012 the OSBTT is working in partnership with the Barbican and the CREATE Festival, and is looking for an individual or company to create a piece of site-responsive non-traditional theatre in the boroughs around the Olympic site in July 2012. For 2013 the guidelines will be on the website from autumn 2011, and the closing date is likely to be the end of that year; the long period between the closing date and the production is because the award gives R&D funds and time to two companies before choosing one of the companies to make a full production. The OSBTT usually funds pieces that are experimental and groundbreaking in form as well as content: the winner in 2010 was *You Me Bum Bum Train*, a highlight of the Barbican BITE season that year.

It is possible to apply for a GRANTS FOR THE ARTS AWARD as an individual, and for awards of less than £10,000 ACE will inform you of the outcome of the application in no more than six working weeks. One of the three 'dimensions' that ACE consider in assessing an application is development: 'the development of the artist, the art form and the arts more widely'. It is possible to apply for funding for the research and development of projects with other artists, as long as the artists are paid properly. The other consideration is ACE's current motto: 'Great Art for Everyone', which implies that projects should have some public outcome, but that could include a showing of the work in progress at the end of the research and development period to peers and possible future collaborators and funders. You will need to read the funding criteria carefully, but it is possible to secure a few thousand pounds of funding to ignite a project: in 2006-7 the average grant to individuals was £5,825.

The director as a business

Even if you do not wish to set up your own company with its own company name, you are in effect becoming a business with a professional profile by joining one of the network organisations for directors, by applying for grants, or by putting on work for professional peers and the public. The name of the business might be your personal name, but there are reasons for considering your professional profile as distinct from you as an individual: for example, if your email address is 'soulanimal' or 'lovewithoutirony' (real examples), this might be the time to change it before putting it on your Young Vic Genesis profile and CV.

First points of contact are CVs, letters and emails. I am grateful to Andrew McKinnon, a director and producer who has mentored many emerging artists, for the following advice on how to construct a professional CV and biography.

Your CV

A CV is a tool for getting jobs. It is not a biography. There is no place for favourite or pet credits if they are not relevant.

A CV is a snapshot of where you are now, and so needs regular revision as your work develops. Always reread it before you send it out, and question whether it clearly gives the facts about you that are relevant for this particular opportunity. Keep a 'master CV' on which absolutely everything you do is listed, with names of collaborators, etc. Update it regularly. It is a resource for you only: never send it out!

When laying out a CV, consider using the header for the name and contact details (you can use the footer for contact details if it doesn't look too crowded). Essentials are name, email and phone. The letters 'CV' and your date of birth are unnecessary. Never use 'risqué' or 'funny' email addresses or Twitter or Facebook names on a professional CV.

Avoid a crowded look. Avoid fancy typefaces. Do not mix different typefaces. A simple 'Personal Statement' at the start can be useful if it says something interesting, but beware 'Mission Statements'; some readers actively dislike them, and they tend to be generalised and cliché-ridden.

Always arrange your work details so that in each section of the CV the most recent event is first – 'reverse chronology'.

Be positive whenever you can be (but don't tell lies – they will always be found out). Don't say 'I was involved in . . .' if you can more truthfully say, 'I took (some) responsibility for . . .'. Don't say 'I helped with / was part of . . .', but 'I helped to co-ordinate / lead / manage . . .'.

A CV shouldn't be more than two pages long, so be economical with words whenever you can. Don't say 'I speak French to a basic standard' when you can say 'basic French'. (Some useful words about languages are basic / competent / conversational / working knowledge of / good / very good / fluent / native speaker. Useful words to sum up degrees of experience are extensive / wide / some.)

Details of professional training should always be included; higher education, possibly; schooling, not. 'Other experience' can be useful if it is relevant or interesting. Hobbies and interests are definitely not essential – only if relevant or interesting.

There is absolutely no excuse – ever – for spelling mistakes in the names or titles of plays or theatres or companies. They will always be noticed.

Your biography

If you are not given a template for biogs in programmes, press releases, etc., remember that they are almost always written in the third person. Either start from your present or recent experience and move back in time or start from training or 'born in' and move forward in time. In either case, put 'future plans' at the end. Beware of 'thanking' anyone or dedicating your work to anyone in a biog; it can look very gauche.

Letters and emails

To this it is useful to add the advice Sue Emmas gives in the interview with her about personalising letters to directors and making the letter the first part of a dialogue between you and the director or theatre: as well as mentioning your own work and experience, try to make and substantiate two or three points of contact you genuinely feel with the work and artistic policies of the theatre to demonstrate that you have seen some of the theatre's or director's work and that you have done some research and thinking; and, of course, attach a CV. Generally, generic letters are a waste of time. As Sue Emmas also notes, it now takes more points of contact and meetings to establish a relationship with a theatre than it used to, so the best outcome from a first letter is probably a 'getting to know you' meeting. Ideally you will have had this meeting before sending an invitation to a show; it is also probably too early in the process of making a relationship to suggest yourself for a production or project; that point may come after the director or theatre has met you or seen your work.

An interview

Gareth Machin offers good advice about how to prepare for a first interview with a peer director and what to expect from it. It is unnecessary to repeat that here, but in terms of thinking of yourself as a professional artist remember his advice that even if an interview is 'billed' as an informal chat, it is never just an informal chat, and even if you casually approach an artistic director to introduce yourself at the bar, it may quickly become a decisive interview on which the artistic director will base their view of you and what they will remember when you send them an invitation to a show. Be prepared: it's never just a chat.

Are you a business? Tax and self-employment

Her Majesty's Revenue and Customs (HMRC) is responsible for the collection of taxes in the UK, and its website now provides so much information on taxation – your status and liability for tax, how to keep records and receipts, how to make up simple accounts, how to calculate and file a tax return, and how to pay your tax – that most directors will find it possible to manage their own tax affairs and not have to hire an accountant, which is expensive. If you work solely and permanently for one or two employers and have your tax and national insurance deducted at source you do not have to concern yourself with filling in a tax return, as your employer(s) will deal with all your tax affairs, and deduct what is needful from your salary; but if you begin to earn money for single fixed-term jobs and work for (or rather supply a service for) several different organisations, and have not had tax or National Insurance deducted for that work, you have become self-employed.

The HMRC website has a useful list of questions to help you determine whether you are self-employed or not:

You're usually self-employed if you can answer 'yes' to the following:

➢ Do you have the final say in how the business is run?
➢ Are you responsible for meeting any losses as well as taking any profits?
➢ Can you hire someone on your own terms to do work for you?
➢ Do you risk your own money?
➢ Do you provide the main items of equipment you need to do your job?
➢ Do you agree to do a job for a fixed price regardless of how long it may take?
➢ Can you decide what work to do, how and when to work and where to provide the services?
➢ Do you regularly work for a number of different people?
➢ Do you have to correct unsatisfactory work in your own time and at your own expense?

For a theatre director the answers to many of the above questions are 'yes'. You may be in a situation where you earn money from a regular employer, perhaps part-time bar or office work, but you are also regularly asked to lead workshops, for which you get paid a fee. It is possible to be simultaneously employed by an employer (as a barista or marketeer) while also being a self-employed director/workshop leader, who receives payment for providing a service (and very often does not have tax or National Insurance deducted), and has to pay for services and equipment (e.g. a rehearsal room) out of your own money in order to develop your craft or in order to earn more money as a freelance director/workshop leader. In a tax return you declare your earnings from your bar work as employment earnings, and fill in a separate section of the tax return to declare your self-employment earnings as a director/workshop leader. If you file your tax return online the form will take into account all your different sources of income and expenses and calculate your tax bill for you.

As you are self-employed you are able to deduct the expenses you incur directly in order to generate income, or turnover: so, if you charge actors £10 a head for a workshop and ten actors turn up, your turnover is £100, but if you have had to pay £50 to hire the hall in order to earn that £100, you can deduct your expenses, £50, from your turnover, £100, and so your profit is £50, and it is only on your profit that you pay tax. And unless you earn over £68,000 a year (and should be thinking about an accountant now you can afford one) that is basically your tax return: everything you have earned as a director (turnover) minus all the expenses directly incurred in creating that turnover, equals the profits of your business. The online tax return will then calculate how much tax you must pay on that profit. HMRC calls it the three-line-account and there are help sheets to download from the website that explain it in more detail.

Equity has guidance for their members about what, as an actor, stage manager, or director, you can legitimately claim as expenses against your turnover, and the following is general advice which you should check with HMRC before submitting a tax return. In principle if you buy or hire something purely for your business you may claim 100 per cent of its cost; if you buy or hire something that you use only partly for your business and also have for personal use, you may claim the percentage that is used for business purposes. So, for example, the hall hire was purely to generate income from the workshop, so you can claim 100 per cent of that, but if you buy the *Guardian* every day to read the reviews and theatre news but also read the general news and sport pages, you can only claim the percentage of the cost that can be assigned to business. The same may apply to your home if you are using half your bedroom as your business office, or to the costs of running a car if you use it for your freelance work. There is detailed information about what can and cannot be claimed on the HMRC website, and if you cannot find the information you can phone and ask for guidance. You will need to keep receipts or bills for anything you wholly or partially claim to substantiate the figures, as well as scrupulous records of all fees and payments received.

However, before you can do any of this you will need to register as self-employed, which you can easily do online or over the phone. When you register you will be given a Unique Tax Reference (UTR) which is the number that will always identify your tax records. Its other significance is that if you do not have a UTR and NI number organisations for whom you lead a one-off workshop may have to deduct tax and NI at source: if you can either supply your UTR and NI number, or better still, provide an invoice with those numbers, your address and bank payment details, it tells the organisation that HMRC allows you to be responsible for your own tax and they should not deduct tax and NI from the fee payment.

Do you need an agent?

Actors without agents find it very difficult to get auditions and work, but for directors it is very different. It is a generalisation which I will later contradict, but broadly speaking directors' agents do not find work for emerging directors. They may act as a point of contact if a theatre or producer wants to discuss possible projects with you, but this is only likely when you have established a considerable professional profile. Agents are very good at negotiating money and contract terms, and it is often very useful to have someone to do that money bargaining for you so that you can retain a primarily artistic relationship with the theatre or producer, but most subsidised theatres pay the agreed going Equity, TMA or ITC rate and there is little to negotiate; it is only when you are discussing a contract with a company which operates outside these agreements or with a commercial producer that there is more room for negotiation, and contracts may be quite complex; then you will really need an agent to negotiate on your behalf. And of course, agents are not philanthropists – they will charge a fee of about 10 per cent plus VAT on any contract they negotiate for you.

Having said that, an agent may act as a valuable confidant and mentor, helping you to guide your career and suggesting ways forward that you may not have considered. An agent with his or her ear to the ground may hear of opportunities you do not, and perhaps an email suggesting you for a project from an established and respected agent may carry more weight than an email from you. Many directors' agents are also literary agents and they may be able to send you scripts by their clients and facilitate relationships with emerging writers, but these opportunities and relationships are more likely to be facilitated by an agent once you have a track record and a profile rather than right at the beginning of your work, and as with theatres and directors, it is unlikely that an agent will 'take you on' until they have seen one or probably two pieces of your work and established a relationship with you. So the same pattern of building relationships applies to agents as it does to directors and theatres.

Are you too old to be emerging?

Many of the competitions and schemes for directors described above have age limits – often twenty-six or thirty – but many of these have either been raised or removed over the past few years, acknowledging, as Sue Emmas mentions, that it now takes longer to establish a career as a director than it did five years ago. Many directors and theatres recognise this, and also that many directors are also actors, stage managers or designers who have established themselves in those fields before turning to directing. Theatres when interviewing directors and considering possible opportunities for them now more frequently look at where they are in terms of the number of pieces they have directed or assisted on rather than their age. Be honest about your experience, try to evaluate critically what are the best next steps for you, and don't worry about your age – and that means not trying to achieve a certain goal by a certain age as an indicator of your progress, as well as not worrying about your actual age.

The director as artist

In the UK there is a culture that leads us to be somewhat reticent about describing as art what we do as directors, and most directors are modest and pragmatic when talking about their work, being wary of not seeming pretentious or pompous – quite rightly. However, as directors we need a range of skills to enable us to think and talk about our work that also acknowledges that our relationship with that work is interpretive and instinctual as well as intellectual, personal as well as objective – and therefore creative and artistic: we each make a connection with *The Tempest* that will make our production of the play unique to us. As independent artists we need to develop ways of critically evaluating our processes with writers, actors and designers; our responses to texts and other projects we may work on; and our responses to others' and our own finished work, in order to evolve as artists and sustain a creative working life as a director. We often have to be our own critics and mentors.

As Gareth Machin says in his interview: 'I'll be interested in finding out why someone wants to become a director, the kind of work that excites them, the kind of work they want to make, what they think they need to do over the next couple of years or so and just start a dialogue.' And: 'Sometimes I'll meet people and be very excited by the work they're talking about and make a real commitment to go see it, sometimes I'll believe somebody hasn't quite arrived at a point where they're clear enough about what their work is to get me excited to go see it, so I might be slightly more hesitant. So that meeting is useful in terms of making the difficult choice about what to go see and what not to go see.'

So, although seeing your work is the ultimate test of whether another director is interested enough in it to build a relationship with you, you will first have to articulate your reasons for wanting to direct. You may have to give a picture of the type of work you are interested in making, by reference to other directors and creative artists; to describe clearly a project you are planning; and perhaps to discuss how you see your work developing over the next two years.

Although you will need to keep those lists of people's work you admire, and have a broad knowledge of the classic and contemporary canon, the real work you might have to do is interrogating your own ideas and finding ways of clearly and economically expressing them. Some directors, when discussing their responses to work and future plans, focus on the 'what' – the product or end result – and may not have asked themselves the question: *why* am I interested in the classics rather than new writing; *why* do I admire Howard Davies's direction or Paule Constable's lighting; *why* do I really want to direct this play. Why me? What do I bring to this project that is grounded in the play but also grounded in my experience and personal responses?

Many of those 'whys' have been explored in the chapters on the director and the actor, author and designer, and although no one expects or would desire a director to know everything about a production before collaborating on it, another director will expect you to have interrogated your responses to a play to the point where your experience and passions have been harnessed to concrete ideas that could be useful to an actor, a writer or designer: they are personal responses that are translatable into real production ideas that can feed the imagination of others.

And if this process of interrogation of your ideas applies to a developed and practical response to a single production, it also applies to your practical philosophy about your work as a whole: what are the preoccupations, passions, tastes, and even ethics which may lie outside theatre as well as within that will guide your choice of projects and collaborators, your decisions and your processes? By posing these questions about your present and future work and discovering and identifying your underlying practical philosophy, you may be able to answer the two most difficult questions on the interview agenda: 'Why do you want to direct?' and 'Where do you see yourself in five years' time?' Asking yourself *why* helps to interrogate the *what*, refine it, and then articulate it more fully and clearly.

Michael Chekhov asks his reader to complete his book by practising his exercises rather than just reading them in order to understand his work, and the most engaging pieces of work are only completed by the creative involvement of an audience. If this book answers some of the questions about what information it might be useful to know, and what factors it might be useful to consider, as an emerging director, it cannot be completed by giving a final answer as to how you become a theatre director, but rather by asking you: 'So, *why* do you want to be a theatre director?'

Over to you. Good luck.

Interviews

Interview with Gareth Machin

Gareth Machin is an associate of the National Theatre Studio, overseeing its engagement with directors. Before coming to the Studio he was artistic director of Southwark Playhouse, where he directed Gaffer!, The Archbishop's Ceiling, The Canterville Ghost, The Chimes *and a site-specific promenade of* The Canterbury Tales. *He was also associate director of Bristol Old Vic, where his work included* The Wizard of Oz, Who's Afraid of Virginia Woolf?, Look Back in Anger, Betrayal, Henry IV Parts 1 and 2 *and the site-specific show* Up the Feeder Down the Mouth and Back Again. *I asked him to tell me what the National Theatre Studio does and explain its relationship to the National Theatre.*

The studio is the research and development side of the National Theatre itself, so our primary function is to engage with a broad range of artists who may be able to produce work for the National Theatre. We're constantly trying to generate new ideas and introduce the National Theatre to new people and to create new work which will play on one of the three stages. We run workshops, which might be a day's or a week's work on a project; we have attachments for artists, primarily writers, but occasionally directors and other practitioners; and then we also do a whole range of work with emerging directors; and we have an international programme – and all of that is feeding into generating new ideas for the main building.

What are the different ways you engage with emerging directors?

There are three formal ways and a whole range of other ways that we might engage with a particular individual. The formal ways are fairly easy to describe: we run a course once a year; we run two bursaries; and then we also have a staff directing programme.

So first, we run a course once a year for two weeks. We invite fourteen directors to take part. We don't charge them, we pay them expenses to be there. One of the things we're looking at when we put the group together is diversity, partly in terms of where they've come from, but also in terms of where they want to go; what we don't want is a group of people who all want to work in a particular part of the theatre industry or make work in the same way. So it tends to be quite a broad range of people taking part. We're not trying to teach any particular system – I suppose you'd describe the course as an explosion of ideas over two weeks. We invite a broad range of leading practitioners to come in and meet the directors, some of whom will, say, do an hour's worth of Q&A, some of whom will do a two-day practical workshop. It's not just directors, there are also writers, designers, lighting and sound designers and key industry people: casting, fundraising, those kind of areas, so it's not just about the art, it's a broader remit.

Then we run two bursaries. The philosophy behind the bursaries is that one of the ways you get better as a director is to work with really good actors. And when we go see things on the fringe quite often they're under-cast, and there's a whole range of reasons why that might be. One of them, of course, is that there's not an awful lot of money to pay actors on the fringe. That may mean you have young or less experienced actors working there, but it's not as simple as that. Sometimes emerging directors feel more comfortable working with their peer group, so you find that people are working with a small group of actors whom they were with at college or drama school; sometimes it's lack of confidence; but sometimes it's also lack of knowledge. I'm always amazed at how few emerging directors really know the acting industry; who make lists of all the actors they like and want to work with. And sometimes it's having the skills, and also the confidence, to pick up the phone and talk to agents, which is a very particular skill. So, I think all those reasons may contribute to fringe shows being quite under-cast. The thinking behind the bursary, therefore, is to give a director six months at the studio, when they will do all the in-house casting for the projects we put on, and also have studio time to themselves so they can also work with some of these actors. So by the end of the six months they should know a fairly broad range of actors who, hopefully, they can carry on working with.

The other bursary, which we call the Leverhulme Bursary, provides the same opportunities as the first, plus funding towards a production at the Finborough Theatre. Clearly, one of the great challenges facing emerging directors is finding the money to put shows on. Previously the award was six months at the studio and six months assisting, but we feel that the opportunities to assist are perhaps greater now than they were ten years ago, and the money is more usefully spent going towards production.

The other thing we do is staff directing. Staff directing at the National usually involves working on three different shows, ideally one in each of the three spaces. The amount of time you're with us for depends on how long your shows end up running for, but ideally it's about a year. As well as assistant directing you're responsible for the understudy work, including sometimes casting the understudies. There's quite a significant amount of work to do with Discover, the education department, and what is really important for us is that it should be an opportunity for directors we're interested in, in their own right. We are looking for the skills and experience required to be an assistant, but we're also looking for something in the work that excites us and makes us want to invest in them as a director. So they also get opportunities in the studio to develop their own work while they're with us.

Those are the three formal things we do. In terms of applying for those positions, apart from the Leverhulme Bursary, there is no formal application process for anything. I suppose there is a danger that would make it feel like a closed shop or a clique. I sincerely hope that's not what it is. The thinking behind it is that we don't feel that by listening to a director talking about directing, or writing about directing, we get any meaningful sense of what a director can do. The only way meaningfully to engage with a director's work is actually to see the work and then, ideally, engage in a dialogue with that director about that work.

So we're not particularly interested in how people write or talk about directing; it's all about seeing the work. We do meet a large number of people as we're always happy to chat informally, but then it's about going to see work and often going to see work over a period of time. So we might see two or three things before one of these opportunities comes up. And we think very hard about finding the right director for particular projects, so we try to marry people up to the best opportunity for them.

The Leverhulme is the one thing you can apply for. We felt that it was important that there was at least one point of access that involved an application, because inevitably some people do get overlooked, or they slip under the radar for whatever reason, so it's great for us to have the opportunity just to see who else is out there. Actually, the person who won the award the first year is someone we didn't know, whose work we hadn't seen, which was great, because otherwise we might never have met her.

So does that happen every year? Is there an application deadline?

At the moment it happens every year. Obviously it's dependent on the continuing support of the Leverhulme Trust. It is happening in 2011, but beyond that I'm not 100 per cent certain. We put an advertisement in the *Guardian* in January and then interviews tend to take place in late February or early March.

But it's a way of engaging with people who maybe haven't had the resources to put on a production?

It's exactly that. It provides an element of support from the Studio and the National Theatre's infrastructure as well. Often that director will be developing their ideas during the time that they're with us, taking advice on casting and other aspects of the production.

There is one other bursary we run. It's not a bursary for an emerging director, but I think there are various glass ceilings that directors seem to have to go through: one of them being trying to get your first show on the fringe, but then also, for a lot of directors who have worked extensively on the fringe and done a lot of assisting, it's finding it difficult to make the transition to working on a main stage or a big stage. So we've launched another bursary called the Quercus Award, which is a joint venture between us and West Yorkshire Playhouse, and gives an opportunity at just that point in a director's career to have a big theatre and say 'Here's a properly funded, properly resourced production with a sensible number of actors', ideally doing a big play. So the first production of that scheme took place in March 2011. Róisín McBrinn directed *Yerma* in the Courtyard in West Yorkshire Playhouse. Again, that is a formal, open application process, and again, we advertise it in the *Guardian*. It's not something that's going to happen at a regular time each year, it'll be slightly more ad hoc than that.

A large number of emerging directors will have heard of the work of the National Theatre Studio and may send you an email saying 'I'm a director.' Would you meet somebody first or would you say 'Let us know when you've got a show on and invite us to it,' and that'll start the conversation? Or is there no rule of thumb?

Generally, we're looking to engage with directors who are a year or two out of formal training. It's not that you have to have trained formally for us to be interested in you, but we're not looking for absolute beginners, people who are just starting out. Part of the skill of being a director is generating work, and it's useful to see the choices someone's making over a year or eighteen months before we start to get meaningfully engaged with them. So if someone sends me their CV and they've just graduated from a drama school or university, what I'll probably say to them is, 'Do keep me informed of your work and, if I haven't had a chance to see anything in a year, do write back,' and then maybe at that point I'll relook at their CV and maybe I'll meet them.

If someone is a bit further on – has started to assist at whatever level and, maybe, has started to put on their own work professionally, wherever that's happening, whether that's on the fringe or outside London – it's quite likely I will meet them. That'll be a very informal meeting for half an hour, where I'll be interested in finding out why someone wants to become a director, the kind of work that excites them, the kind of work they want to make, what they think they need to do over the next couple of years or so, and just starting a dialogue. And often, on the strength of that meeting I'll say, 'You just have to let me know when you have work on.' Sometimes I'll meet people and be very excited by the work they're talking about and make a real commitment to go to see it, sometimes I'll believe somebody hasn't quite arrived at a point where they're clear enough about what their work is to get me excited to see it, so I might be slightly more hesitant. So that meeting is useful in terms of making the difficult choice about what to go see and what not to go see.

What are the factors that go into deciding what you see? If someone put on a rehearsed reading for example, would you go see that? Or do you tend to try and see fully resourced or realised productions?

There are a number of factors. In terms of where work takes place, I'm happy to go see work anywhere. It doesn't have to be work that's taking place in a formal theatre environment. It doesn't have to be happening in London, I'm very happy to be travelling around, but if it is outside London then that takes a bit more organising, so more notice is probably needed. What is important is that someone needs to have had a meaningful rehearsal period. That means if something has just been thrown together over a week, or indeed if it is a rehearsed reading, that's going to be of less interest to me because what I want to see is evidence of what the director's process has led to. It's also about being able to see an aesthetic on view, because, clearly, an enormous part of directing is the choices you make with a designer. So with a rehearsed reading I'm not going to get any sense of what that might be.

I'm also keen to see directors working with actors who are of such calibre that they can recognise what it is the director's asking them to do. That doesn't mean I wouldn't go to see a director's work at a drama school for example, but working with drama students is a slightly different exercise, so I'm probably more interested in seeing someone's work with a professional cast. But those are really the criteria: it needs a proper rehearsal process; it needs to have been resourced to a level so there's at least a chance of seeing what a director's aesthetic vision is. Beyond that, there aren't really any criteria in terms of genre.

What is just as useful as going to see the show is the conversation with the director afterwards, because that can be very revealing about the choices the director has made – and that degree of self-analysis is very useful. Sometimes we go to see a show and maybe something hasn't quite worked, so it's always useful to see if the director knows that, or if they think it was fine.

Or if something is the result of compromises or the budget and they would like to have done it differently had they been able?

Absolutely. I'm very reluctant to make a decision just after seeing a production; I then want to have the conversation, and often see a director's work over a period of time before inviting them on the course or to be a staff director.

In terms of the etiquette of inviting people to shows, what's a good notice period and how often is it useful to badger someone to see your show?

If you've already got a relationship with the person, I think it's probably worth just dropping a line saying, 'This is going to be happening whenever,' once a production is confirmed, and the time frame of that can be different every time. Then I think it's worth sending an email saying, 'This is happening, here's the date,' about a month before. Probably at that point you'll have the casting information and the marketing information, so at that point send a more detailed invitation. And then, I think, there's one more time that you can invite somebody. That might be just before you open or just after you open. I think anything beyond that and it starts to feel like you're hassling. Most people are sensible about it, but occasionally people get fixated on one person, or a couple of people, attending their production and then start to behave a little erratically; at that point you're doing yourself a disservice, because then it's less likely someone will come if they feel like they're being hassled.

One of the problems is that some directors assume their work is going to be terrible until it's open, so they put off inviting industry people because they want to know that the show is going to be all right. The problem then is that if you don't invite people until halfway through the run it can be hard to get those people in because their diaries are full. So it's always good to give the month-before invitation and then, if for any reason the production doesn't quite realise itself in the way you'd imagined or hoped, it's perfectly acceptable to uninvite people, and say, 'I don't know if you were planning to come and see the show, but actually this probably isn't the best example of my work.' And most people will be grateful for the excuse not to go see your show, and be quite impressed by the level of discernment you've shown. And then the next time you do a show you say, 'This one I really want you to see.' There are a whole range of reasons why productions don't work out the way we'd imagined them, so it's perfectly fine to acknowledge it. What's worse is having someone there and knowing that this isn't truly representative of what you want to achieve.

And then it's just a question of seeing where the relationship might go from there and what possibilities there might be, in terms of the ways you've outlined that the Studio engages with directors?

Yes. And there is no order that you might do things at the Studio. It might be that you did the course then became a staff director; you might be a staff director, then do the course. And often we're looking for people to work on one-off projects. One of the things we are careful about, because we have all these formal schemes, is that sometimes people don't fit neatly into these boxes and it's wrong to try and force people into them. We're interested in people's work and thinking, 'What is the best way of accommodating this person and helping this person take their work on to the next level?' So for example, Analogue are a very interesting emerging theatre company who work in a very collaborative, collective way, and as individuals, perhaps wouldn't particularly benefit from any of the formal ways of working, but actually, what they acknowledge they need to do as a company is to work with a little bit more dramaturgical rigour and to challenge themselves with the range of actors they're working with. That is something the Studio can help with. So they've been working with us over the last few months developing a new piece, working with the in-house team at the Studio and also with the literary department on the dramaturgical structure of what they've done, and with actors from the National Theatre company. So we've created an opportunity that's tailored to their specific needs rather than saying, 'Well, you need to become a staff director for a year,' which isn't what they're looking for at the moment.

Have you got any advice about how to prepare for that half-an-hour meeting where you meet a director, in terms of how to give an impression of your work, your passions and interest that that person can easily take away with them?

I think that there is a range of things you can do to prepare, and although meetings can go off in all kinds of different directions, there are questions that are likely to come up. Whoever you're talking to will want to get a sense of what your taste is, what kind of theatre excites you, so it's quite likely the question of 'Who are the directors who excite you?' will come up. And most people think that question is an excuse to list twelve names of people they've heard of. Actually, that's not what that question's about: it's about identifying particular aspects of a director's work that excite you and why. So it's much better to talk about one or two people and say what your connection is, because no two directors are the same.

If someone says 'I really like the work of director A,' it's not that I think they're going to direct plays exactly like that person; I just want to know what it is about that work which inspires them, but what would they do slightly differently? It's about trying to define yourself in relation to other people, because it's helpful for someone who hasn't seen your work to get a sense of what it is you're trying to make. I think it's important to convey a sense of enthusiasm and excitement. Sometimes in interviews people can be a bit too reserved or slightly non-committal. It's fine to say, 'I've not exactly worked out what the work is I want to make, but I do like these things.' Sometimes people will say 'I like everything,' and that's not necessarily helpful.

I think one of the biggest mistakes people make in a meeting is that they're so keen to show you what they know that they don't actually listen. They'll ask a question, but not actually listen to what it is that you're saying because they're as keen as they can be to show you what they know. And my feeling is that a massive part of being a director is the ability just to listen, and they're not giving me any evidence that they're able to do that.

Sometimes what happens, because directing can be such an isolating job, just being able to go in a room and talk to someone about directing, it all sort of piles out. I'm always interested when people come in and say, 'I really want your advice on this', but then don't ever really give you a chance to give your advice, but at the end of the meeting they say, 'Thank you, that was really helpful,' and I'm thinking, 'I said nothing there.' And that's a strange feeling because you realise someone just needed to get something off their chest, which is fine, but probably not what those meetings are about.

I think, also, you have to go into those meetings with a positive energy. I think there's a temptation sometimes to express your frustration that this or that hasn't happened, and that's not particularly helpful. It's fine to say, 'I'm having this particular problem, have you got any points?' but that's very different from saying, 'I'm really fed up,' because I'm also thinking, 'Do I want to work with this person? Do I think other people want to work with this person?' One of the things that can happen in theatre interviews is that it doesn't feel like an interview. It feels like a nice cosy chat, and everybody's very, very nice, but actually it's absolutely an interview. However at ease someone is making you feel, however relaxed, however informal it feels, you need to be thinking, 'How do I want this person to respond to me?' Just as you would in any other job interview, it's just we're not doing it in such a formal, self-conscious way. But I think that informality seduces people into thinking . . .

'It's just a chat.'

'It's just a chat.' But it's never just a chat.

Interview with Sue Emmas

Sue Emmas is the Associate Artistic Director of the Young Vic and has been directly responsible for the Young Vic's engagement with directors since the inception of the Genesis Directors' Project and the Jerwood Award. Before joining the Young Vic Sue worked at the Arts Council and as a youth theatre director. I asked her to give me a brief history of the Young Vic's engagement with directors, and why they developed that engagement.

It really started with David Lan's arrival as artistic director in 2000. When a new artistic director arrives you are naturally inundated with people wanting to come and work, both as assistants and as directors, and it's a challenge to respond positively and effectively to all that interest. David's own particular circumstance was that he'd been working at the Royal Court, where there was so much support for new writers, and he was aware that at that time nothing existed for directors. There was no sense of community for directors. It was very isolating; it was very competitive; and there was a lot of suspicion among directors. He felt that the Royal Court, the Bush Theatre and the Soho Theatre and others supported writers but no one gave similar support to directors.

So we got together all the emerging directors who had expressed an interest in the Young Vic and asked, 'If we were to create a network, would that be something of interest to you?' It started with thirty people and then grew to 200, then 400 and now it's about 750. Through that time the programme has undergone various different incarnations. In the early stages it was very ad hoc and without financial support, but then the Jerwood came on board and we created the Jerwood Award, which each year enabled two directors to produce a show in the Clare Theatre. This has now come to an end, and we work with them on the Jerwood Assistant Director Programme. Then we had five years of very intense and incredibly supportive funding from the Genesis Foundation. This was then extended by a further two years, and they continue to fund our work with directors but in a less extensive way.

The focus of the work Genesis has supported has ebbed and flowed over the years, but it has included one-off workshops, master classes with international directors, research-and-development opportunities, international exchanges, and so on. But at the heart of the directors' programme has been the Genesis Directors' Network. Essentially this is a website which acts both as a database and a communication hub. The directors all have a profile which can be publicly accessed, but they also have a way to communicate with each other. It's an online community which acts as a forum to seek advice from peers and professionals, to create discussion and debate, and to exchange experience and contacts. This is also how we advertise all the activities we run and a way of advertising job opportunities from the Young Vic, outside companies and individual practitioners. Individuals, theatres, producers, writers who are looking for a director advertise through the network so it is a genuine way of hearing about and getting work.

Personally I think the network has played a part in changing how directors work together. It's created a forum for talking to each other, sharing ideas, asking advice and getting to know each other. Directors are always going to be competitive but I think the network and the projects we run have opened up the chance to share process, methodology, artistic taste and not to be so isolated. Ten years ago getting directors in a room and asking them to work practically together was fraught with tension and distrust, now it's a much more regular and therefore a more natural experience – though the edge never goes!

The programme of activity that we have run focuses on developing both a craft and a career as a director. So workshops are led by core Young Vic team members such as Daniel Kramer, Carrie Cracknell, Joe Hill-Gibbins, or David Lan, or by other directors who have a strong relationship with the Young Vic such as Rufus Norris or Matthew Dunster. But there are also events about how to cast, how to acquire rights, directing in drama schools, etc.

We have also provided research and development opportunities for directors to develop plays and ideas – and not necessarily with the intention of programming them. Having the chance to create work without the pressure of performance is a rarity, and for a young director finding their artistic feet this can be a great opportunity.

The range of activities may change, but essentially it's giving the directors a community. There's a support system internally so they receive peer-to-peer support; access to all the Young Vic shows and access to the artists who work here, primarily directors; skill-based workshops; opportunities to make work when we can provide them; and looking at the career of the director in terms of getting people in to talk about how you make a proposal, including getting the Arcola, the Gate Theatre, ourselves and the Royal Court to talk about how you approach them. So I think it's a very wide and varied group of work, but it's all related to the Young Vic: we're not trying to be an institution of education or training – everything we do relates to what we put on stage.

So if you are an emerging theatre director and you've had no contact with the Young Vic, what is the portal to everything you've described?

The first thing is to go online, check the network is something that is going to be of use to you then you make an online application and send us a letter and your CV. After that we have a welcome meeting, usually of between ten and twenty-five people, so that we get to meet everybody who has expressed an interest in the programme and they get to meet other directors who are joining at the same time. Especially when you're starting out in directing it can be very isolating and lonely. It feels like everyone else is 'in the know' and that every door is shut to you. There's no one to ask seemingly stupid questions, or to get advice from.

The initial group meeting enables new members to meet other young directors and also get a sense of the breadth of membership. At the meetings I try to give an honest summary of the project so we're not over-promising what they are likely to get from joining. It can be a bit brutal telling potential new members this isn't an immediate way to get a Young Vic show, but I want directors to join for the right reason: an interest in sharing with their peers and developing their craft.

After they've attended the introductory meeting they are activated, so they have a profile on the website. Individuals and companies do go to the website to search for directors or assistant directors for projects, so it's a way of making connections and getting work. Once they're on the website they can start talking to each other, so they can ask for casting suggestions, publicise their work etc. They also hear of everything we do at the Young Vic and then it's up to them to select which projects might be of interest to them.

Many of the initiatives are open, but some are selective. For example, if we need an assistant director through the Jerwood Assistant Director Programme we send the information out to everybody and then it becomes a selection process like any other; if we do an intensive week which is only open to ten people and fifteen express an interest, then again we have to go through the process of selection – so it's transparent but it's competitive.

Do you have any advice about how initially to approach a theatre or director with a letter and CV?

Yes, I do think that a lot of people don't know how to write effective letters and they don't know how to get into contact with theatres. Often silly things like putting 'Dear Sir or Madam' instead of taking the time to find out the person's name – or how to spell the person's name correctly. What should be in letters is a huge area of uncertainty and each recipient is going to have their own likes and dislikes, so it's hard to generalise, but for me letters are often so much about the sender and not enough about the theatre or director they are writing to. Personally I want to know why are you interested in the Young Vic, what shows have you seen, why do you think you and the Young Vic would make a good fit? For me, letters that detail clearly, passionately, intelligently and articulately their response to a show or the artistic vision of the theatre are much more interesting. Anyone can be flattering and say the Young Vic has a great reputation and they'd love to work here but you have to go on to substantiate what you're saying. It feels like some directors don't know who they should be writing to, or indeed why, so they just write a letter to about fifty theatres without doing any research beforehand.

It should be more like having a relationship: when you want someone to go out with you, you don't pitch up to your blind date and talk for 90 per cent of the time about yourself. You should really spend about half the time asking about the other person – and that's what should be in your letter. You have to know why you want to go somewhere and it has to be a personal choice that the Young Vic was of interest to you for three or four really good reasons. It would be better to write two really good letters than fifty uninformed ones. If someone writes in and they have something interesting to say about the Young Vic because they have seen a show, you're always going to be more interested in them.

It's surprising how many letters we get from directors who express an interest in the Young Vic but haven't seen a show here, or want to assist a director whose work they've not seen. Going to meet with someone if you've never seen their work seems to me a pointless exercise.

Because you've got no basis to communicate?

Exactly, there's nothing to talk about. The director would think, 'If you're not interested in me enough to see my shows, why would you want to assist me for five weeks?'

Would you normally meet somebody one to one before you actually go and see their work, or does it just depend on what the project might be?

I don't think there's any hard and fast rule really. The likelihood is that at some stage I will have had a brief chat with them, but that wouldn't necessarily have been a meeting. They might have taken part in a project, whether it was a one-off discussion or something more practical, or they might have come to one of the question-and-answer sessions with one of our directors. Equally, it could be that they have a show that sounds intriguing and the invite comes at a time I've got a free night, so I just go through the invitations and find whoever sounds interesting, even if I haven't met them before. So it's a bit of a lottery, but certainly if you've met someone you're going to be more interested to go and see what they've put on.

We are sitting in the Young Vic and 'young' is the first word, but it seems that more emerging directors are coming to directing later, and there are some schemes which cut off at twenty-six years old. Do you think it's taking longer for directors to get to the same place that they might have been a few years ago?

Yes but no. Rufus Norris said he was in his early thirties before he even started to eke out a living as a director. Other directors like Matthew Dunster have been writers or actors before they move into directing. But it does feel that for the great majority of people it takes longer. When we started off doing the Jerwood Directors Award we had thirty as the age limit, then that shifted to under thirty-five, and then we took the age limit off completely because the age of people seemed irrelevant to who they were as directors.

The 'young' relates to where you are in your career, not where you are in your chronological age. I think it's interesting that some things still have ages attached and I sometimes wonder whether that is relevant to a career structure – or relevant to a funding structure in terms of where the money comes from.

I think everything we try and do is not age related, but equally I have noticed increasingly people saying, 'I'm twenty-two and I'm not where I want to be' and you think, 'Calm down! It takes time and don't try and put pressure on yourself.' That's partly because hitting thirty is a definite milestone: you start thinking, 'Am I going to have a family? Am I going to get to be in a position where I really can earn a living through being a director?' People have always had different means of earning money – directing isn't always going to be the way they make their living and they'll have to find different ways to pay the mortgage or have a family.

So someone who is only two years out of university can't reasonably expect to make all those connections and get all those paid jobs by the time they're twenty-five, so it's more of a marathon than a sprint?

Often people don't do the things that could help them develop at a quicker pace: people don't go and see work, saying that they can't afford it. Well, you could get £1 standing seats at the Royal Court, you can go to the Globe Theatre for £5, and so many theatres have pay-what-you-can nights – there are so many things that you can get to see in the theatre really cheaply. Going to the theatre can help build up a knowledge base and also help with making connections – and it's not just going to every press night and hanging about, it's actually developing your theatre muscles in ways which aren't just about making work but also about seeing work and finding a vocabulary to convey your reactions.

It really is just seeing every opportunity as a chance to flex your muscles: if you don't like a show, fine, but don't just sit there thinking, 'Well that was rubbish.' Ask yourself what would your notes be? If you were the artistic director what notes would you give that director that you feel they could benefit from – not ditch the set and start again because that's not realistic, but, say, what notes to give the actors to move it forward?

You have to stop looking at other people, you have to stop measuring your own achievements by anything more than where you want to be and what you want to be doing, and stop worrying that someone else has just done an assistantship when you really wanted to do it, and stressing that other people are where you want to be. It is a long race – it is a marathon in the sense that as a long-distance runner you do it against yourself and you're on your own, you're not in a pack. But it's not a sprint either, and therefore you should know what you want to do and remain true to who you are, the work you want to make, and how you want to get to where you want to be.

Has a sense of competition become less relevant because the paths to directing have become even more individual than they were a few years ago?

This has been true for a long time, but I do think it is more so now, with career paths so completely varied. All the time I have meetings with people who say, 'Should I be doing more as an assistant director? Is assisting the way to get me where I want to be?' and I think, 'It might be but then again it might not.' There is no single pattern – there never has been – but increasingly it's a mixed economy: it's a complex theatre ecology and you have to find your own path.

People do need to look at that terrible question, 'What do I want to be doing in five years' time?' and look to see the various different paths that they can take. Do they want to be an artistic director or does the freelance life suit them better? Do they want to also move into opera at some stage? Do they fancy having a year as a resident director on a West End show and actually earn a living wage?

I also think that it was true that people felt they had to specialise. For example, you had to be all about new writing, classical work or physical theatre; or if you worked in children's theatre you might get stuck. I think it's much easier these days to move between those different areas and not feel that you need to categorise yourself. People now actually look to people who may be able to move between new writing and Shakespeare, while also having an understanding of how to utilise a movement director or choreographer within their work.

So in some ways that frees up your movement, but then people feel under pressure to make inroads on three fronts: trying to keep in with the new writing; trying to keep in with the Young Vic classics; and making sure they go to Battersea to see some work by somebody who's making work from a movement-based starting point. But even if you have an interest in a particular area I do think you shouldn't ignore other ways of making work as there isn't that clear division any more.

Some people go on the fringe and make work and others choose the route of an MA and then make connections both as assistant directors and as a director in their own right. Also, I think with the professionalisation of the fringe in the last ten years the opportunities to make work in quite a rough-and-ready and immediate way have decreased. The financial demands are much greater and getting good deals so much harder, and the amount of money you need to put a piece of work on is so much greater than it used to be. There has always been a risk, it's just that now people are risking more and therefore it takes longer to get the resources together and develop work. Also I think there's a growing appetite for research-and-development periods where in the past people just got on and did it!

The increased difficulty of securing Grants for the Arts funding has also changed the landscape: there was so much more project funding about maybe fifteen years ago, so the likes of Katie Mitchell could start her company Classics on a Shoestring, and you could move much more quickly into making resourced work that was funded. It's always been tough, but it feels that now the process is more complex, the level of individual grants so much smaller and the overall pot of money much reduced, so getting money to fund a show on the fringe is very difficult.

With the idea of actually getting people to see your work?

Well, yes, the whole purpose of getting people to see your work is essentially what is going to get you your next job – going to see your work, enjoying it, feeling a connection, and then thinking, 'I can see now that you are the person to do this play in my studio.' A director has to have a mixed ecology of many different relationships and increasingly people are expecting you to self-produce. That used to be more of a rarity. Directors like Katie Mitchell, Dominic Cook, Rufus Norris and Matthew Dunster created their own companies, but there were many more of their generation who didn't; whereas now I think you'd be hard pressed to find many directors who haven't at some stage found their own money and produced their own work, and that just takes a lot longer now.

Some of the directors I've spoken to don't give themselves the permission to think that they can go and make their own work yet. They seem to think that they're not quite ready, or worry that they need to train a bit more, or wonder if they need to go and assist before they actually take a leap, whereas previously there was a much more gung-ho generation who had been told by the previous generation of directors that you are born a director – you can't teach it, you can't train in it, you can't develop your craft, you're either good at it or you're not, so the only way to prove that you were any good was to go and do it.

Now I have various disagreements with that theory because I think it's quite elitist – it was quite Oxbridge-oriented, in that some people felt that they had the right and the privilege to direct. Whereas now I think directing is seen as something that you should be developing and changing. So there was a generation who just did it, but now we've over-developed a generation who never feel they are ready. The thing is, you'll never know if you're ready until you do it – no amount of training or thinking or reading or assisting is actually going to place you in a better place than just going and doing it.

Do you think, with producing or directing on the fringe being financially a higher stake than it used to be, as well as there being so many directors around, that directors think, 'If it's my first show and it's not very good then I've lost my one shot,' whereas in the past people thought they were going to get two or three hits and people would still take them seriously?

Yes, I think there is a definite feeling of 'Oh my God this is my one shot,' which creates too much anxiety and therefore you end up censoring yourself before you even start. But having said that, there are other directors who just proliferate – they make work on £300 and they find ways to make it happen and they progress by doing that. Yet other people do that and they keep inviting you to things and then you get there and they say, 'It's not very good but I thought I'd let you know,' and I think, 'Oh no, do as many things as you like, but only invite me to the things that you think really demonstrate your taste and talent.'

So it really is about trying to get a balance. For the most part, making work will always be a good thing: but it's how you then use that work to build up your toolbox as a director and your craft; and also how you use it to make the connections that you need in order to get the opportunities to make more work in the future. You need to be a bit canny about that and know who you are inviting to what and why.

Given the difficulties in funding we are going to face over the next few years, do you think it might make directors more collaborative than competitive?

I hope so. Some directors get so paranoid, and it's just not helpful. It is much better now, and I would like to think that it's partly because of the directors' programme that we run here: people are a lot more open to being in a room together and sharing their processes and discussing their fears and anxieties, or their triumphs, and what they don't know. I don't think this was true ten or fifteen years ago. This means that there's an openness and a vivaciousness and a robustness that there hasn't been previously. There are more directors who have come together to create companies so that they can produce each other's work.

I'm not sure the cuts will create camaraderie, but I do think they will mean that people have to think of different structures and use each other in different ways. We've created something called the Theatre Network which is thirty directors who wanted to create relationships with other people like critical friends or mentors, and talk about their concerns and uncertainties. That feels like a great use of each other, like a real movement forward. And I think in the generation just above the emerging directors there is a real desire to pass on their skills, to nurture and support younger directors.

Interview with Allison Troup-Jensen

Allison Troup-Jensen relocated to New York from London and has directed, choreographed and produced work internationally featuring artists such as Harold Pinter, Eve Best, Henry Goodman, Joanna Lumley, Samuel West, Bekah Brunstetter, James Saito and Shaun Parkes. Her US credits include the English-language premiere of Count Cagliostro's Animals *by Andrzej Bursa at the Martin E. Segal Theatre Center; After Hours at The Bowery Electric; So the Arrow Flies by Esther Chae at the Bennett Media Studios, NYC; the West Coast premiere of* I Used to Write on Walls *by Bekah Brunstetter at the Tenth Annual Women on the Way Festival; the US premiere of* Mannequins' Ball *by Bruno Jasienski at Performa 09, Ellebasch Hall, NYC; and* Material Man *by Ji-Woo Hwang for Prelude 09. UK credits include work at Tristan Bates Theatre, Jermyn Street Theatre, Theatre503, DryWrite, Cambridge Arts Theatre, Savoy Theatre, Chichester Minerva Festival Theatre and the Crucible Theatre, Sheffield. From 2006 to 2007 Allison was Resident Director at the Crucible Theatre, Sheffield, under the artistic direction and mentorship of Samuel West, where she directed the regional premiere of* Topdog/Underdog *by Suzan-Lori Parks. She has been a member of the Bush Associates since 2007, and is the artistic director of Counterpoint, an international, interdisciplinary theatre company based in New York.*

What are the main centres of theatre activity in the US, and how do US directors manage to network across such a vast landscape?

Theatre in the US is broken up into regions. You have the East Coast hub with New York obviously being the most significant point, along with important theatre centres in Connecticut, Boston, and Washington, DC. On the West Coast, cities like San Francisco, Berkeley, Seattle and Portland maintain strong theatre communities, while Los Angeles focuses more on TV and film, although there is a smaller but thriving theatre scene developing there. Other important regions include Chicago and Louisville, Kentucky, home of the amazing Actors Theatre of Louisville and the Humana Festival, and in Texas there's exciting work happening in Austin, Dallas, and Houston.

But in terms of bridging the gaps and networking for US directors, I'm still working it out myself, but I believe it comes down to initiative. In my case, I did it the same way we did it in London. I decided to travel to the West

Coast because I had a desire to work there. I did my research and sent my CV out, with a letter introducing myself, letting them know that I was going to be on the West Coast – I put a sense of urgency in it, saying, 'I'm here in San Francisco for a week and I'd like to meet with you and talk to you about your company, and here's why . . . ', and I tailored my letter to their company and the interest it held for me. It's very much about researching and figuring out what your links are to people before writing the letter. American practitioners, in my opinion, seem genuinely interested to know you and open to meet with you if you have done your homework and can show some good experience.

The fact you have to travel 3,000 miles doesn't alter that relationship – it's exactly the same as it would be in the UK?

Well, not exactly, of course distance has an impact. Regional theatres here are interested in investing in people who want to invest in their communities. So even though I was meeting with a variety of companies in different cities who were interested in my work, they also wanted to know how serious I was about investing in their community long term. Because I was interested in being a bi-coastal director, and willing to spend the money and time to go over there and make it happen, they were more interested in meeting with me.

Additionally, they were also very interested in all my London experience. I know that what I bring to the table is different from other US directors, and for a British theatre director coming here, that's useful to know. I think American practitioners have a high respect for the English theatre tradition and practice, and that is helpful in opening up the lines of communication.

For an emerging director, what is the theatre scene like in New York? In terms of off-Broadway, off-off-Broadway, how do you get going in New York?

The New York theatre scene is the most diverse I've ever experienced. As in the UK, relationships are really important: you have to be willing to network. And emerging artists have to be willing to do that in this city more than anywhere else. They have to be willing to sell themselves and really know how to self-promote. Emerging directors have to go to every kind of event they possibly can, meet every artistic director and producer in the city that they can, and be able to speak intelligently and knowledge-ably about the work that's happening in those theatres. But beyond that, like anywhere else, you find a way to make your work and then let the work speak for itself.

What about getting your work on: is it easy, is it expensive?

You can find hundreds of tiny venues that are being rented for vast sums of money. Real estate in New York for rehearsal space and performance space is much higher than in the UK, and of course theatres are not subsidised in America the way they are in the UK. Everyone in New York is fighting for space and if you have the cash you can put on a show, but it is expensive. A lot of self-producing does occur and artists band together and form their own companies to try and deal with the costs, and again that is why relationships are so important. But there is a downtown theatre scene where the more emerging and more experimental work happens and where emerging artists can find resources to develop their work. A good example would be Here Arts, a company committed to supporting cross-disciplinary and experimental artists. Here Arts provides space, residencies and resources to develop new work .

This city is also filled with readings. Every day you can find multiple readings happening for commercial and non-commercial theatre. It can prove to be an effective way for an emerging director, or writer, to get their work heard and to get producers in the room – which then may lead to a chance of getting it developed by a producer or larger, non-profit theatre.

Do emerging directors put on readings in the hope that the show, and therefore they, might get picked up by a producer?

Yes, but there are two different kinds of producers in this city: there are commercial producers, interested in supporting a Broadway show that's going to make back its investment and then some; and then there is a rarer breed of producer who will invest in the show, knowing they may not get their money back, because they have a passion for the story or helping the director find a home for it at a larger, non-profit company. Usually you'll find many emerging directors involved with readings and showcase productions throughout the summer festivals.

The New York International Fringe Festival is open to US and international submissions and grows larger every year, with several productions each year finding a longer run after the festival. NYMF – the New York Musical Theatre Festival – is specifically for musical theatre, and there is also the

Midtown International Theatre Festival, which draws many emerging directors because you end up paying half the costs you would normally need to get your show on in New York, with a limited run of, on average, about five performances.

And it's helpful for an emerging director to do a festival because it's more likely you would get a review from an important critic. Reviews are extremely important here, and because there is always so much work being produced it can be a challenge to get a critic in when you're a new voice in the city.

Also a lot of emerging directors do a 'showcase code' production. This is an agreement you have with Equity, which means you can do your production on a much smaller budget, casting Equity actors who agree to do the show with only their travel costs being reimbursed. You're limited to twelve performances, though you can apply for an extension to do sixteen. Most of the critics won't review you unless you are running for three or four weeks at least, so there is this tricky balance between trying everything you can to get the critic in the room so they will press your show, but only doing twelve or sixteen performances. Hiring a publicist, with an established relationship with the press here, is a worthwhile investment and can make the difference between getting a review or not.

So if you are an emerging theatre director in London and you put a production on in a fringe theatre, it's actually more important to get artistic and peer directors and producers in to see it than a review in The Times, or the Guardian – but in New York it's much more important to get the critics in?

I think you have to try and get the critics in. Of course you want a balance: you want to impress Oskar Eustis, the artistic director at the Public Theater, and you try your best to get him to come and see your show, along with countless other artistic directors. But the reality is that there are hundreds of shows being produced every week, which means hundreds of directors trying to get the same artistic directors and producers to see their work. Having the right critics in who can speak in an articulate manner about your work means you have a press package you can present when it's been impossible to get that artistic director or producer in the room. Of course a review will also help to get the audiences coming to see your show and hopefully to fall in love with you and your company.

For you, who are the interesting companies in New York at the moment?

Well, the Amoralists Theatre Company for one, a group of actors and a writer, Derek Ahonen, who went to drama school together at the American Academy of Dramatic Arts, and decided to start their own company after being a bit disgruntled by the work they were doing individually. Their work is bold, fearless and engaging, with incredibly visceral performances and writing that is intelligent and heartfelt. They have become the darlings of the critics, but what is so impressive is their commitment to stay accessible to their audiences. I'm also a big fan of Rattlestick, a new-writing theatre company that is fantastic; the wonderful Soho Rep, who produce new work by established and emerging writers; and ps122, which is more of an arts centre, but esteemed for supporting provocative and emerging artists.

How do you go and seek writers? Are there places where emerging directors can meet writers?

Overall, I feel there is a more of a focus on developing young writers than there is on developing young directors. You just have to take the initiative in some cases. When I first came to New York I researched theatres that have programmes for young writers and wrote to them expressing my interest in being introduced. I immediately connected with the Public Theater's literary department. They select a group of young writers every year called the Emerging Writers Group, and I have been developing work with several of their writers over the last two years.

I also connected with the writers from the Old Vic New Voices Network, which is open to actors, writers, directors and producers aged between twenty-one and thirty who are based in New York. This is how I first started working with Bekah Brunstetter, whose work I've now directed in San Francisco and New York and who is now my company's Resident Playwright. New Georges is another theatre company with an artist development programme for female playwrights, directors and actors, and Soho Rep has a yearly Writer/Director Lab, which is an important programme for putting directors and writers together for early-stage development.

What advice would you give to a British director coming to New York, and what advice would you give to a US director coming to London?

To a British director I would say, before you come here try and figure out what networks you may already be connected to. Who do you know who has really good contacts in the city? Who could introduce you, via email introduction or whatever, to the bigger people in the business in New York – the artistic directors, the literary managers – to set up meetings? Go through that list first, then do your research on theatre companies via the internet. Who are the people you want to meet? Write to them. If you're not connected to them by some degree of separation, then the fact alone that you're coming from London and you've got some legitimate experience on your résumé means there is a good chance they'll set up a meeting.

I think the same advice can be given to the American director going to London, but the turn-around time in terms of getting replies to emails can take a bit longer in London than in New York, so it's even more important to have all your meetings set up before you go, particularly if it's only for a short period. And if possible it's really important that you have friends or colleagues that can connect you with UK contacts when you get there, so that you can connect with the right theatre communities. For both cities, you need to have done your research before you leave home, because otherwise you can spend your whole visit just finding your way around rather than meeting the right people.

Of course in the end you have to be good at what you do, whether that's in London or New York. But communication style is quite a bit different. How you present yourself as an artist is important – professionalism, passion and vision are appreciated on both sides of the pond, but in the UK you have to be more understated. In New York I think you have to have a little more bravado, in a positive way. You have to be willing to sell yourself with confidence, in a bigger way.

Practical exercises

Exercise one

Read the advice offered by Andrew McKinnon on how to construct a CV and rewrite your own CV using these guidelines. Read the advice in the interview with Sue Emmas and write a letter to the artistic director of a theatre where you have recently seen work, using her advice that the letter should be a 50–50 encounter between your knowledge of the artistic director's work (or their associates or guest directors) and the artistic policy of the theatre, and your own tastes and artistic aims; and address it personally with your new CV.

Exercise two

Think about the questions in the interview with Gareth Machin and Sue Emmas: why do you want to direct; whose work do you admire (including all creative practitioners); describe the type of work you wish to make; where you see yourself in five years' time; and what you see as the next steps towards achieving this; and how may we help?

Another way to answer these questions might be to think of yourself as a theatre company and ask the questions you would ask in a Grants for the Arts application about a company, but as yourself. To begin this exercise you may wish to write a 200-word mission statement about the work you wish to make. You might visit the websites of theatre companies who have mission statements to decide what a mission statement should include, but, broadly speaking, it should concretely describe the work the company wishes to make, and why. Using words such as innovative, accessible, collaborative and immersive are just meaningless unless they are backed up by specifics: be specific, not generalised, in order to nail your colours to a mast and stick to them – if not for ever, then until you feel passionate about something else.

Then describe a piece of work you feel passionate about and would like to make in the next two years, if you had the resources: be bold and idealistic but also honest and realistic. Perhaps choosing a company whose work you really admire and thinking in terms of their artistic policy, budgets and audiences may help: it is ambitious and wishful thinking but you have also thought about the reality of cast sizes, budgets and finding a real audience for the work.

Imagine that this might be your first ACE project grant in two years' time and your National Portfolio Organisation in five years' time; and then create the first steps towards that by completing a Grants for the Arts application for you, as an individual, for about £5,000 (the average grant for an individual being between £5,000 and £6,000) for a piece of research and development that might lead to a full project, which you will submit in the next three months.

You may wish to be an assistant director for the next few years, or the artistic director of an existing company, rather than pursuing this path, but you now have a means of defining your tastes and ambitions so that someone can get a sense of you as a director. You may never create this company or work, but you now have a credo, or a mission statement; you have a realistic but passionate idea of the work you wish to create in two and five years' time; you have reference points to indicate the type of work you wish to make; and you have the first practical steps towards it: a modest, personal, Grants for the Arts application. You have a vision, a plan, and some practical sense of how you might achieve those plans. You are ready to make some work – and ready for the interview, because you are being proactive about your future.

Weblist

Actors Theatre of Louisville	actorstheatre.org
The Amoralists, New York	www.theamoralists.com
Counterpoint Theatre	www.counterpointtheatre.org
Devoted and Disgruntled	devotedanddisgruntled.ning.com
Directors Guild of Great Britain	www.dggb.org
Donmar Warehouse	www.donmarwarehouse.com
Grants for the Arts	www.artscouncil.org.uk/funding/grants-arts
Her Majesty's Revenue and Customs (HMRC) Self-assessment	www.hmrc.gov.uk/sa/index.htm
Here Arts, New York	www.here.org
Humana Festival	actorstheatre.org/humana-festival
IdeasTap	www.ideastap.com
Independent Theatre Council (ITC)	www.itc-arts.org
JMK Trust	www.jmktrust.org
Midtown International Theatre Festival	www.midtownfestival.org
National Theatre Studio	www.nationaltheatre.org.uk/studio
New Georges, New York	www.newgeorges.org
New York International Fringe Festival	www.fringenyc.org
New York Musical Theatre Festival	www.nymf.org
Old Vic New Voices	www.ideastap.com
Oxford Samuel Beckett Theatre Trust	www.osbttrust.com/award.html
Performance Space 122 (ps122)	www.ps122.org
Public Theater, New York	www.publictheater.org
Rattlestick Playwrights Theater, New York	www.rattlestick.org
The Regional Theatre Young Director Scheme	itvtheatredirectorscheme.org

Royal Shakespeare Company (RSC)   www.rsc.org.uk

Shift Happens   shifthappens.ning.com

Soho Rep, New York   www.sohorep.org

State of the Arts Conference
www.thersa.org/events/rsa-conferences/state-of-the-arts-conference

Young People in the Arts   www.ypia.co.uk

Young Vic Genesis Directors' Network   www.youngvic.org

Index